AF745970

HUMAN-ROBOT INTERACTION - THEORY AND APPLICATION

Edited by **Gholamreza Anbarjafari**
and **Sergio Escalera**

Human-Robot Interaction - Theory and Application
http://dx.doi.org/10.5772/intechopen.68231
Edited by Gholamreza Anbarjafari and Sergio Escalera

Contributors

Oscar Chang, Momina Moetesum, Imran Siddiqi, Kourosh Meshgi, Shigeyuki Oba, Önsen Toygar, Ayman Afaneh, Esraa Alqaralleh, Georgia Koukiou, Takashi Kuremoto, Masanao Obayashi, Shingo Mabu, Kunikazu Kobayashi, Fatima Isiaka, Kassim Mwitondi, Adamu Ibrahim, Gholamreza Anbarjafari

© The Editor(s) and the Author(s) 2018
The rights of the editor(s) and the author(s) have been asserted in accordance with the Copyright, Designs and Patents Act 1988. All rights to the book as a whole are reserved by INTECHOPEN LIMITED. The book as a whole (compilation) cannot be reproduced, distributed or used for commercial or non-commercial purposes without INTECHOPEN LIMITED's written permission. Enquiries concerning the use of the book should be directed to INTECHOPEN LIMITED rights and permissions department (permissions@intechopen.com).
Violations are liable to prosecution under the governing Copyright Law.

Individual chapters of this publication are distributed under the terms of the Creative Commons Attribution 3.0 Unported License which permits commercial use, distribution and reproduction of the individual chapters, provided the original author(s) and source publication are appropriately acknowledged. If so indicated, certain images may not be included under the Creative Commons license. In such cases users will need to obtain permission from the license holder to reproduce the material. More details and guidelines concerning content reuse and adaptation can be found at http://www.intechopen.com/copyright-policy.html.

Notice

Statements and opinions expressed in the chapters are these of the individual contributors and not necessarily those of the editors or publisher. No responsibility is accepted for the accuracy of information contained in the published chapters. The publisher assumes no responsibility for any damage or injury to persons or property arising out of the use of any materials, instructions, methods or ideas contained in the book.

First published in London, United Kingdom, 2018 by IntechOpen
IntechOpen is the global imprint of INTECHOPEN LIMITED, registered in England and Wales, registration number: 11086078, The Shard, 25th floor, 32 London Bridge Street
London, SE19SG – United Kingdom
Printed in Croatia

British Library Cataloguing-in-Publication Data
A catalogue record for this book is available from the British Library

Additional hard copies can be obtained from orders@intechopen.com

Human-Robot Interaction - Theory and Application, Edited by Gholamreza Anbarjafari and Sergio Escalera
p. cm.
Print ISBN 978-1-78923-316-2
Online ISBN 978-1-78923-317-9

We are IntechOpen, the world's leading publisher of Open Access books

Built by scientists, for scientists

3,550+
Open access books available

112,000+
International authors and editors

115M+
Downloads

151
Countries delivered to

Our authors are among the
Top 1%
most cited scientists

12.2%
Contributors from top 500 universities

CLARIVATE ANALYTICS BOOK CITATION INDEX INDEXED

WEB OF SCIENCE™

Selection of our books indexed in the Book Citation Index
in Web of Science™ Core Collection (BKCI)

Interested in publishing with us?
Contact book.department@intechopen.com

Numbers displayed above are based on latest data collected.
For more information visit www.intechopen.com

For EU product safety concerns:
IN TECH d.o.o., Prolaz Marije Krucifikse Kozulić 3, 51000 Rijeka, Croatia,
info@intechopen.com or visit our website at intechopen.com.

Meet the editors

Gholamreza Anbarjafari heads the iCV Research Lab at the University of Tartu. He is an IEEE senior member and the chair of the SP/CAS/SSC Joint Societies Chapter of the IEEE Estonian section. He is an expert in computer vision, human-robot interaction, graphical models, and artificial intelligence. He is an associate editor of several journals and has been a lead guest editor of several special issues.

Sergio Escalera leads the HUPBA Group at University of Barcelona and Computer Vision Center at Campus UAB. He is an expert in human behavior analysis in temporal series, statistical pattern recognition, visual object recognition, and HCI systems. He is the vice president of ChaLearn Challenges in Machine Learning, leading ChaLearn Looking at People events.

Contents

Preface

Robots and computers have become a prominent aspect of our lives and their presence will give rise to unique technologies. There are many difficulties to overcome before robots can interact fluidly with human beings. Human-robot interaction would be greatly enhanced if the robotic agent had a module that could interpret the socio-communicative intentions of the users by recognizing their moods and attitudes. The systems developed for the foregoing purpose consider combinations of different modalities, based on vocal and visual cues. This book project takes the foregoing modalities and applications into account by considering three main aspects, namely, social and affective robotics, robot navigation and risk event recognition. We are hoping that this book can be a very good starting point for the scientists who are about to start their research work in the field of human-robot interaction.

Finally, we would like to thank all members of iCV Research Lab at University of Tartu and Human Pose Recovery and Behavior Analysis Group at University of Barcelona for providing sufficient support for making this book come true.

Gholamreza Anbarjafari
iCV Research Lab
Institute of Technology
University of Tartu
Tartu, Estonia

Sergio Escalera
Computer Vision Center and University of Barcelona
Barcelona, Spain

Section 1

Social and Affective Robotics

Chapter 1

Socially Believable Robots

Momina Moetesum and Imran Siddiqi

Additional information is available at the end of the chapter

http://dx.doi.org/10.5772/intechopen.71375

Abstract

Long-term companionship, emotional attachment and realistic interaction with robots have always been the ultimate sign of technological advancement projected by sci-fi literature and entertainment industry. With the advent of artificial intelligence, we have indeed stepped into an era of socially believable robots or humanoids. Affective computing has enabled the deployment of emotional or social robots to a certain level in social settings like informatics, customer services and health care. Nevertheless, social believability of a robot is communicated through its physical embodiment and natural expressiveness. With each passing year, innovations in chemical and mechanical engineering have facilitated life-like embodiments of robotics; however, still much work is required for developing a "social intelligence" in a robot in order to maintain the illusion of dealing with a real human being. This chapter is a collection of research studies on the modeling of complex autonomous systems. It will further shed light on how different social settings require different levels of social intelligence and what are the implications of integrating a socially and emotionally believable machine in a society driven by behaviors and actions.

Keywords: social robots, human computer interaction, social intelligence, cognitive systems, anthropomorphism, humanoids, roboethics

1. Introduction

Robots have been an important part of the industrial setups around the globe for many years now. For many industrial operations, robots have completely or partially replaced the human operators and their involvement is likely to grow manifolds in the years to come. Nevertheless, in most cases, these robots operate in a controlled work environment and their interaction with humans remains fairly limited. The recent advancements in the hardware (actuators, sensors, etc.) and software technologies (computer vision, artificial intelligence, etc.), however, have paved way for involvement of robots in our daily life, both at work place and home. Such

IntechOpen

© 2018 The Author(s). Licensee IntechOpen. This chapter is distributed under the terms of the Creative Commons Attribution License (http://creativecommons.org/licenses/by/3.0), which permits unrestricted use, distribution, and reproduction in any medium, provided the original work is properly cited. (cc) BY

robots, contrary to the industrial robots, naturally require more interactions with humans and have to be designed accordingly. The term "social robot" was coined jointly by researchers in artificial intelligence and robotics in the early 90s and refers to the robots engaging in social interactions with the humans. Studies [1, 2] define social robots as autonomous agents designed to interact with humans and possibly other robots exhibiting the expected social behaviors of the assigned role. Such interactions, in addition to the primary expected tasks, involve communication, recognition of individuals, familiarization with the environment and adapting accordingly to the variety of situations encountered. In order to enable them to interact socially, these robots need to be equipped with what is generally termed as "social intelligence". Lazzeri et al. [3] argue that this social intelligence enables robots not only to converse with humans (and other robots) but also interpret the emotional signals and react accordingly hence producing an impression of a real human being. In addition to the conventional role of serving humans, other typical roles include providing guidance or assistance at homes, offices or public places, provide companionship and care services and serve as pets. The expectations from a social robot naturally vary as the function of the role it takes.

Breazeal [4] argues that humans tend to anthropomorphize robots for interaction and identifies four classes of social robots. These include "socially evocative", "social interface", "socially receptive" and "sociable robots". Socially evocative robots, for instance toy robots, are designed to engage in entertaining interactive sessions with the humans. According to him,

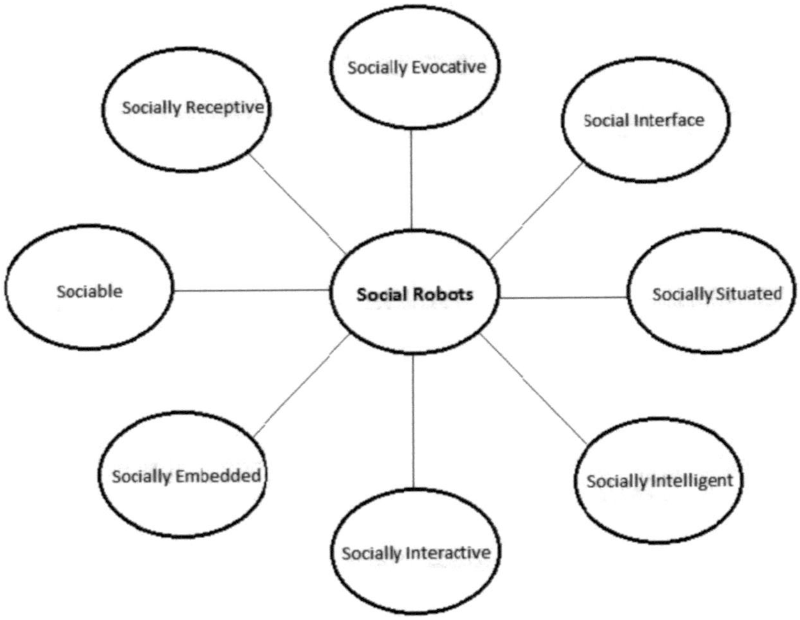

Figure 1. Taxonomy of social robots in literature.

socially interfaced robots, for instance guides at the airports, provide human-like conversational interaction that in addition to speech also involves body language and facial expressions. Socially receptive robots learn and enhance their social intelligence through interactions while sociable robots are highly participative to satisfy their own social aims. In addition to these four categories, Fong et al. [1] have identified three further categories including "socially situated", "socially embedded" and "socially intelligent" robots. They further describe a new breed of social robots called "socially interactive robots" that comprise of some common attributes with additional distinctive characteristics of their own. Based on the different categorizations suggested in the literature, we can identify taxonomy of social robots as illustrated in **Figure 1**. This chapter is dedicated to a discussion on the design considerations and applications of socially believable robots with a discussion on the associated challenges and the future prospects. Case studies and examples of social robots in entertainment, health and education will also be discussed.

2. Design considerations

Every passing decade is forcing robot designers and engineers to push their skills to the limit. As robots integrate further into our lives, high expectations are posing new challenges in their creation. All robots, whether industrial, field or social, must address a number of design issues. However factors of social believability and social intelligence increase the complexity of designing a socially interactive robot. One of the foremost conditions of believability in a social robot is its near realistic embodiment, to which users can relate without reluctance or discomfort. Secondly a socially interactive robot is expected to be expressive in terms of rich dialog, emotions and gestures. In addition to expressiveness, a social robot is required to manifest social behavior which includes perception of its surroundings and ability to plan and execute appropriate goal oriented actions. Variance in social situations and expected performance outcomes make it difficult to generalize design strategy for a social robot. Nevertheless designers broadly divide design approaches into two categories i.e. Bio-inspired and Function-inspired [1]. Bio-inspired design strategies are a multitude of disciplines like anthropology, cognition, psychology and sociology. On the other hand function-inspired approaches focus on task oriented designs. However, realizing the gap between available technology and performance expectations is of prime significance.

2.1. Embodiment and expressiveness

According to Fong et al. [1], a robot's visual appearance is the first projection of its believability. People establish performance expectations based on a robot's outlook. In a way, physical embodiment influences human robot interactions as people interact with humanoids differently from non-humanoids. Other than expectations, a robot's morphology plays a vital role in its usability, acceptability and expressiveness. Therefore it is required that a robot's morphology should correlate to its proposed functionality. For instance, robots that are intended to

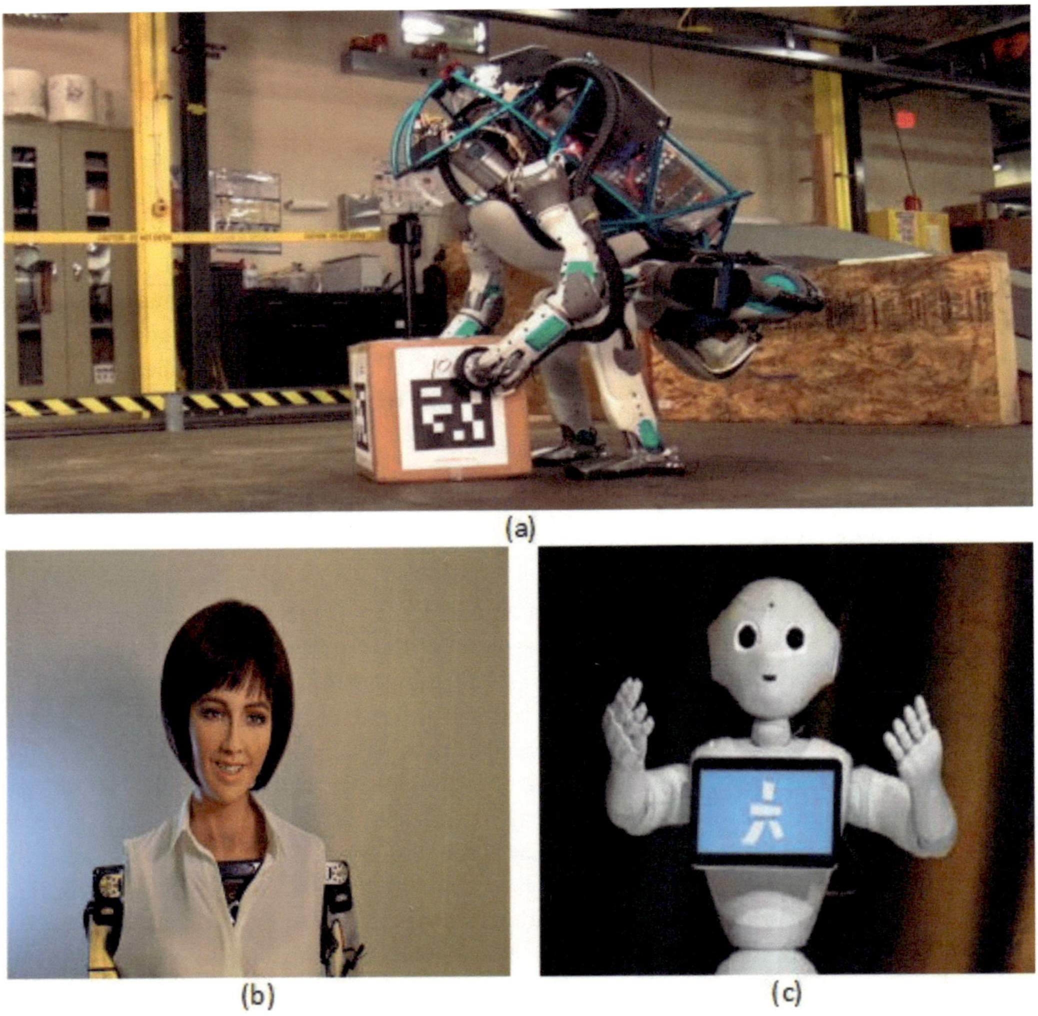

Figure 2. Advance humanoids: (a) ATLAS, (b) Sophia, (c) Pepper.

carry out human like tasks must be equipped accordingly; visual human likeness may not be of much importance in such cases as in the case of ATLAS and similar humanoids (**Figure 2a**). On the other hand those designed for interaction purposes must be more human like, with distinct facial expressions (e.g. Sophia) (**Figure 2b**) or with emotional speech capabilities (e.g. Pepper) (**Figure 2c**).

With the aim to achieve a naturalistic embodiment, designers get inspiration from nature itself. Morphological design of natural looking social robots can be attributed to anthropomorphism. Based on their area of application, morphological inspirations for a robot's outlook can also be taken from zoomorphism (e.g. pets or creatures), caricature (e.g. animations or fictional characters) and functional expectations (e.g. assistive or service robots etc.). Nevertheless most social robots are intended to work with humans; thus the general notion is to give them a human-like appearance. Therefore we will emphasize more on anthropomorphism.

2.1.1. *Anthropomorphism*

Anthropomorphism is the provenance of human characteristics in something non-human. According to Fink [5], anthropomorphism can be introduced in all three aspects of a robot's design i.e. morphology, behavior and interaction.

2.1.1.1. *Humanoid head*

The most effective anthropomorphic feature of a robot is its head. To project human likeness and better expressiveness, the simplest kind of humanoid robot heads are equipped with RGB LEDs, cameras, microphones and speakers. These mechanical parts are mostly cost-effective and provide a variety of expressions for more naturalistic human robot interaction. DARwIn-OP, HOAP-3, Pepper, NAO, UXA-90, Roboy and ASIMO are some of the examples of humanoids with faces equipped with LEDs and speakers. Perception of emotions by humans, while interacting with these robots is at times difficult due to limited modes of expressions giving unrealistic or mechanical effect. Some humanoids are provided with kinematic heads. These humanoid heads can perform transformations from one emotional state to another by tilting head, moving eyes and mouth etc. In contrast to LEDs, these heads are equipped with actuators and moving parts which work in intense coordination. Romeo, iCUB, Simon, RoboThespian, MERTZ and KOBIAN RII, are some of the humanoids featuring kinematic head with moving eyelids, eyebrows, jaws and neck. In quest to manifest ultimate humanness, roboticists experimented with animatronic heads with flexible skin. Alice, Albert HUBO, Roman and Actroid are some of the examples of robots with animatronics head consisting of several DC motors and artificial skin made of special material called Frubber. **Figure 3** shows three different kinds of humanoid heads with their ability to express emotions. Nevertheless such humanoid heads have a tendency to make users uncomfortable, as suggested in Mori's "Uncanny Valley" theory [6].

2.1.1.2. *Whole-body dynamics and control*

The idea of substituting humans with surrogates for tasks like search and rescue in challenging scenarios has been prevailing for some time now [8]. With the introduction of socially interactive and socially assistive robots, designing humanoids to be autonomous has become inevitable. In a rich social setup, robots require high level of autonomy including extended physical mobility. Although robots are becoming more sophisticated both mechanically and emotionally, yet they are still far from achieving agile human-like manipulation and interaction, thus providing significant research potential in these areas. Dimensions of robot's body (i.e. height and weight etc.), Degree of Freedom (DoF), tactile sensors, number and flexibility of joints are the design factors that determine its mobility (i.e. walking, sitting, standing and turning etc.) and manipulation (i.e. reaching and grasping, pulling and pushing and holding etc.) capabilities. Whole-body control techniques [9, 10] have matured over the past few years enabling various humanoids to interact with their environment in a more robust manner. There is a steady transition of robot's actions in predictable contacts to unpredictable ones. Forums like DARPA Robotics Challenge (DRC)[1], RoboCup[2] and other international robotic challenges [11]

---

[1] https://en.wikipedia.org/wiki/DARPA_Robotics_Challenge

[2] www.romela.org/robocup/

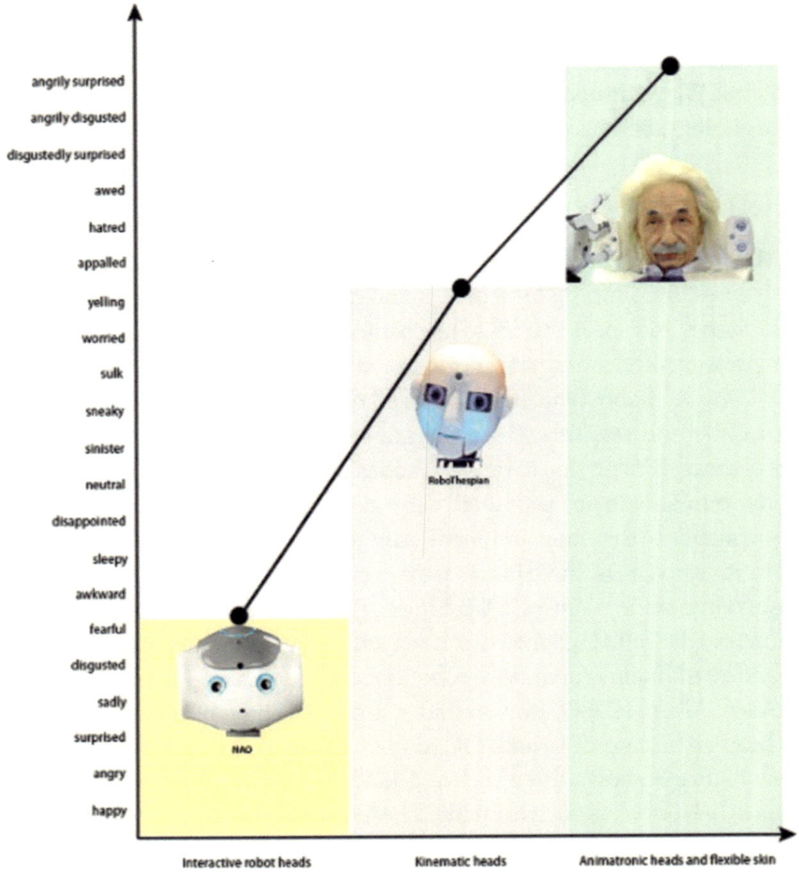

Figure 3. Comparison of three humanoid faces based on emotion expression capabilities [7].

are providing a platform for innovative researches in this area. Nevertheless there is always room for further improvement especially in the out-of-routine challenging situations, multiple and diverse contacts etc. The concept of sight in robots is now possible due to various components like servo-motors, actuators, 2D or 3D cameras and embedded optical sensors. Computer vision techniques for object recognition, human gestures, gaze and speaker tracking and collision or obstacle avoidance mimics sense of sight for the humanoids [12]. Distant communication with a robot using voice in an unconstrained environment is a highly challenging task. Methods to improve the auditory and speech recognition of a robot are being given much attention by the researchers [13–15].

2.2. Speech and linguistics

Speech is the most effective and natural mode of communication and interaction. From the view point of social robots, not only the robots need to be equipped with state-of-the-art automatic speech recognition (ASR) software [14], language models for interaction [16, 17] are also required to make semantic sense of what is being communicated to the robot. While ASR has its own challenges (noisy environments, multiple individuals talking, etc.), natural language processing has emerged as an important component of social robots which are expected to converse rather than simply accept keywords as commands. Such language models are important for the robot not only to understand what is being spoken but also to respond. Lee et al. [18] investigated the speech and language technologies involved in educational social robots and studied their impact in language learning. Brick and Scheutz [19] argue that robots must carry out their language processing incrementally with the ability to comprehend the context in order to meet the expectations of humans. Authors propose an interesting interaction engine (RISE) which incrementally processes the syntactic and semantic information. User **modeling** for effective natural language processing in long term human-robot interactions has also been proposed [20].

2.3. Cognition and perception

As we try to make machines that look and behave like people, we need to equip them with perceptual abilities similar to that of humans. As user expectations exceed, a robot's perception must go beyond basic functionalities (e.g. localization, navigation or obstacle avoidance etc.). A key mechanism to achieve this is user modeling. Comparative studies of humans and robots can lead to new approaches [21–23]. The classical approach is to deliberately abstract computational instructions from physical realization of a human's cognitive system. Such robots that can perceive, infer and learn to mimic human behaviors are called cognitive robots. Intelligence, in a cognitive robot is the ability to transform sensed information into behavior. Human beings exhibit multitude of communicative signals while interacting. For a successful social interaction, a socially interactive robot should recognize the interaction roles, verbal and non-verbal cues and situation; thus exhibit a considerable degree of "social intelligence".

Speech signals contain information about who is saying, what is being said and how it is being said. Context, tone, pitch and loudness all combine to convey information. Research regarding speech understanding in robotics include works like [24, 25], etc. In addition to vocalization, facial expressions, also give an insight into the intent of the social agent. Detection of human face and recognition of facial expressions is being incorporated in a socially believable robot. Cognitive empathy [26] is the phenomenon which models perception of emotions in robots. Gaze tracking [27] is another important aspect of perceiving the intentions of people while interaction, as it can indicate the focus of their attention. However gaze tracking involves detection of both face and eye orientation. Work is being carried out in this area but there are still numerous challenges that need to be addressed. Gestures and activity recognition [28], is also a promising area of research that can contribute to designing a socially intelligent robot.

2.4. Emotions and personality

Emotions play a significant role in human interaction; thus it was inevitable to induce emotions in socially interactive robots. The use of artificial emotions in social robots helps enhance believability and provides feedback to the users regarding the internal state of the robot, its goals and intentions. Artificial emotions [29], can also act as a control mechanism to understand robots perception of its surroundings. Numerous architectures have been proposed for introduction of artificial emotions but the most popular ones are based on bio-inspired models that include ethology, structure and psychology [30]. As mentioned in the previous section, there are several ways in which a robot can be made to express its emotions. Robots are now equipped with LEDs, motors and actuators beneath a flexible artificial skin to mimic various primary and secondary emotions. Aside mechanical actuation, computer graphics and animation techniques can also be applied to project emotions. Aside from facial gestures, robots are being designed to display emotions by other non-verbal cues like sound tone and pitch and body movements. The main purpose of expressing emotions is to convey readable signals to human for providing feedback and giving insight about robots intended plan of action.

Psychology defines personality as distinctive traits that distinguish an individual [31]. It is mainly the observers who define a person's personality. In terms of robots, five types of personalities are usually considered, i.e. Tool like, Pet or Creature, Cartoon, Artificial being and Human-like based on its morphology and functionality. According to studies [32], personality of a robot can also be determined based on its ability to interact, express emotions and react in a given situation. Much has been done to make a believable human replica, however our biological and psychological complexities are still not fully discovered or understood, making it extremely difficult to project them into a robot.

3. Human robot interaction

Human robot interaction (HRI) is an emerging research area, originating from the fast increasing integration of robots in our daily lives. In contrast to conventional human computer interaction models which usually involve interaction between users and a passive machine, human robot interaction is influenced by several factors. Researchers have tried to categorize HRI approaches. Goodrich and Schultz [33], divided HRI into two broad categories i.e. remote interaction and proximate interaction, based on the proximity level of both human and robot during interaction. According to Sheridan [34], HRI can be divided based on nature of application, i.e. tele-robots, tele-operators and social robots. HRI model for tele-robots mainly consists of human supervisory control of robots in performance of routine tasks. Such robots have limited capability of automation and rely on commands of their human supervisor. Tele-robots are mostly used in assembly lines, packaging, mail sorting, offices, and hospitals. They are capable of sensing their environment and reporting back to a human operator. HRI model for tele-operators involves remote control of robots in challenged environments like space, air, terrestrial, and under water for non-routine tasks. Both of these interaction models are basically master–slave in nature. Interaction with social robots is different from that of tele-robots and tele-operators mainly because it perceives robots not just as slaves but as peer-to-peer collaborators.

3.1. Human robot social interaction

According to Dautenhahn [35], human robot social interaction approaches can be divided into three general categories, i.e. robot-centered approaches, human-centered approaches and robot cognition-centered approaches. In robot-centered HRI model, social robots are pre-programmed to interact with humans. Sociable robots are usually designed based on such approaches. They proactively engage people in a social manner and the interaction is designed to be mutually beneficial for both participants i.e. humans can be motivated to perform a specific task (e.g. for therapeutic purposes etc.) whereas robots can use the conversation for learning purposes. On the other hand, socially evocative robots are designed to interact with humans based on human-centered perspective. Anthropomorphism plays a key role in such kind of interaction. In a way, human participant attributes social responsiveness to the robot participant. Reasoning and consequently learning capabilities of the robot are not central objective in this HRI model. Socially interactive robots have instigated another HRI approach which is centered on robot cognition. These robots aim to intelligently interact with their human counterparts. Nevertheless such type of HRI models are greatly influenced by various factors and mainly require deep modeling of human cognition.

3.1.1. Factors influencing human robot social interaction

Significant efforts are being made to model HRI with the objective to inculcate social intelligence in robots. Some suggest modeling of human behaviors and cognition as a sequence of instructions which are pre-programmed into the robots while the other approach is to imitate human behaviors and learn from interactions. Irrespective of the approach selected for designing a social HRI model, several common factors play vital role in shaping it and thus should be given due consideration.

3.1.1.1. Robot autonomy

According to Beer et al. [36], HRI is greatly influenced by levels of robot autonomy (LORA). From tele-operators to humanoids, LORA influences the way in which humans and robots interact. Hence in order to model HRI, we must first identify the variables that influence and are influenced by robot autonomy.

3.1.1.2. Robot intelligence and cognitive ability

A robot's intelligence and learning capabilities are important considerations as they influence what tasks a robots performs and how it performs them. A robots learning process may require a number of interactions with its human counterpart. Robots with high intelligence require lesser frequency of interactions than those with comparatively lesser intelligence.

3.1.1.3. Proxemics

Distance and orientation in social encounters between humans and robots is an important aspect [37]. A robot in close proximity may be able to hear human voice and detect facial expression clearly but might not be able to detect human gestures due to limitation in vision. On the other hand, a robot at a distance may detect full body gestures but is unable to carry out facial expressions and speech recognition.

3.1.1.4. Social and situation awareness

An important aspect of day-to-day interaction is the ability to perceive and abstract information from the environment. This phenomenon is termed as situation awareness and it helps in decision making, planning and responding accordingly while interaction. By use of various sensors a robot can be designed to sense its surroundings or perceive emotional condition of its interacting partner. Based on this information it can create a goal oriented understanding of its environment and finally respond either based on past experience, mimicry or adaptation. Nevertheless it is not surprising that human robot interactions might fail when at times even human-human interactions do. Giuliani et al. [38], described two types of failures in HRI, i.e. social norm violations and technical failures. Any deviation from the social script or the usage of the wrong social signals (i.e. correct action execution but inappropriate for the given situation) due to incorrect judgment of the robot is usually considered as social norm violation. On the other hand if a robot judges the situation correctly and selects the appropriate action but the action is poorly executed then this is termed as technical failure.

3.1.1.5. Verbal and non-verbal communication

Interaction between two or more participants is usually termed as a dialog. Exchange of information is the prime objective of a dialog. When humans engage in a dialog, they usually rely on a variety of para-linguistic social cues (i.e. facial expressions and gestures, etc.) in addition to words. Research [39], has proven such non-verbal cues to be highly effective for controlling human robot dialog. However robot's inability to fully interpret speech signals (e.g. pitch and tone etc.) alone, for complete comprehension of human emotions during an interaction can cause interaction failure. Gestures, facial expression and body movements add extra clues for the robot to understand the mental state of the participant and respond accordingly.

3.1.1.6. Cognitive or affective empathy

Empathy plays a vital role in interactions among people. It must therefore be an important consideration in the case of social robots and their interactions with humans [40]. It covers both a robot's capacity to understand human mental state and its ability to respond to that state appropriately.

3.1.1.7. Social influence and roboethics

User acceptance is the most important element in the success of any technology. In case of social robots, demographics, psychology and comfort of the human participant must be kept in mind while designing the HRI model. Another issue in human interactions is their being abided by certain rules called "social norms". These social attitudes approve or disapprove social interactions. A violation of social standards is considered a failure of interaction in both cases of human-human and human-robot interaction [41]. Roboethics is a field which incorporates various aspects of communication and social sciences to chalk out norms of human robot interaction. Keeping these ethics in view, while designing a social HRI model is vital for its acceptance.

3.1.2. Assessment and evaluation methodologies

As social HRI is gaining attention of the research community, a growing need is occurring for strong and efficient methods of its assessment and evaluation. Currently most of the assessment and evaluation criterion used in HRI are adapted from HCI either per se or with slight modifications. According to Beer et al. [36], assessment methodologies for HRI can be commonly characterized as process-oriented, diagnostic approach, ongoing and continuous. Similarly the evaluation methodologies include product-oriented, judgmental approach, final and discrete evaluations. Once again the factors that model HRI also decide which assessing methodologies are most suitable for it. Assessments can however be carried out in combination as well. Beer et al. [36] grouped existing assessment methodologies into three basic groups i.e. Social models which mainly involve assessment of emulation of empathy during HRI; technology acceptance model (TAM) and similar methodologies which represent user acceptance; behavioral adaptation model. Both the assessment and evaluation methodologies can be objective (e.g. task success, dialog quality and dialog efficiency etc.) or subjective (UTAUT model, Godspeed questionnaire etc.). Existing evaluation methodologies on HRI can also be divided as primary and non-primary based on how (i.e. directly or indirectly) they evaluate the HRI model. Popular primary evaluation methodologies used for human studies HRI include methods like self-assessments and subjective evaluations, behavioral measurements,

Evaluation methodologies	Description	Strengths	Weaknesses
Self-assessments and subjective evaluation	Includes psychometric measures, questionnaires, and/or surveys for personal assessment of participants in response to the robot and interaction.	Easily implemented, easily quantified.	Possibility of inaccuracy due to mental state and interpretation capabilities of the human participant; oriented towards engineering and leaves out social interaction perspective.
Behavioral measurements	Includes observation of human participants behavior while interacting with the agent.	Can be implemented in combination with other methodologies, e.g. self-assessment and subjective evaluation and psycho-behavioral measures.	Can be biased due to "Hawthorne effect".
Psycho-physiological measures	Observation of user behavior towards the agent repeatedly over a period of time.	Objective hence less biased; non-invasively measures stress and response of participants; video based reduces Hawthorne effect.	Can lead to misinterpretations due to complexity; requires prior knowledge of human participants; time consuming due to longitudinal in nature.
Task performance metrics	Involves more than one person or one robot; pre-set variables in the selection criteria for task performance.	Good for team scoring; less biased; good for evaluating HRI involving humanoids; good for HRI involving non-verbal behaviors in addition to verbal ones.	Not suitable for one-to-one HRI; less flexible method; not generalized enough for every HRI model; not suitable for robots other than humanoids or HRI which involves mainly verbal behaviors and not non-verbal cues; limited application areas.

Table 1. Existing evaluation methodologies for HRI.

psycho-physiological measures and task performance metrics. Strengths and weaknesses of these methods are summarized in **Table 1**.

Efforts have been done to outline some secondary methodologies like ease of classification, passive-social medium, numerical analysis of body movements and proximity theories for improved evaluation of HRI. Nevertheless due to the complexity of human robot social interaction researchers suggests the use of combination of more than one of the existing methodologies till empirical research can be mapped in theoretical concepts.

4. Application areas

In addition to research purposes, social robots find applications in a variety of problem areas including education, health care and entertainment.

4.1. Social robots in research

While a number of social robots have been designed to serve as test beds to evaluate the technological advancements in the design of social robots, a number of robots have been used as test subjects to replace humans. Social robots present an attractive alternative to humans to serve as test subjects in a number of experimental settings especially those involving risks, privacy or ethical issues [42, 43]. Likewise, operations which are difficult or controversial to carry out on humans can be performed on social robots. Not only human biasness can be avoided but evaluations can be repeatedly performed under identical conditions. Such social robots can serve as subjects to evaluate social interactions and study their influence on cognition. Among one of the early contributions, Kismet, a robot head designed by Breazeal [44] in the late 90s for affective computing, has been employed to study caregiver behavior among infants. Likewise, infanoid is an infant-like humanoid robot that has been used to study social development in the children. Its abilities to detect humans and objects, extract emotions of the interacting partner and imitate human voice allows its usage in investigating the development of social learning skills. Similarly, Cog, a well-known humanoid robot has been employed to evaluate the behavioral and learning models. Another widely used humanoid robot test bed is iCub that articulates a 3.5 years old child and has been designed to support research in cognitive functioning and artificial intelligence.

4.2. Entertainment

Entertainment robots (autonomous or remote controlled) include toys, pets, companions, cars and drones etc. While the interactions with robots like cars or drones are not expected to be humanoid, toys and pets (companions) are expected to interpret and behave as close as possible to their real world equivalents. Such robots directly target the consumers and hence cost is the most important parameter in designing entertainment robots. Optimizing the cost in the competitive robot market, in some cases, may result in comprising on the technology. Among popular toy robots is 'My Real Baby' developed by iRobot in partnership with a toy manufacturer. The robot is an expressive and responsive toy doll which can smile, laugh and

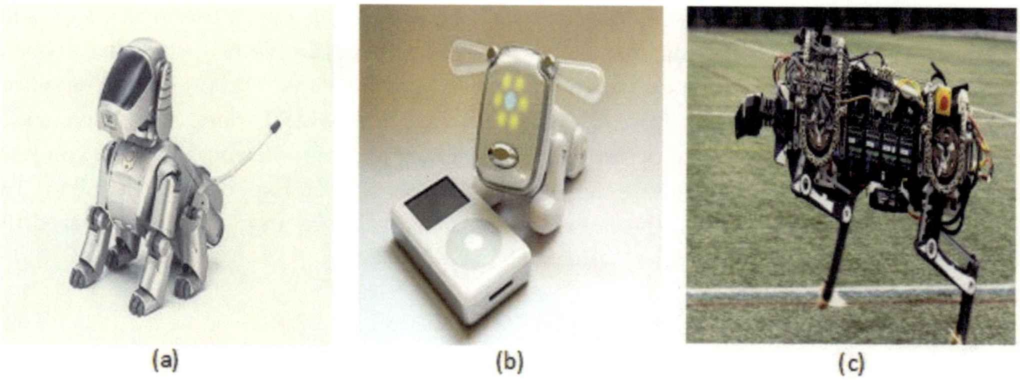

Figure 4. Zoomorphic robots: (a) AIBO, (b) iDog, (c) Cheetah.

imitate infant sounds. While such animated toy robots require their human masters to look after them, pet or companion robots are more autonomous. Mobility is one of the prime concerns in such companion (quadruped and wheeled) robots. Among these, AIBO [45] by Sony is one of the most advanced pet robots in the market that imitates the relationship between man and a pet dog. First introduced in 1999 in the market, different models were produced till 2005. One of the most sophisticated consumer robots, AIBO could respond to over 100 voice commands, learn to walk and play with a ball. Other similar pet robots include Poo-Chi, Pleo, iDog, Genibo and FIDO. In addition to entertainment, companion robots have also been designed for military and research purposes. Examples include Rhex, Canid, Cheetah, SCARAB, Rise and Titan. **Figure 4** shows some of the popular zoomorphic robots.

4.3. Healthcare

While surgical robots have been serving the medical sector for a long time, the relatively recent idea of employing social robots in the health sector has also been widely employed [46] for application like rehabilitation, elderly assistance and therapy etc. (**Figure 5a**). Researchers have investigated the possibilities of employing robots to educate and enhance the communication

Figure 5. Social robots in: (a) health care, (b) service, (c) education.

skill of children with disabilities. Likewise, social robots have also been useful as coaches for physical exercises and following diet plans. A well-known example of a coaching robot is Autom [47] that is designed to be a weight loss coach. Another similar robot, iRobiQ, monitors hypertension, manages medication and issues reminders. A wide variety of assistive social robots for elderly care have also been designed ranging from robotic wheelchairs to companion robots attempting to compensate the loss of a family member. Experiments with Paro, the therapeutic robot, revealed that the presence of a social robot in an old home increased the number of interactions among the elderly residents.

4.4. Service

Service robots are designed to assist human beings in doing everyday tasks including household chores (**Figure 5b**). Examples of these robots include PatrolBot for delivery, security, monitoring and guidance, Gita for cargo carrying, Roomba that serves as a vacuum cleaner, Sanbot that provide passenger services at airport and many more. Likewise, social robots like Rhino and Mobot have been designed to serve as guides for tourists. Severinson-Eklundh et al. [48] discuss the interaction models between humans and service robots using Cero as an example. The authors conclude that for satisfactory interactive sessions, the design considerations, in addition to the primary user of the service robot, should also take into account the group of people in the environment where the robot is intended to provide its services. Likewise, authors in [49] discuss the design issues interaction between humans and domestic robots using Roomba vacuum cleaner as a case study. The authors investigate the possibilities of smoothly 'fitting' such service robots in the home environment. A multi-modal design based on vision and speech is proposed in [50]. Though the models are discussed with service robots as applications, the authors claim that the proposed interaction cycle can be applied to general man-machine interaction scenarios as well.

4.5. Education

Beyond health care and services, robots have increasingly been used in the education sector as well. While introduction of robots in class room teaching makes the lectures interesting in the elementary schools, robots have been effectively employed in the higher educational institutes as well. Students of medicine, for instance, can perform complicated medical procedures on humanoid robots. Likewise, engineering students can use robots in complex or dangerous experimental or real world scenarios. One such popular educational robot is NAO (**Figure 5c**) developed by SoftBank Robotics. In addition to general education, NAO robots have also been employed to interact with autistic children. Robots can also serve as proxies both for students and teachers in case they are not able to attend the classes. A well-known series of such education robots has been designed by VGoRobotics. A key concern in using robots as teachers is the replacement of interpersonal relationships. Such robots also need to detect and adapt to the social mood of the environment they are deployed in. Some researchers argue that robots at elementary schools must change their behavior as a function of the activities of the children. A comprehensive review of the applicability of robots in education can be found in [51].

5. Challenges

Despite the emergent technological solutions at hand and conceptualizations regarding acceptability, there are considerable challenges to be addressed before social believability in robots can be considered a success. Literature [52, 53] suggests that the integration of social robots in human society poses both social and technical problems.

5.1. Complexity of social situations and ethics

In contrast to their successors, the industrial robots that are designed to carry out routine tasks in controlled environments and the field robots that work in places beyond human reach, social robots are expected to operate in a highly unpredictable and diverse habitat with its habitants that share the same traits. According to **S**alter et al. [54], real-world environments can prove to be both beneficial as well as challenging test grounds for assessing the capabilities of a robotic device. A gap still exists between the performance of an intelligent agent in a controlled environment and that in a real-world scenario. Limitations in replication of most **h**uman **r**obot **i**nteraction (HRI) scenarios greatly attribute in average adaptation of social robots in real-world situations. Empirical studies like [55], which investigate robots' acceptability and usability, explain the complexity of social situations and dimensions of HRI beyond the domestic vacuum cleaning robots. The capacity of a social robot to contextually understand the **behaviors** of the real world, its response to subjective experiences and user feedback

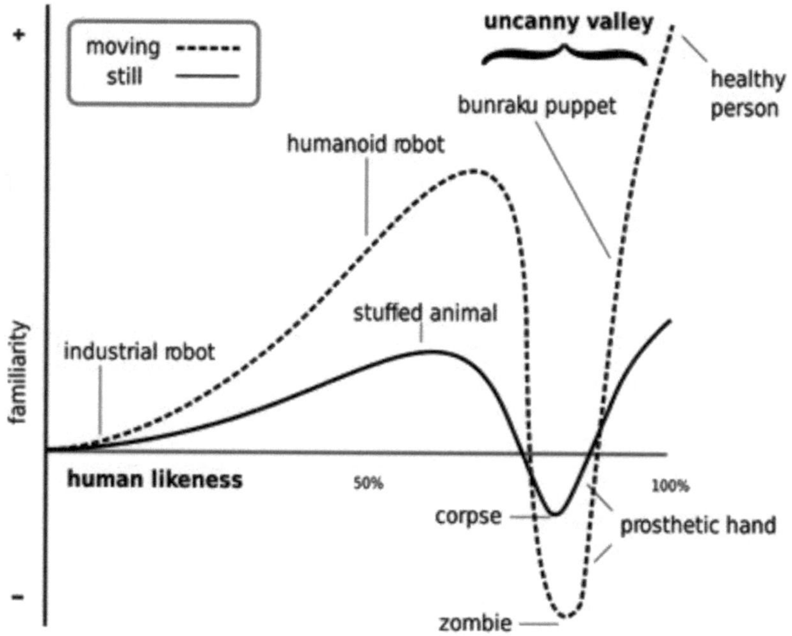

Figure 6. Mori's Uncanny Valley theory [8].

are actual performance parameters rather than technical capabilities alone. Despite its significance, context awareness in the design and development of social robots is still in its infancy.

Another limiting factor the integration of social robots in society is ethics. Interaction in social groups and relationship of a single individual with a machine is influenced by a variety of meta-principles and paradigms; thus making roboethics a challenging task. Diversity of cultures and religions make modeling of sensitive issues like human dignity and integrity, respect and family, privacy and protection, a complex task. Preservation of common principles of humanity and human rights in occasions which involve robotic intervention must be assessed keeping ethical sensitivity in view.

5.2. Hardware limitations vs. human expectations

The ultimate goal of anthropomorphism is to replicate a human being. Nevertheless our pursuit of making realistic humanoids might experience Mori's "Uncanny valley effect" at some point (**Figure 6**). Human expectations increase with a sophistication in design of a humanoid. This can attribute to people's rejection of anthropomorphic robots and other intelligent agents. On the other hand, recent studies like [56] suggest that shortcomings like mismatch between appearance and movement or voice can also create an uncanny or eerie feeling.

Despite great progression in the synthetic industry and mechatronics, we are still decades away from providing richer support for speech, gestures or expressions to machines. A look at the latest generation of humanoids reveals the gap between reality and fiction. The expressive behavior of robotic faces is still not life-like due to limitations of mechatronic design and control. Even for the most sophisticated generation of robots, displaying emotions reflects a certain degree of artificiality.

A robot's body is a mechanical structure composed of several rigid parts, connected to each other by joints. Currently each active joint has a restricted range of motion generated by actuators. Due to the complexity of design, manufacturing cost and mechanical dynamics, even the latest line of humanoids can imitate only basic tasks in a coordinated manner.

In contrast to conventional interactive systems, an interactive social robot must take its physical environment into consideration while communicating with users. Most real-world environments are unstructured, dynamic and noisy, making it challenging for robots. Although synthesized voice quality has improved over a period of time nevertheless communication between a human and a humanoid is still constrained by several factors like speech localization, language understanding, dialog management and non-verbal cues like gaze tracking etc.

5.3. Standard models and comparability issues

An essential prerequisite to designing an intelligent system is to outline its functional requirements. Same holds true for the field of cognitive robotics. Nevertheless, the fact that cognitive science, as a discipline, is yet to establish normative models itself that can be realized in well-engineered systems, makes it difficult to give robots a capacity for cognition [57]. Research in cognitive architectures for biologically inspired agents suffers from a significant void. This has resulted in modeling and trial of such agents in a controlled environment with most demonstrated results as mere proof-of-concept. Lack of relevant HRI models is another issue limiting the interaction capacity of a socially believable robot. The field of HRI incorporates contributions from both engineering sciences (communications, computer science and engineering) and human sciences (psychology and sociology). Due to its multidisciplinary nature it is difficult to generalize a standard HRI model. This is the reason that currently most HRI models are inspired by conventional HCI models. However there is a particular need for a dedicated social human robot interaction model as human interaction with social robots differs significantly from interaction with traditional passive computer based systems or agents.

Need for a comparison criterion is equally significant as the existence of benchmark architecture in the field of social robotics. Nevertheless it is not an easy task considering the dimensions of the test environment and diversity of outcome expectations. According to Bartneck et al. [58], "quick and dirty" methods adopted by most robot developers, result in questionable success of targeted goals. Recent studies like [59], suggest introduction of "Human in the loop" approach. Application and modification of User Experience Design (UXD) evaluation techniques in addition to relevant criteria of evaluation in HCI must be considered for designing performance comparability metrics suitable for HRI. However research in this area is still in its infancy.

6. Conclusion

As we progress, the reality of socially believable robots in our daily lives is becoming more vivid. The relationship between humans and robots has crept beyond Master–Slave but instead has become that of peers. Social robots are already assisting us in health care, education and entertainment. They are serving as our tour guides and office assistants. Soon they will be our companions in our homes. Nevertheless our optimism can dampen if we are unable to overcome the challenges and limitations, we face today. It is evident that technological advancement alone cannot contribute fully without complete understanding of humans and society. Efforts must be taken to reduce the complexity of human psychology and society in order to model effective human robot social interactions.

In order to achieve success, human in the loop concept must be incorporated as frequently as possible. Defining roles and rules might make it easier for a social robot to comprehend its surroundings and respond appropriately. Furthermore a socially interactive robot requires frequent interactions with a wide range of users: different genders, different cultural and social backgrounds, different ages, etc. for it to understand the needs and dimensions of various social situations. In many current applications and experimentations, social robots engage only in short-term interactions with their human counterparts and thus treat all humans in the same manner. This usually results in a failure in HRI as perceived by its users. As robot designers and engineers tackle with issues like cost effectiveness, user acceptance and social awareness, mass integration of these mechanical companions in our everyday life might take a while.

Author details

Momina Moetesum* and Imran Siddiqi

*Address all correspondence to: reach.momina@gmail.com

Department of Computer Sciences, Bahria University, Islamabad, Pakistan

References

[1] Fong T, Nourbakhsh I, Dautenhahn K. A survey of socially interactive robots. Robotics and Autonomous Systems. 2003;**42**:143-166

[2] Dautenhahn K, Billard A. Bringing up robots or—The psychology of socially intelligent robots: From theory to implementation. In: Proceedings of the Third Annual Conference on Autonomous Agents; ACM; 1999. pp. 366-367

[3] Lazzeri N, Mazzei D, Zaraki A, De Rossi D. Towards a believable social robot. In: Conference on Biomimetic and Biohybrid Systems; Spring; 2013. pp. 393-395

[4] Breazeal C. Toward sociable robots. Robotics and Autonomous Systems. 2003;**42**(3):167-175

[5] Fink J. In: Ge SS, Khatib O, Cabibihan J-J, Simmons, editors. Anthropomorphism and Human Likeness in the Design of Robots and Human-Robot. Berlin, Heidelberg: Springer Berlin Heidelberg; 2012. pp. 199-208. DOI:10.1007/978-3-642-34103-8_20

[6] Mori M. The uncanny valley. Energy. 1970;**7**(4):33-35

[7] Introrobotics. 3 different humanoid robot head designs to generate facial expressions [Internet]. February 27, 2015. Available from: https://www.intorobotics.com/3-different-humanoid-robot-head-designs-to-generate-facial-expressions/

[8] Cubber GD, Doroftei D, Rudin K, Berns K, Matos A, Serrano D, Silva E. Introduction to the Use of Robotic Tools for Search and Rescue. In Search and Rescue Robotics-From Theory to Practice. InTech; 2017. DOI: 10.5772/intechopen.69489

[9] Balderas D, Rojas M. Human Movement Control. In Automation and Control Trends. InTech; 2016. DOI: 10.5772/intechopen.63720

[10] Dai H, Valenzuela A, Tedrake R. Whole-body motion planning with centroidal dynamics and full kinematics. In: 2014 14th IEEE-RAS International Conference on Humanoid Robots (Humanoids); 2014. pp. 295-302

[11] Fontana G, Matteucci M, Amigoni F, Schiaffonati V, Bonarini A, Lima PU. RoCKIn Benchmarking and Scoring System. In RoCKIn-Benchmarking Through Robot Competitions. InTech; 2017. DOI: 10.5772/intechopen.70013

[12] Kılıç V, Wang W. Audio-visual speaker tracking. Motion Tracking and Gesture Recognition. InTech; 2017. DOI: 10.5772/intechopen.68146

[13] Ishi CT, Matsuda S, Kanda T, Jitsuhiro T, Ishiguro H, Nakamura S, Hagita N. Robust speech recognition system for communication robots in real environments. In: 2006 6th IEEE-RAS International Conference on Humanoid Robots; IEEE; 2006. pp. 340-345

[14] Wang N, Broz F, Di Nuovo A, Belpaeme T, Cangelosi A. A user-centric design of service robots speech interface for the elderly. In: Recent Advances in Nonlinear Speech Processing. Springer International Publishing; 2016. pp. 275-283

[15] Noda K, Yamaguchi Y, Nakadai K, Okuno HG, Ogata T. Audio-visual speech recognition using deep learning. Applied Intelligence. 2015;**42**(4):722-737

[16] Lauria S, Bugmann G, Kyriacou T, Bos J, Klein A. Training personal robots using natural language instruction. IEEE Intelligent Systems. 2001;**16**(5):38-45

[17] Kaigorodova L, Rusetski K, Nikalaenka K, Hetsevich Y, Gerasuto S, Prakapovich R, Sychou U, Lysy S. Language modeling for robots-human interaction. In: International NooJ Conference; Spring; 2015. pp. 162–171

[18] Lee S, Kim C, Lee J, Noh H, Lee K, Lee GG. Affective effects of speech-enabled robots for language learning. In: Spoken Language Technology Workshop (SLT), 2010 IEEE; 2010. pp. 145-150

[19] Brick T, Scheutz M. Incremental natural language processing for HRI. In: Human-Robot Interaction (HRI), 2007 2nd ACM/IEEE International Conference on; IEEE; 2007. pp. 263-270

[20] Hameed IA. Using natural language processing (NLP) for designing socially intelligent robots. In: 2016 Joint IEEE International Conference on Development and Learning and Epigenetic Robotics (ICDL-EpiRob); IEEE; 2016. pp. 268-269

[21] Karapinar S, Sariel S. Cognitive robots learning failure contexts through real-world experimentation. Autonomous Robots. 2015;**39**(4):469-485

[22] Borghi AM, Cangelosi A. Action and language integration: From humans to cognitive robots. Topics in Cognitive Science. 2014;**6**(3):344-358

[23] Belpaeme T, Adams S, de Greeff J, di Nuovo A, Morse A, Cangelosi A. Social development of artificial cognition. In: Toward Robotic Socially Believable Behaving Systems-Volume I. Spring; 2016. pp. 53-72

[24] Noda K, Yamaguchi Y, Nakadai K, Okuno HG, Ogata T. Audio-visual speech recognition using deep learning. Applied Intelligence. 2015;**42**(4):722-737

[25] Ding Ing Jr, Shi J-Y. Kinect microphone array-based speech and speaker recognition for the exhibition control of humanoid robots. Computers & Electrical Engineering. 2017;**62**:719-729

[26] Tisseron S, Tordo F, Baddoura R. Testing empathy with robots: A model in four dimensions and sixteen items. International Journal of Social Robotics. 2015;**7**(1):97-102

[27] Palinko O, Rea F, Sandini G, Sciutti A. Eye gaze tracking for a humanoid robot. In: 2015 IEEE-RAS 15th International Conference on Humanoid Robots (Humanoids); IEEE; 2015. pp. 318-324

[28] Rautaray SS, Agrawal A. Vision based hand gesture recognition for human computer interaction: A survey. Artificial Intelligence Review. 2015;**43**(1):1-54

[29] Novikova J, Watts L. Towards artificial emotions to assist social coordination in hri. International Journal of Social Robotics. 2015;**7**(1):77-88

[30] Wehle, Marko and Weidemann, Alexandra, Boblan IW. Research on human cognition for biologically inspired developments: Human-robot interaction by biomimetic AI. In: Advanced Research on Biologically Inspired Cognitive Architectures; IGI Global; 2017. pp. 83-116

[31] Boyce CJ, Wood AM, Powdthavee N. Is personality fixed? Personality changes as much as "variable" economic factors and more strongly predicts changes to life satisfaction. Social Indicators Research 2013;**111**(1):287-305

[32] Lee KM, Peng W, Jin S-A, Yan C. Can robots manifest personality? An empirical test of personality recognition, social responses, and social presence in human-robot interaction. Journal of Communication. 2006;**56**(4):754-772

[33] Goodrich MA, Schultz AC. Human-robot interaction: A survey. Foundations and Trends in Human-Computer Interaction. 2007;**1**(3):203-275

[34] Sheridan TB. Human-robot interaction: Status and challenges. Human Factors. 2016;**58** (4):525-532

[35] Dautenhahn K. Socially intelligent robots: Dimensions of human-robot interaction. Philosophical Transactions of the Royal Society of London B: Biological Sciences. 2007;**362** (1480):679-704

[36] Beer J, Fisk AD, Rogers WA. Toward a framework for levels of robot autonomy in human-robot interaction. Journal of Human-Robot Interaction. 2014;**3**(2):74

[37] Mead R, Matarić MJ. Proxemics and performance: Subjective human evaluations of autonomous sociable robot distance and social signal understanding. In: 2015 IEEE/RSJ International Conference on Intelligent Robots and Systems (IROS); IEEE; 2015. pp. 5984-5991

[38] Giuliani M et al. Systematic analysis of video data from different human-robot interaction studies: A categorization of social signals during error situations. In: Frontiers in psychology. 2015;**6**. ISSN: 1664-1078

[39] Mavridis N. A review of verbal and non-verbal human-robot interactive communication. Robotics and Autonomous Systems. 2015;**63**:22-35

[40] Leite I, Pereira A, Mascarenhas S, Martinho C, Prada R, Paiva A. The influence of empathy in human-robot relations. International Journal of Human-Computer Studies. 2013;**71**(3):250-260

[41] Thellman S, Ziemke T. Social attitudes toward robots are easily manipulated. In: Proceedings of the Companion of the 2017 ACM/IEEE International Conference on Human-Robot Interaction; ACM; 2017. pp. 299-300

[42] Hayashi K, Sakamoto D, Kanda T, Shiomi M, Koizumi S, Ishiguro H, Ogasawara T, Hagita N. Humanoid robots as a passive-social medium—A field experiment at a train station. In: 2007 2nd ACM/IEEE International Conference on Human-Robot Interaction (HRI); 2007. pp. 137-144

[43] Scassellati B. Investigating Models of Social Development Using a Humanoid Robot. Biorobotics. CiteSeer; 2000

[44] Breazeal C, Scassellati B. Infant-like social interactions between a robot and a human caregiver. Adaptive Behavior. 2000;**8**(1):49-74

[45] Steels L, Kaplan F. AIBO's first words: The social learning of language and meaning. Evolution of Communication. 2000;**4**(1):3-32

[46] Lu EC, Wang RH, Hebert D, Boger J, Galea MP, Mihailidis A. The development of an upper limb stroke rehabilitation robot: Identification of clinical practices and design requirements through a survey of therapists. Disability and Rehabilitation: Assistive Technology. 2011;**6**(5):420-431

[47] Ricks DJ, Colton MB. Trends and considerations in robot-assisted autism therapy. In: 2010 IEEE International Conference on Robotics and Automation (ICRA). 2010; pp. 4354-4359

[48] Severinson-Eklundh K, Green A, Hüttenrauch H. Social and collaborative aspects of interaction with a service robot. Robotics and Autonomous Systems. 2003;**42**(3):223-234

[49] Forlizzi J, DiSalvo Carl. Service robots in the domestic environment: a study of the roomba vacuum in the home. In: Proceedings of the 1st ACM SIGCHI/SIGART Conference on Human-Robot Interaction; ACM; 2006. pp. 258-265

[50] Ido J, Matsumoto Y, Ogasawara T, Nisimura R. Humanoid with interaction ability using vision and speech information. In: 2006 IEEE/RSJ International Conference on Intelligent Robots and Systems; IEEE; 2006. pp. 1316-1321

[51] Mubin O, Stevens CJ, Shahid S, Al Mahmud A, Dong J-J. A review of the applicability of robots in education. Journal of Technology in Education and Learning. 2013;**1**:209-0015

[52] Tapus A, Maja M, Scassellatti B. The grand challenges in socially assistive robotics. IEEE Robotics and Automation Magazine. 2007;**14**(1):35-42

[53] Salem M, Lakatos G, Amirabdollahian F, Dautenhahn K. Towards safe and trustworthy social robots: Ethical challenges and practical issues. In: Tapus A, André E, Martin JC, Ferland F, Ammi M, editors. Social Robotics. Lecture Notes in Computer Science. Springer, Cham. ICSR. 2015;**9388**:584-593

[54] Salter T, Michaud F, Larouche H. How wild is wild? A taxonomy to characterize the 'wildness' of child-robot interaction. International Journal of Social Robotics. 2010;**2**(4): 405-415

[55] Sung JY, Grinter RE, Christensen HI. Domestic robot ecology. International Journal of Social Robotics. 2010;**2**(4):417-429

[56] Mitchell WJ, Szerszen KA Sr, Lu AS, Schermerhorn PW, Scheutz M, KF MD. A mismatch in the human realism of face and voice produces an uncanny valley. I-Perception. 2011; **2**(1):10-12

[57] Lieto A. Representational limits in cognitive architectures. Cognitive Robot Architectures. 2017;**16**

[58] Bartneck C, Kulić D, Croft E, Zoghbi S. Measurement instruments for the anthropomorphism, animacy, likeability, perceived intelligence, and perceived safety of robots. International Journal of Social Robotics. 2009;**1**(1):71-81

[59] Alenljung B, Lindblom J, Andreasson R, Ziemke T. User experience in social human-robot interaction. International Journal of Ambient Computing and Intelligence (IJACI). 2017; **8**(2):12-31

Chapter 2

A Control System for Detecting Emotions on Visual Interphase Stimulus

Fatima Isiaka, Kassim Mwitondi and
Adamu M. Ibrahim

Additional information is available at the end of the chapter

http://dx.doi.org/10.5772/intechopen.75873

Abstract

Complex dynamic contents of visual stimuli induce implicit reactions in a user. This leads to changes in physiological processes of the user which is referred to as stress. Our goal is to model and produce a system that represents the mechanical interactions of the body and eye movement behavior. We are particularly concerned with the skin conductance response (SCR) and eye fixations to visual stimulus and build a dynamic system that detects stress and its correlates to visual widgets. The process consists of the following modules: (1) a hypothesis generator for suggesting possible structural changes that result from the direct interaction with visual stimulus, (2) an information source for responding to operator querying about users' interactive and physiological processes, and (3) a continuous system simulator for simulating and illustrating physiological reactions during interaction. This model serves as an infrastructure for modeling physiological processes and could be of benefit in usability laboratory, web developers, and designers of interactive systems, enabling evaluators to visualize interface as a better access to identifying areas that cause stress to users.

Keywords: physiological process, widgets, control systems, cognitive load, SCR, eye fixations

1. Introduction

A common finding in cognitive neuroscience [1] states that a person's perception of their behavior does not always relate to their neural activity. Experiments have shown that people do not always know what is going on inside their minds. For instance, in an eye-tracking study that involved reading [2], real-time quantitative measures of eye movements revealed longer fixation times for reading text with transposed letters as compared to reading normal

IntechOpen

© 2018 The Author(s). Licensee IntechOpen. This chapter is distributed under the terms of the Creative Commons Attribution License (http://creativecommons.org/licenses/by/3.0), which permits unrestricted use, distribution, and reproduction in any medium, provided the original work is properly cited.

text even though readers claimed to spend just a few seconds on text with transposed letters. Also, electroencephalography (EEG) of language processing [3] has concluded that phrases judged as easy to comprehend and highly acceptable sometimes entail a larger processing effort on the part of the readers.

Control systems are sometimes used to understand the mechanism behind human computer interaction to provide industry-standard algorithms and applications that systematically analyze, design, and tune linear control systems. In this aspect, a system can be specified as a state-space model, transfer function, frequency-response model, or zero polegain. Some applications and functions, such as step response plot and Bode plot, let us visualize system behavior in time domain and frequency domain, which was observed in the result section of the chapter to analyze the behavior of our final system response. The compensator parameters are tuned using automatic, Bode loop shaping method in MATLAB; this was used to validate the design by verifying the rise time, settling time, phase, and gain margins. To understand the systems dynamics between eye movement and the visual stimuli, we adopt the second differential equation Eq. (1), which represents the prediction focus, 4 min from the detected fixations, and visual contents that induce stress. Therefore, the main objectives of this chapter include:

- reviewing some related works,
- development of a control system for detecting emotions,
- testing the performance of process on multiple orders, and
- simulating the physiological processes.

2. Related works

More work has been carried out in developing comprehensive web-based and software interfaces that can adapt to significant end-user needs. Some of this work requires the development of adaptive algorithms to learn about changes in user interests or emotions [4]. A flawless user interface (UI) would automatically adapt or change its layout and web content elements to suit the needs of the users and similarly allow for users themselves to alter the contents of the UI [5].

Users easily adapt to the less com plex applications due to the cognitive ability to easily familiarize themselves with friendly and well-designed interphases, such as those used as a means of information distribution and learning [6]. Visually complex applications change the way users view content [7]. Reactions from the users can relay quantitative information when physiological sensors are part of the equipment used to study and interpret perception.

Other state-of-the-art techniques, such as that written by Dean C Karnopp et al. [8] and that of Franziska Kretzschmar and Simon P Liversedge et al. [9, 10], try to find the mystery surrounding emotions, how they work, and how they affect our lives have which not yet been unraveled. But recent techniques such as [11–13] developed a system and method provided for detecting emotional states, one of which uses statistics. A speech is first received and then an acoustic parameter is extracted from the speech signal. Then statistics or features from samples of the voice are calculated from extracted speech parameters. The features serve as inputs to a classifier, which can be a computer program, a device, or both. The classifier assigns at least one emotional state from a finite number of possible emotional states to the speech signal. Such techniques enable scientists to further debate the real nature of emotions, whether they are evolutionary, physiological, or cognitive to explain affective states. Results from applying this methodology on real-time data collected from a single subject demonstrated a recognition level of 71.4% which is comparable to the best results achieved. The detection mechanism outlined in this chapter has most of the characteristics required to perform emotion detection on real-time visual stimulus.

3. Methods

An experiment was conducted [14, 15] in which a single participant interacted with three different visual interphases—games, webpage, and a textbook. The user's physiological readings were taken alongside the eye movement measured with an eye tracker. The rationale for choosing these interphases is derived from the fact that all stimuli contain dynamic contents and involve cognitive workload on the user that induces slight stress. For creating a system control capable of identifying users' emotion on an interphase, MATLAB was used for its signal processing and system identifiable toolbox capable of developing dynamic systems. The following sections discuss these visuals and tasks involved.

3.1. Adera

Adera is a story-driven adventure game that involves a single player; it allows to solve puzzles, collect artifacts, and explore the environments to reveal the mysteries of a new-found civilization. The episodic story involved begins when the player receives a message from a missing person known as the grandfather (Hawk). The game involves some cognitive processing on the part of the user. The user interacts with the first episode, while his eye movement was taken.

3.2. Yahoo webpage

The Yahoo homepage is a very popular site where most regular users frequent for currents news and entertainment widgets. The user was simply asked to locate news or entertainment contents that were of interest and interact with while the physiological measures were taken.

3.3. Textbook

The textbook (The Designer) incentive involves locating an interesting phrase from a stimulus page that captures the reader's attention at a single glance. All the tasks are contrived, simply to induce slight stress so we can observe the amplitudes or increase in physiological response in reaction to the visual interphase.

3.4. Physiological measures

The physiological measures adopted for the experiment includes SCR, skin temperature (ST), and eye movement (saccade and fixations). These user attributes are used to measure changes in reaction to dynamic contents on the visual interphase.

1. SCR/ST: The SCR measures the electrical changes of the skin; it provides a functional signal of emotional responses by measuring the electrodermal (EDA) changes of the skin, caused because of sweat [16]. The skin temperature (ST) changes according to blood circulation at the surface of the skin through body tissue. In a state of increased emotion, such as interest or stress, muscle fibers contract and cause a stenosis of the vasculature [17, 18].

2. Eye movement: This is the behavior of the eye during interaction; the eye-gaze pattern is a measure of behavior. The movement of a user's eyes is based on fixations (location of a user's eye gaze), saccades (rapid movements of the eye from one fixation to another) as indicated in **Figure 1**.

3.5. Hypothesis generator

The concepts behind modeling physiological processes involve setting to get a significant accuracy and a prediction focus close to original data model; the model adopts the concepts for physical processes on dynamic systems [8], a least squares technique applied to system controls. For a user attribute saved from the sensors, the entire system is represented by the expression in Eqs. (1) and (2); the model fit to data represents prediction focus, 4 min from the detected fixations, and corresponding stress levels.

$$\frac{du}{dy} = Cu(y) + Fr(y) + e \tag{1}$$

$$y(m) = Gr(y) + Hr(y) + e \tag{2}$$

where $y(m)$ is the response variables (stress levels) that determine coefficients of physiological reactions with computed variables $r(y)$, C, F, G, and H are the estimated coefficients with noise

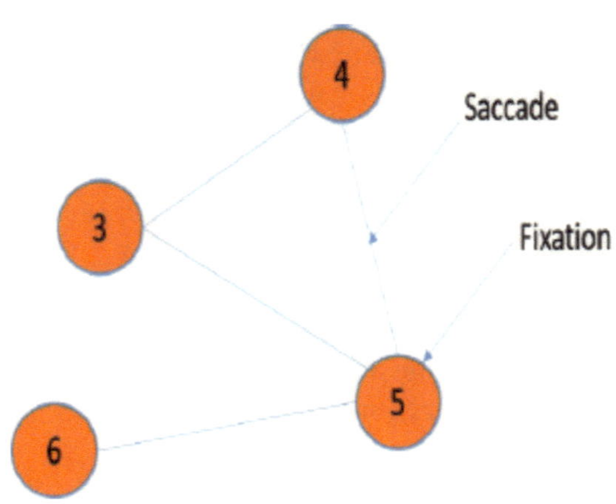

Figure 1. Fixations and saccades of eye movement.

e. The input generator is a discrete time-identified model fit representing the set of values the physiological reaction processes can take in response to dynamic visual stimuli. The primary data sources are measured in frequency (Herz and rads) and contain both categorical and numeric variables that contribute to making predictions on the multiple response output using multiple inputs (MIMO), for this case, $y \ and \ y_m$ are the response outputs (**Figure 2**). This represents the affects' states and fixations. The model is tested on the different estimated polynomial orders of the differential equation u(y). An identity state space object is created with C as the estimated initial state for the model, that is, the possible set of values the process can take, F is the estimated coefficients as a product of physiological parameters, G is the estimated output, and H the transformation matrix with noise e; y(m) is used to represent other response variables like the eye movement (fixations on the interphases). The threshold is set based on unique baseline such that:

$$thresh = 0.5\left(mean_{amplitude} - minimum_{SCR}\right) \tag{3}$$

The alternate hypothesis is chosen if the rules does not apply to the null hypothesis, that is, H0: stress is constant if $thresh < mean_{amplitude}$, Ha: stress fluctuates if thresh $> mean_{amplitude}$. The affect states to identify are stress, relaxed, and a neutral mood on the interphase. To detect the affect state, control is directed to a logical output in a loop which has a place holder for the dimensions of the physiological response.

The module to identify the optimal responses correlating to user's mood is given in the following steps (Algorithm 1), the 'FINDPEAKS' function detects and finds phasic changes in physiological signals and high-level tonic phases (Appendix 1). Red indicates stress; blue and purple indicate relaxed and a neutral mood, respectively. The predicted fixations on the visual interphase indicate possible moves or positions for the user to reach their goal.

Algorithm 1. Algorithm to detect affect state on visual interphase.

```
procedure FINDPEAKS
        [peaks, locs] ← findpeaks(Response.eda, magenta'minpeakdistance', 15;)
        m ← length(locs) ;
        thresh ← 0.5*(mean(amplitude) − min(eda)) ;
top:
        if mean(peaks) > = thresh < = baseline then return false
                disp('stressed')
elseif mean(peaks) < = thresh > = baseline.

                disp('neutral')
else.
                disp('relaxed')
end.
end.
```

```
loop:
    if size(emotion2) = [0, 1] ; then
            emotion2 ← 1. else
            emotion2 ← emotion2.
end.
            emotion1 = strmatch('stressed', PP12.Affectate(locs(m)));
            emotion2 = strmatch('neutral', PP12.Affectate(locs(m)));
            goto loop.
            close;
    X ← Response.MappedFixationPointX(locs(emotion1)) ;.
    Y ← Response.MappedFixationPointY(locs(emotion1)) ;.
    XX ← Response.MappedFixationPointX(locs(emotion2)) ;.
    YY ← Response.MappedFixationPointY(locs(emotion2)) ;.
    goto top.
```

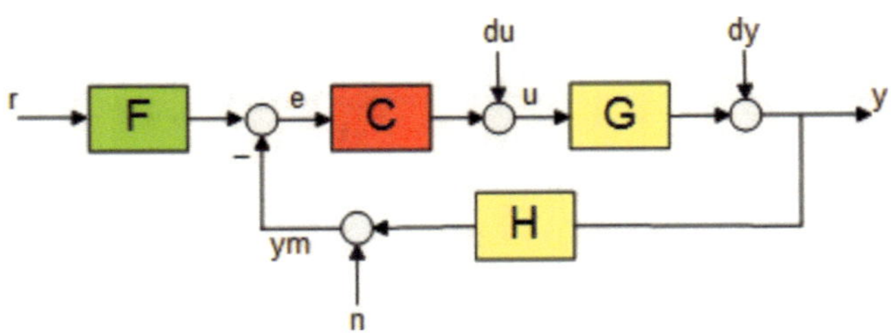

Figure 2. Control system feedback configuration.

3.6. Operator querying

The mechanism involved is a direct synchronization of the two-sensor port while there is a querying model for the system output. This helps to identify optimal responses in the physiological measure that correlates to visual attention on the part of the user. The next exposition discusses analysis and findings from the control system.

4. Analysis and implementation

Possible strategies to locate the missing person in the Adera interphase is indicated by the predicted fixations. Rather than following the original eye movement (pink circles), the player can retrace the steps and identify the missing person by following the predictions. Four areas indicating stress mood were detected. One of these is on a commercial widget at the right upper edge of the interphase. The neural point is detected inside the game interphase. The predicted and original (natural) response lying in the same cartesian coordinate of the Adera game interphase (**Figure 3**) shows possibility of a high performance of the control model. The stress and neutral mood are indicated of the three affect states generated. One interesting aspect is the stress point at the area where a question mark is located on the interphase just close to the position where we have a pointing black arrow. This icon (question mark) is there to provide suggestions on which direction/strategy to take in locating the missing person. The user was seen to be undecided whether to make a move on and make use of the lifeline

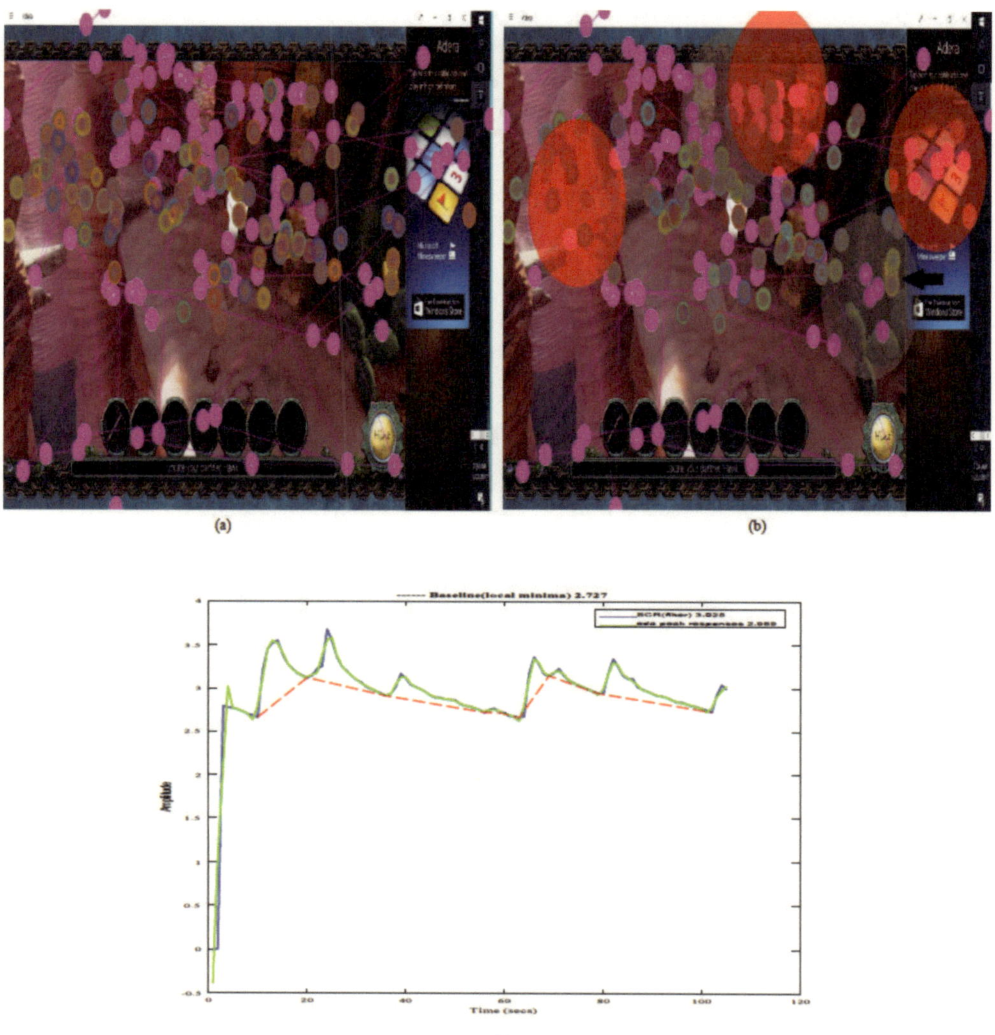

Figure 3. Detected affect state and correlating physiological reaction to Adera episode 1.

or simply ignore this icon, hence, the appearance of a stress indicator (neutral mood) on that area. The pattern or arrangement of fixations toward that direction indicates it might be the right strategy to take; these predicted points are indicated close to the question mark content. The user also experienced a stress mood, while looking at the advert section on the right side of the interphase. The participants' physiological reaction toward that phase indicates more phasic changes, hence, there is a higher emotion indicator (stress and neutral moods) toward the interphase with an average baseline response of $2.72\mu s$. At the point where a stress and a relaxed indicator intersects, a neutral indicator is produced (purple indicator).

On the yahoo interphase (**Figure 4**), there are different dynamic and static contents that can distract the user and induce both positive and negative emotions. The user feels a neutral mood toward the dynamic picture content having the headline "Silicon Vas reacts to Trump inauguration" which is indicated by the neutral points close to and on the picture content. The user's physiological reaction toward the interphase suggests an increase in amplitude between 20 and 40 s in the interaction. This interval correlates to the convoluted fixation points close to the dynamic picture content. The pattern for the predicted response lies in the same convoluted pattern as the original response.

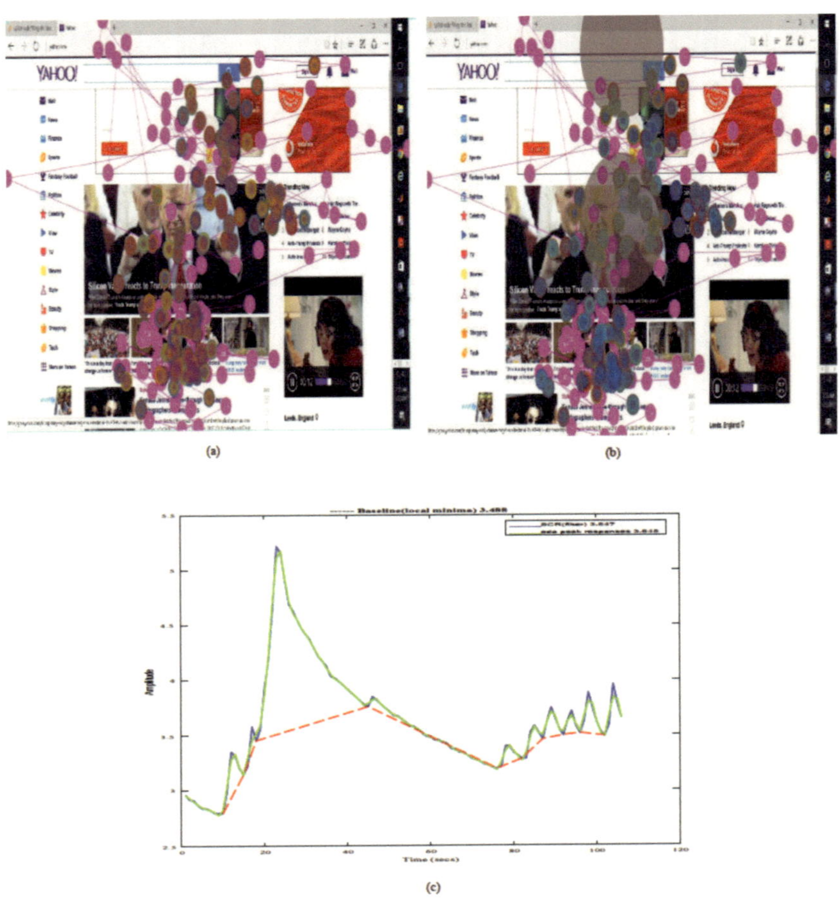

Figure 4. Detected affect state and correlating physiological reaction to yahoo page.

http://dx.doi.org/10.5772/intechopen.75873

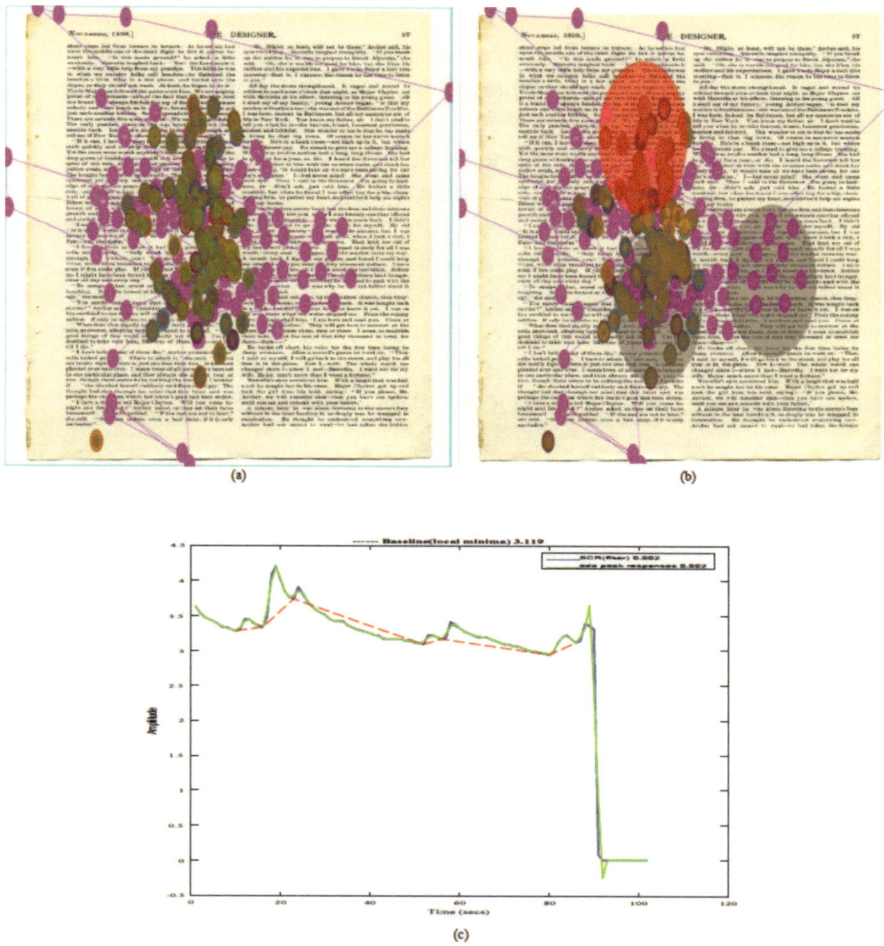

Figure 5. Detected affect state on Adera episode 1. (a)Textbook with original fixation and prediction fixation,(b)Detected emotion on Textbook,(c)Detected affect state and correlating physiological reaction to Textbook.

The reaction of the user to the book interphase stimulus suggests confusion and an undecided strategy to take when locating an interesting peace of phrase he might find interesting. This is with an average baseline on 3.1μ which is quite high for this interphase. The natural law of attention is that the gaze is directed to the center of the book, as seen by the convoluted arrangement of fixations of both the predicted and natural eye movement on one point at the center of the book interphase stimuli. The pattern of the predicted eye movement suggests the possible strategy he could take on that area to locate an interesting piece of phrase. Three affect indicators were located on this interphase, two of which are neutral and the other a stress mood. The emotion of the user can be seen and is indicated by the three-emotion detector on the spot (**Figure 5**).

5. Results

The state variables used to estimate the coefficient of the control systems were defined by the input parameters which the signal provided. The sensors were used to generate the primary data that serves as the user attributes. These are the SCR, ST, and eye movement represented as fixations. Multiple polynomial orders were chosen to run the model. The best of these include polynomial order 1–3; this gives a precise representation of the physiological reaction to the dynamic contents on the interphase. This concept represents that which is applied to physical systems. This is very appropriate, if the goal is to predict and indicate emotion on visual interphase. We have to go beyond the normal approach to apply a multidimensional procedure to achieve the targeted objective. For the Adera Episode 1 interphase, both polynomial order one and three have the same phasic change when compared to polynomial order one. The phasic response of the MappedFX (input 3) with MappedFY (response variable) has the same but opposite reaction to the systems control; this is a positive and negative effect to the connection between the user and the Adera interphase. The SCR (input 1) has a positive effect in the connection, and this implies that it is a good indicator of the emotional response for the Adera interphase (**Figure 6**).

The magnitude of the response on all inputs has a positive impact to the systems' interphase between the webpage (**Figure 7a**) and the user. For this case, applying polynomial order one and two have the same phasic change compared to three. The input ST have the same magnitude and phasic change for all polynomial order. The different variations in phasic changes are indicated in the input 3 and input 4 to the response output. On the other hand, all inputs have the same magnitude and phasic change for the polynomial orders used in the text-user interphase interaction; using order three and two runs on the system on average signifies

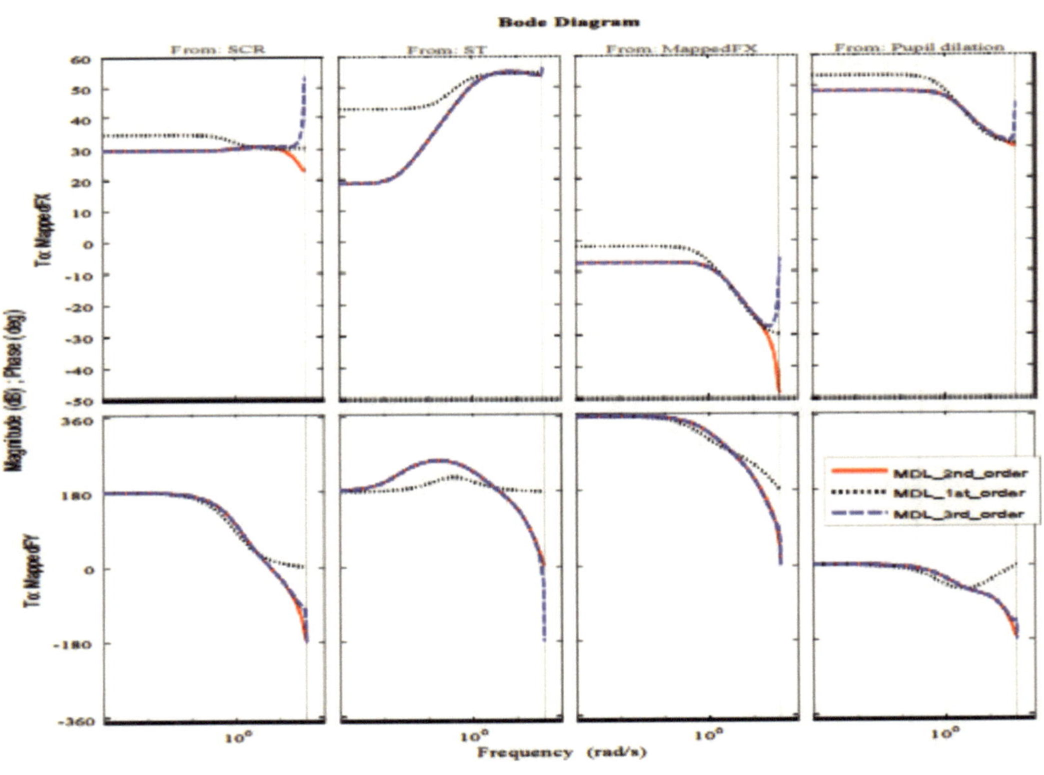

Figure 6. Bode plot of the system on Adera interphase.

http://dx.doi.org/10.5772/intechopen.75873

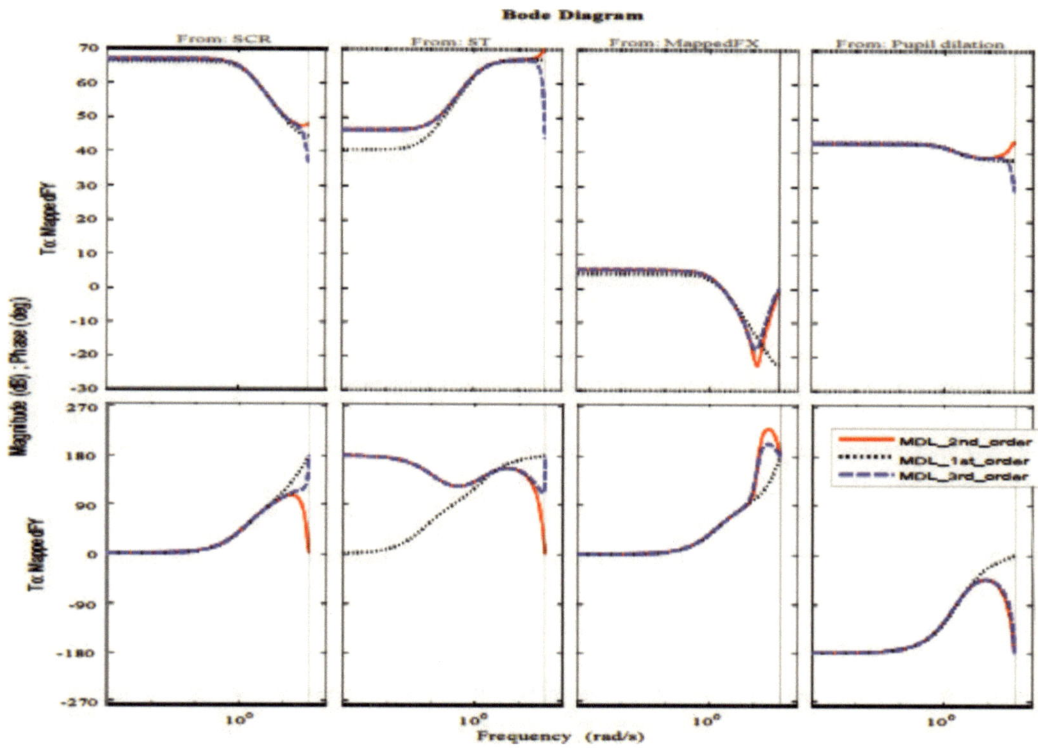

Figure 7. Bode plot of the system on webpage interphase.

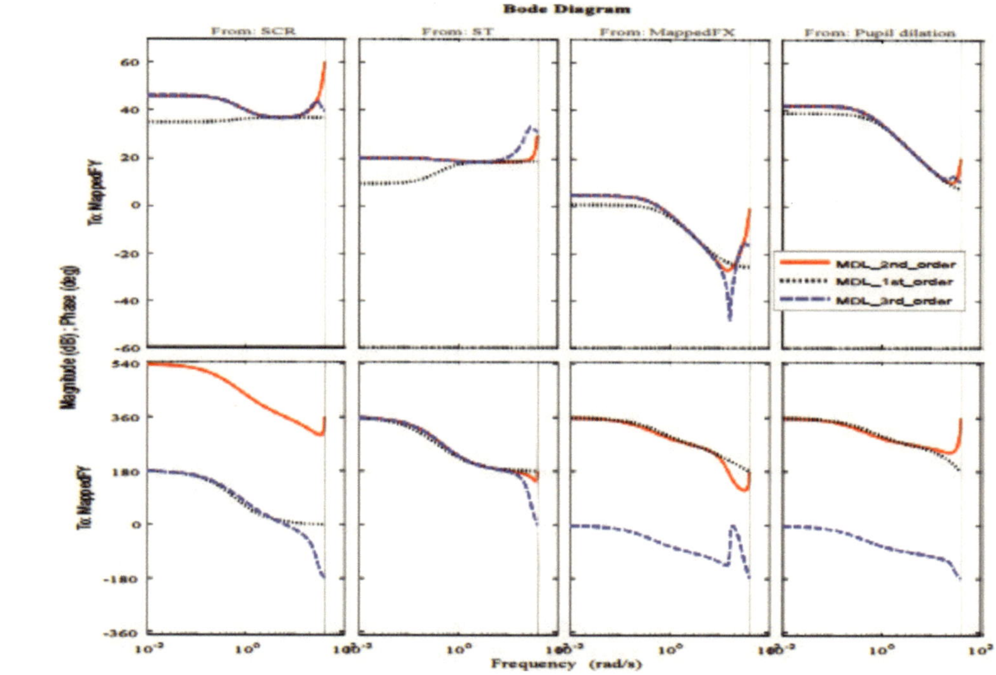

Figure 8. Comparing original and predicted response.

possibility of a good performance on the system model. The response output illustrates the most significant response magnitude at order 3 (**Figure 8b**).

6. Conclusion

This chapter has offered an evaluative perspective on an important aspect in user interphase on game, web, and text. By introducing a novel approach to user interaction and user physiological response, we integrated eye movement and physiological response to determine correlates that serve as tertiary indicators of the stress levels of a user based on attributes obtained from their physiological response. The benefits of the proposed model have proved to be reliable, given the results and findings from the response output of the system and the model has offered some solutions to the persistent user interaction and physiological association, which may be sustainable in the long-term with further evaluations and validations. The method used here provides an automated way of assessing human stress levels when dealing with specific visual contents. This is an important achievement and in that it is able to predict what contents on a visual interphase course stress-induced emotion in users during interaction. This could be applied to other areas like Internet security, triggering alarm for unauthorized access, or abnormal activities online which is the basis for our future work and also in testing performance. This chapter opens the way to possible benefits in terms of predicting human behavior in respect to Internet security by using the process as an alarm trigger for sending alerts on unauthorized access or abnormal activities online; this can be done by detecting user emotion on the visual interphase.

Author details

Fatima Isiaka[1], Kassim Mwitondi[1] and Adamu M. Ibrahim[2*]

*Address all correspondence to: scami@leeds.ac.uk

1 Department of Computing, Sheffield Hallam University, UK

2 University of Leeds, UK

References

[1] Andreassi JL. Psychophysiology: Human Behavior and Physiological Response. Psychology Press; 2000

[2] Cooley R, Mobasher B, Srivastava J. Data preparation for mining world wide web browsing patterns. Knowledge and Information Systems. 1999;**1**(1):5-32

[3] De Santos A, Sanchez-Avila C, Guerra-Casanova J, Pozo GB-D. Real-time stress detection by means of physiological signals. In: Recent Application in Biometrics. Rijeka: InTech; 2011

[4] Demiral SB, Schlesewsky M, Bornkessel-Schlesewsky I. On the universality of language comprehension strategies: Evidence from turkish. Cognition. 2008;**106**(1):484-500

[5] Isiaka F, Mwitondi K, Ibrahim A. Window based model for simulation of integrative human physiological response to webpages. In: Computing and Communication (IEMCON), 2015 International Conference and Workshop on. IEEE; 2015. pp. 1-8

[6] Isiaka F, Mwitondi KS, Ibrahim AM. Detection of natural structures and classification of HCI-HPR data using robust forward search algorithm. International Journal of Intelligent Computing and Cybernetics. 2016;**9**(1):23-41

[7] Kamon E, Pandolf K, Cafarelli E. The relationship between perceptual information and physiological responses to exercise in the heat. Journal of Human Ergology. 1974;**3**(1): 45-54

[8] Karnopp DC, Margolis DL, Rosenberg RC. System Dynamics: Modeling, Simulation, and Control of Mechatronic Systems. John Wiley and Sons; 2012

[9] Kretzschmar F, Pleimling D, Hosemann J, Fussel S, Bornkessel-Schlesewsky I, Schlesewsky M. Subjective impressions do not mirror online reading effort: Concurrent eeg-eyetracking evidence from the reading of books and digital media. PLoS One. 2013;**8**(2):e56178

[10] Liversedge SP, Blythe HI. Lexical and sublexical influences on eye movements during reading. Lang & Ling Compass. 2007;**1**(1-2):17-31

[11] Mindfield. eSence temperature, mindfield biofeedback sytems. eSence Skin Temperature-Handbook. 2014;**1**(1):1-12

[12] Mizokawa T.Control system for controlling object using pseudo-emotions and pseudo-personality generated in the object, US Patent 6,230,111, May 8 2001

[13] Niedenthal PM, Ric F. Psychology of Emotion. Psychology Press; 2017

[14] Paulson LD. Building rich web applications with ajax. Computer. 2005;**38**(10):14-17

[15] Petrushin VA. Detecting emotions using voice signal analysis, US Patent 7,222,075, May 22 2007

[16] Ramakrishnan S. Recognition of emotion from speech: A review. In: Speech Enhancement, Modeling and Recognition-Algorithms and Applications. Rijeka: InTech; 2012

[17] Schneider-Hufschmidt M, Malinowski U, Kuhme T. Adaptive User Interfaces: Principles and Practice. Elsevier Science Inc.; 1993

[18] Widyantoro DH, Ioerger TR, Yen J. An adaptive algorithm for learning changes in user interests. In: Proceedings of the Eighth International Conference on Information and Knowledge Management. ACM; 1999. pp. 405-412

Chapter 3

Review on Emotion Recognition Databases

Rain Eric Haamer, Eka Rusadze, Iiris Lüsi,
Tauseef Ahmed, Sergio Escalera and
Gholamreza Anbarjafari

Additional information is available at the end of the chapter

http://dx.doi.org/10.5772/intechopen.72748

Abstract

Over the past few decades human-computer interaction has become more important in our daily lives and research has developed in many directions: memory research, depression detection, and behavioural deficiency detection, lie detection, (hidden) emotion recognition etc. Because of that, the number of generic emotion and face databases or those tailored to specific needs have grown immensely large. Thus, a comprehensive yet compact guide is needed to help researchers find the most suitable database and understand what types of databases already exist. In this paper, different elicitation methods are discussed and the databases are primarily organized into neat and informative tables based on the format.

Keywords: emotion, computer vision, databases

1. Introduction

With facial recognition and human-computer interaction becoming more prominent with each passing year, the amount of databases associated with both face detection and facial expressions has grown immensely [1, 2]. A key part in creating, training and even evaluating supervised emotion recognition models is a well-labelled database of visual and/or audio information fit for the desired application. For example, emotion recognition has many different applications ranging from simple human-robot computer interaction [3–5] to automated depression detection [6].

There are several papers, blogs and books [7–10] fully dedicated to just describing some of the more prominent databases for face recognition. However, the collection of emotion databases is disparate, as they are often tailored to a specific purpose, so there is no complete and thorough overview of the ones that currently exist.

IntechOpen

© 2018 The Author(s). Licensee IntechOpen. This chapter is distributed under the terms of the Creative Commons Attribution License (http://creativecommons.org/licenses/by/3.0), which permits unrestricted use, distribution, and reproduction in any medium, provided the original work is properly cited.

Even though there already are a lot of collected databases out there that fit many specific criteria [11, 12], it is important to recognize that there are several different aspects that affect the content of the database. The selection of the participants, the method used to collect the data and what was in fact collected all have a great impact on the performance of the final model [13]. The cultural and social background of participants as well as their mood during recordings can sway the results of the database to be specific to a particular group of people. This can even happen with larger sample pools, like the case with the Bosphorus database [14], which suffers from a lack of ethnic diversity compared to databases with a similar or even smaller size [15–17].

Since most algorithms take an aligned and cropped face as an input, the most basic form of datasets is a collection of portrait images or already cropped faces, with uniform lighting and backgrounds. Among those is the NIST mugshot database [18], which has clear gray-scale mugshots and portraits of 1573 individuals on a uniform background. However, real-life scenarios are more complicated, requiring the authors to experiment with different lighting, head pose and occlusions [19]. For example in the M2VTS database [20], which contains the faces of 37 subjects in different rotated positions and lighting angles.

Some databases have focused on gathering samples from even less controlled environments with obstructed facial data like the SCface database [21], which contains surveillance data gathered from real world scenarios. Emotion recognition is not solely based on a person's facial expression, but can also be assisted by body language [22] or vocal context. Unfortunately, not many databases include body language, preferring to completely focus on the face, but there are some multi-modal video and audio databases that incorporate vocal context [11, 23].

2. Elicitation methods

An important choice to make in gathering data for emotion recognition databases is how to bring out different emotions in the participants. This is the reason why facial emotion databases are divided into three main categories [24]:

- posed
- induced
- spontaneous

Eliciting expressions can be done in several different ways and unfortunately, they yield wildly different results.

2.1. Posed

Emotions acted out based on conjecture or with the guidance from actors or professionals are called posed expressions [25]. Most facial emotion databases, especially the early ones i.e. Banse-Scherer [26], CK [27] and Chen-Huang [28], consist purely of posed facial expressions, as it is the easiest to gather. However, they also are the least representative of real world authentic emotions as forced emotions are often over-exaggerated or missing subtle details, like in **Figure 1**. Due to this, human expression analysis models created through the use of posed databases often have very poor results with real world data [13, 30]. To overcome the problems related to authenticity, professional theatre actors have been employed, e.g. for the GEMEP [31] database.

2.2. Induced

This method of elicitation displays more genuine emotions as the participants usually interact with other individuals or are subject to audiovisual media in order to invoke real emotions. Induced emotion databases have become more common in recent years due to the limitations of posed expressions. The performance of the models in real life is greatly improved, since they are not hindered by overemphasised and fake expressions, making them more natural, as seen in **Figure 2**. There are several databases that deal with audiovisual emotion elicitation like the

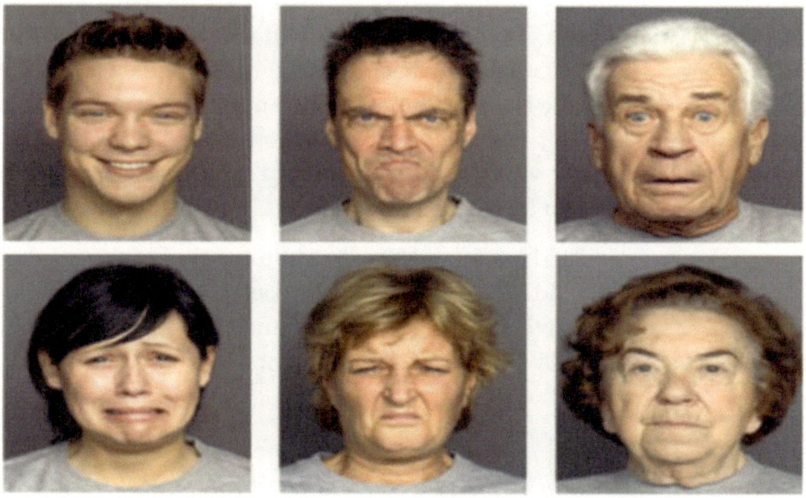

Figure 1. Posed expressions over different age groups from the FACES database [29].

Figure 2. Induced facial expressions from the SD database [32].

SD [32], UT DALLAS [33] and SMIC [34], and some that deal with human to human interaction like the ISL meeting corpus [35], AAI [36] and CSC corpus [37].

Databases produced by observing human-computer interaction on the other hand are a lot less common. The best representatives are the AIBO database [23], where children are trying to give commands to a Sony AIBO robot, and SAL [11], in which adults interact with an artificial chat-bot.

Even though induced databases are much better than the posed ones, they still have some problems with truthfulness. Since the emotions are often invoked in a lab setting with the supervision of authoritative figures, the subjects might subconsciously keep their expressions in check [25, 30].

2.3. Spontaneous

Spontaneous emotion datasets are considered to be the closest to actual real-life scenarios. However, since true emotion can only be observed, when the person is not aware of being recorded [30], they are difficult to collect and label. The acquisition of data is usually in conflict with privacy or ethics, whereas the labelling has to be done manually and the true emotion has to be guessed by the analyser [25]. This arduous task is both time-consuming and erroneous [13, 38], having a sharp contrast with posed and induced datasets, where labels are either predefined or can be derived from the elicitation content.

With that being said, there still exist a few databases out there that consist of data extracted from movies [39, 40], YouTube videos [41], or even television series [42], but these databases have inherently fewer samples in them than their posed and induced counterparts. Example images from these databases are in **Figures 3–5** respectively.

Figure 3. Images of movie clips taken from the AFEW database [39, 40].

Figure 4. Spanish YouTube video clips taken from the Spanish Multimodal Opinion database [41].

Figure 5. TV show stills taken from the VAM database [43].

3. Categories of emotion

The purpose of a database is defined by the emotions represented in it. Several databases like CK [27, 44], MMI [45], eNTERFACE [46], NVIE [47] all opt to capture the six basic emotion types: anger, disgust, fear, happiness, sadness and surprise as proposed by Ekman [48–50]. In the tables, they are denoted as primary 6. Often authors tend to add contempt to these, forming seven primary emotions and often neutral is included. However, they cover a very small subcategory of all possible emotions, so there have been attempts to combine them [51, 52].

Several databases try to just categorise the general positive and negative emotions or incorporate them along with others, e.g. the SMO [41], AAI [36], and ISL meeting corpus [35] databases. Some even try to rank deception and honesty like the CSC corpus database [37].

Apart from anger and disgust within the six primary emotions, scientists have tried to capture other negative expressions, such as boredom, disinterest, pain, embarrassment and depression. Unfortunately, these categories are harder to elicit than other types of emotions.

TUM AVIC [53] and AVDLC [12] databases are amongst those that try to label levels of interest and depression while GEMEP [31] and VAM [43] attempt to divide emotions into four quadrants and three dimensions, respectively. The main reason why most databases have a very small number of categories (mainly, neutral and smile/no-smile) is that the more emotions added, the more difficult they are to label and also more data is required to properly train a model.

Relatively newer databases have begun recording more subtle emotions hidden behind other forced or dominant emotions. Among these are the MAHNOB [51] database, which focuses on emotional laughter and different types of laughter, and others that try to record emotions hidden behind a neutral or straight face like SMIC [34], RML [54], Polikovsky's [55] databases.

One of the more recent databases, the iCV-MEFED [52, 56] database, takes on a different approach by posing varying combinations of emotions simultaneously, where one emotion takes the dominant role and the other is complimentary. Sample images can be seen in **Figure 6**.

3.1. Action units

The Facial Affect Sorting Technique (FAST) was developed to measure facial movement relative to emotion. They describe the six basic emotions through facial behaviour: happiness, surprise and disgust have three intensities and anger is reported as controlled and uncontrolled [57]. Darwin [58], Duchenne [59] and Hjortsjo [60], Ekman and Friesen [61] developed the Facial Action Coding System (FACS), a comprehensive system, which catalogues all possible visually distinguishable facial movements.

FACS describes facial expressions in terms of 44 anatomically based Action Units (AU). They are meant for facial punctuators in conversation, facial deficits indicative of brain lesions, emotion detection, etc. FACS only deals with visible changes, which are often induced by a combination of muscle contractions. Because of that, they are called action units [61]. A small

Figure 6. Combinations of emotions from the iCV-MEFED [52].

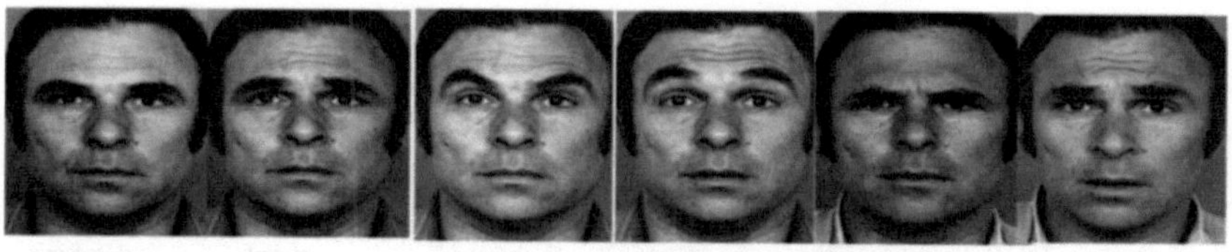

Figure 7. Induced facial action units from the DISFA database [62].

Database	Participants	Elicitation	Format	Action units	Additional information
CMU-Pittsburgh AU-Coded Face Expression Database [27] 2000	210	Posed	Videos	44	Varying ethnic backgrounds, FACS coding
MMI Facial Expression Database [63, 64] 2002	19	Posed and audiovisual media	Videos, images	79	Continuously updated, contains different parts
Face Video Database of the MPI [65, 66] 2003	1	Posed	Six viewpoint videos	55	Created using the MPI VideoLab
D3DFACS [67] 2011	10	posed	3D videos	19–97	Supervised by FACS specialists
DISFA [62] 2013	27	audiovisual media	Videos	12	

Table 1. Action unit databases.

sample of such expressions can be seen in **Figure 7**. A selection of databases based on AUs instead of regular facial expressions is listed in **Table 1**.

In 2002, the FACS system was revised and the number of facial contraction AUs was reduced to 33 and 25 head pose AUs were added [68–70]. In addition, there is a separate FACS version intended for children [71].

4. Database types

Emotion recognition databases may come in many different forms, depending on how the data was collected. We review existing databases for different types of emotion recognition. In order to better compare similar types of databases, we decided to split them into three broad categories based on format. The first two categories separated still images from video sequences, while the last category is comprised of databases with more unique capturing methods.

4.1. Static databases

Most early facial expression databases, like the CK [27], only consist of frontal portrait images taken with simple RGB cameras. Newer databases try to design collection methods that incorporate data, which is closer to real life scenarios by using different angles and occlusion (hats, glasses, etc.). Great examples are the MMI [45] and Multi-PIE [72] databases, which were some of the first well-known ones using multiple view angles. In order to increase the accuracy of the human expression analysis models, databases like the FABO [22] have expanded the frame from a portrait to the entire upper body.

Static databases are the oldest and most common type. Therefore, it's understandable that they were created with the most diverse of goals, varying from expression perception [29] to neuropsychological research [73], and have a wide range of data gathering styles, including self-photography through a semi-reflective mirror [74] and occlusion and light angle variation [75]. Static databases usually have the largest number of participants and a bigger sample size. While it is relatively easy to find a database suited for the task at hand, categories of emotions are quite limited, as static databases only focus on six primary emotions or smile/neutral detection. In the future, it would be convenient if there were databases with more emotions, especially spontaneous or induced, because, as you can see in **Table 2**, almost all static databases to date are posed.

4.2. Video databases

The most convenient format for capturing induced and spontaneous emotions is video. This is due to a lack of clear start and end points for non-posed emotions [93]. In the case of RGB Video, the subtle emotional changes known as microexpressions have also been recorded with the hope of detecting concealed emotions as in USF-HD [94], YorkDDT [95], SMIC [34], CASME [96] and Polikovsky's [55] databases, the newest and most extensive among those being CASME.

Posed video databases in **Table 3** suggest that they tend to be quite small in the number of participants, usually around 10, and often professional actors have been used. Unlike with still images, scientists have tried to benefit from voice, speech or any other type of utterances for emotion recognition. Many databases have also tried to gather micro-expressions, as they do not show up on still images or are harder to catch. The posed video databases have mainly focused on six primary emotions and a neutral expression.

Media induced databases, as in **Table 4**, have a larger number of participants and the emotions are usually induced by audiovisual media, like Superbowl ads [107]. Because the emotions in these databases are induced via external means, this format is great for gathering fake [108] or hidden [34] emotions.

Interaction induced video databases have more unique ways of gathering data, like child-robot interaction [23] or reviewing past memories [36]. This can be seen in **Table 5**. This type of databases takes significantly longer time to create [113], but this does not seem to affect the sample size. Almost all of the spontaneous databases are in video format from other media sources, purely because of how difficult they are to collect. Spontaneous databases are also some of the rarest, compared to other elicitation methods. This is reflected in **Table 6**, which has the lowest number of databases among the different elicitation methods.

4.3. Miscellaneous databases

Apart from the formats mentioned above, 3D scanned and even thermal databases of different emotions have also been constructed. The most well-known 3D datasets are the BU-3DFE [15],

Database	Participants	Primary 6	Neutral	Contempt	Embarrassment	Pain	Smile	Positive	Negative	Other	Additional information
JACFEE [76] 1988	4	X	X								Eight images of each emotion
POFA (or PFA) [73] 1993	14	X									Cross-cultural studies and neuropsychological research
AT-T Database for Faces (formerly ORL) [77, 78] 1994	40						X			X	Dark homogeneous background, frontal face
Yale [75] 1997	15		X								Frontal face, different light angles, occlusions
FERET [79] 1998	1199		X				X				Standard for face recognition algorithms
KDEF [80] 1998	70	X	X								Psychological and medical research (perception, attention, emotion, memory and backward masking)
The AR Face Database [81] 1998	126	✓[1]	X				X		X		Frontal face, different light angles, occlusions
The Japanese Female Facial Expression Database [74] 1998	10	X	X								Subjects photographed themselves through a semi-reflective mirror
MSFDE [82] 2000	12	X	X								FACS coding, ethnical diversity
CAFE Database [83] 2001	24	X	X								FACS coding, ethnical diversity
CMU PIE [84] 2002	68		X				X		X		Illumination variation, varying poses
Indian Face Database [85] 2002	40	✓					X				Indian participants from seven view angles
NimStim Face Stimulus Set [86] 2002	70	X					X			X	Facial expressions were supervised
KFDB [87] 2003	1920						X		X		Includes ground truth for facial landmarks
PAL Face Database [88] 2004	576	✓							X		Wide age range
UT DALLAS [33] 2005	284	✓					X				Head and face detection, emotions induced using audiovisual media
TFEID [89] 2007	40	X							X		Taiwanese actors, two simultaneous angles
CAS-PEAL [90] 2008	1040	X	X				X				Chinese face detection
Multi-PIE [72] 2008	337		X				X				Multiple view angles, illumination variation
PUT [91] 2008	100		X							X	High-resolution head-pose database
Radboud Faces Database [92] 2008	67	X	X	X							Supervised by FACS specialists
FACES database [29] 2010	154	X									Expression perception, wide age range, evaluated by participants
iCV-MEFED [52] 2017	115	X	X								Psychologists picked best from 5

[1]A selection of six primary emotions has been used in databases with this symbol.

Table 2. Posed static databases.

BU-4DFE [16], Bosphorus [14] and BP4D [17]. BU-3DFE and BU-4DFE both contain posed datasets with six expressions, the latter having higher resolution. Bosphorus tries to address the issue of having a wider selection of facial expressions and BP4D is the only one among the four using induced expressions instead of posed ones. A sample of models from a 3D database can be seen in **Figure 8**.

Database	Participants	Primary 6	Neutral	Contempt	Embarrassment	Pain	Smile	Positive	Negative	Other	Additional information
University of Maryland DB [97] 1997	40	X									1–3 expressions per clip
CK [27] 2000	97	X									One of the first FE databases made public
Chen-Huang [28] 2000	100	X									Facial expressions and speech
DaFEx [98] 2004	8	X	X								Italian actors mimicked emotions while uttering different sentences
Mind Reading [99] 2004	6		X				X				Teaching tool for children with behavioural disabilities
GEMEP [31] 2006	10	✓								X	Professional actors, supervised
AONE [100] 2007	75										Asian adults
FABO [22] 2007	4	✓								X	Face and upper-body
IEMOCAP [101] 2008	10	✓	X							X	Markers on face, head, hands
RML [54] 2008	8	X									Suppressed emotions
Polikovsky's database [55] 2009	10	X	X								Low intensity micro-expressions
SAVEE [102] 2009	4	X	X								Blue markers, three images per emotion
STOIC [103] 2009	10	X	X			X					Face recognition, discerning gender, contains still images
YorkDDT [95] 2009	9	X	X								Micro-expressions
ADFES [104] 2011	22	X		X	X				X		Frontal and turned facial expressions
USF-HD [94] 2011	16	✓								X	Micro-expressions, mimicked shown expressions
CASME [96] 2013	35	✓	X							X	Micro expressions, suppressed emotions

Table 3. Posed video databases.

With RGB-D databases, however, it is important to note that the data is unique to each sensor with outputs having varying density and error, so algorithms trained on databases like the IIIT-D RGB-D [115], VAP RGB-D [116] and KinectFaceDB [117] would be very susceptible to hardware changes. For comparison with the 3D databases, an RGB-D sample has been provided in **Figure 9**. One of the newer databases, the iCV SASE [118] database, is RGB-D dataset solely dedicated to headpose with free facial expressions.

Even though depth based databases, like the ones in **Table 7**, are relatively new compared to other types and there are very few of them, they still manage to cover a wide range of different emotions. With the release of commercial use depth cameras like the Microsoft Kinect [120], they will only continue to get more popular in the future.

Database	Participants	Elicitation	Primary 6	Neutral	Contempt	Embarrassment	Pain	Smile	Positive	Negative	Other	Additional information
IAPS [105] 1997	497–1483	Visual media									X	Pleasure and arousal reaction images, subset for children
SD [32] 2004	28	AVM[1]	✓	X							X	One of the first international induced emotion data-sets
eNTERFACE'05 [46] 2006	42	Auditory media	X									Standard for face recognition algorithms
CK+ [44] 2010	220	Posed and AVM	X									Updated version of CK
SMIC [34] 2011	6	AVM	✓									Supressed emotions
Face Place [106] 2012	235	AVM	X	X							X	Different ethnicities
AM-FED [107] 2013	81–240	AVM		X				X				Reactions to Superbowl ads
MAHNOB [51] 2013	22	Posed and AVM	✓								X	Laughter recognition research
SASE-FE [108] 2017	54	AVM	✓		X							Fake emotions

[1]Audiovisual media.

Table 4. Media induced video databases.

As their applications are more specific, thermal facial expression datasets are very scarce. Some of the first and more known ones are IRIS [123] and Equinox [121, 122], which consist of RGB and thermal image pairs that are labelled with three emotions [124], as can be seen in **Figure 10**. Thermal databases are usually posed or induced by audiovisual media. The ones in **Table 8** mostly focus on positive, negative, neutral and six primary emotions. The average number of participants is quite high relative to other types of databases.

4.3.1. Audio databases

There are mainly two types of emotion databases that contain audio content: stand-alone audio databases and video databases that include spoken words or utterances. The information extracted from audio is called context and can be generally categorized into a multitude, wherein the three important context subdivisions for emotion recognition databases are the semantic, structural, and temporal ones.

Semantic context is where the emotion can be isolated through specific emotionally marked words, while structural context is dependent on the stress patterns and syntactic structure of longer phrases. **Temporal context** is the longer lasting variant of the structural context as it involves the change of emotion in speech over time, like emotional build-up [42].

Database	Participants	Elicitation	Primary 6	Neutral	Contempt	Embarrassment	Pain	Smile	Positive	Negative	Other	Additional information
ISL meeting corpus [35] 2002	90	Human-human interaction		X					X	X		Collected in a meeting fashion
AAI [36] 2004	60	Human-human interaction			X				X	X	X	Induced via past memories
AIBO database [23] 2004	30	Child-robot interaction	✓	X							X	Robot instructed by children
CSC corpus [37] 2005	32	Human-human interaction									X	Honesty research
RU-FACS [109] 2005	90	Human-human interaction	X	X								Subjects were all university students
SAL [11] 2005	24	human-computer interaction	✓	X								conversations held with a simulated "chat-bot" system
MMI [45] 2006	61/ 29	Posed/child-comedian interaction, adult-audiovisual media	X									Profile views along with portrait images
TUM AVIC [53] 2007	21	Human-human interaction									X	Commercial presentation
SEMAINE [110, 111] 2010/2012	150	Human-human interaction	X		X						X	Operator was thoroughly familiar with SAL script
AVDLC [12] 2013	292	Human-computer interaction									X	Mood disorder and unipolar depression research
RECOLA [112] 2013	46	Human-human interaction									X	Collaborative tasks. Audio-video, ECG and EDA were recorded

Table 5. Interaction induced video databases.

Database	Participants	Primary 6	Neutral	Contempt	Embarrassment	Pain	Smile	Positive	Negative	Other	Additional information
Belfast natural database [42] 2003	125	X	X	X						X	Video clips from television and interviews
Belfast Naturalistic Emotional Database [114] 2003	125	X								X	Studio recordings and television program clips
VAM [43] 2008	47									X	Video clips from a talk-show
AFEW [39, 40] 2011/2012	330	X	X								Video clips from movies
Spanish Multimodal Opinion [41] 2013	105							X	X		Spanish video clips from YouTube

Table 6. Spontaneous video databases.

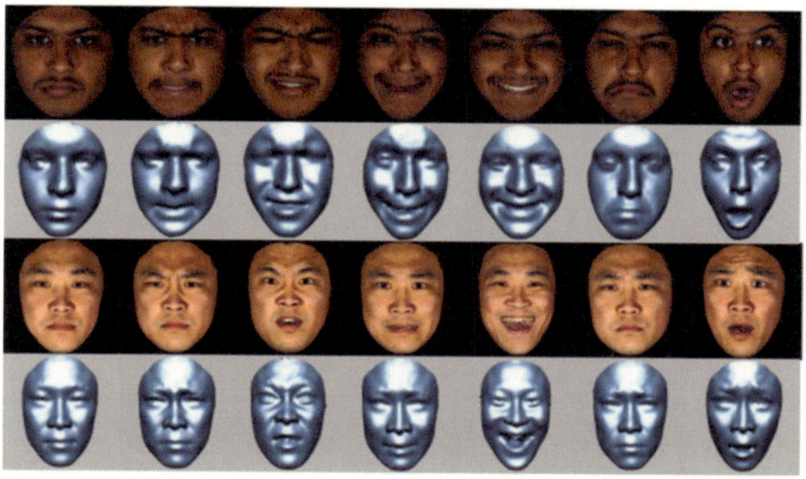

Figure 8. 3D facial expression samples from the BU-3DFE database [15].

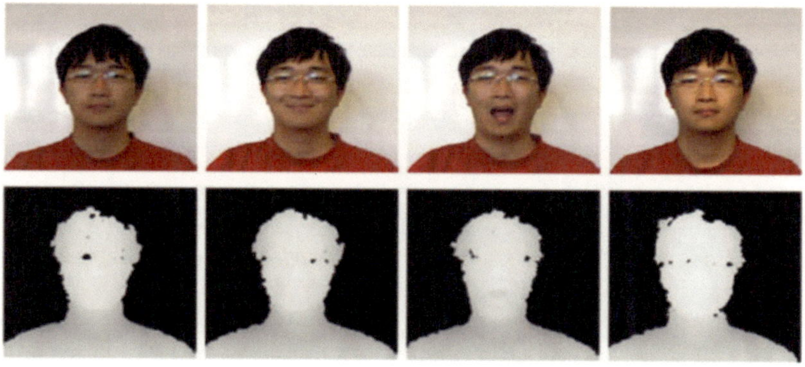

Figure 9. RGB-D facial expression samples from the KinectFaceDB database [117].

In case of multimodal data, the audio component can provide a semantic context, which can have a larger bearing on the emotion than the facial expressions themselves [11, 23]. However, in case of solely audio data, like the Bank and Stock Service [126] and ACC [127] databases, the context of the speech plays a quintessential role in emotion recognition [128, 129].

The audio databases in **Table 9** are very scarce and tailored to specific needs, like the Banse-Schrerer [26], which has only four participants and was gathered to see whether judges can deduce emotions from vocal cues. The easiest way to gather a larger amount of audio data is from call-centres, where the emotions are elicited either by another person or a computer program.

Even with all of the readily available databases out there, there is still a need for creating self-collected databases for emotion recognition, as the existing ones don't always fulfil all of the criteria [130–133].

Database	Participants	Format	Primary 6	Neutral	Contempt	Embarrassment	Pain	Smile	Positive	Negative	Other	Additional information
BU-3DFE [15] 2006	100	3D images	X									Ethnically diverse, two angled views
Bosphorus [14] 2008	105	3D images	X									Occlusions, less ethnic diversity than BU-3DF
BU-4DFE [16] 2008	101	3D videos										Newer version of BU-3DFE, has 3D videos
VAP RGB-D [116] 2012	31	RGB-D videos						X			X	17 different recorded states repeated 3 times for each person
PICS [119] 2013	—	Images, videos, 3D images										Includes several different datasets and is still ongoing
BP4D [17] 2014	41	3D videos	X			X	X					Human-human interaction
IIIT-D RGB-D [115] 2014	106	RGB-D images		X				X				Captured with Kinect
KinectFaceDB [117] 2014	52	RGB-D images, videos		X				X				Captured with Kinect, varying occlusions

Table 7. 3D and RGB-D databases.

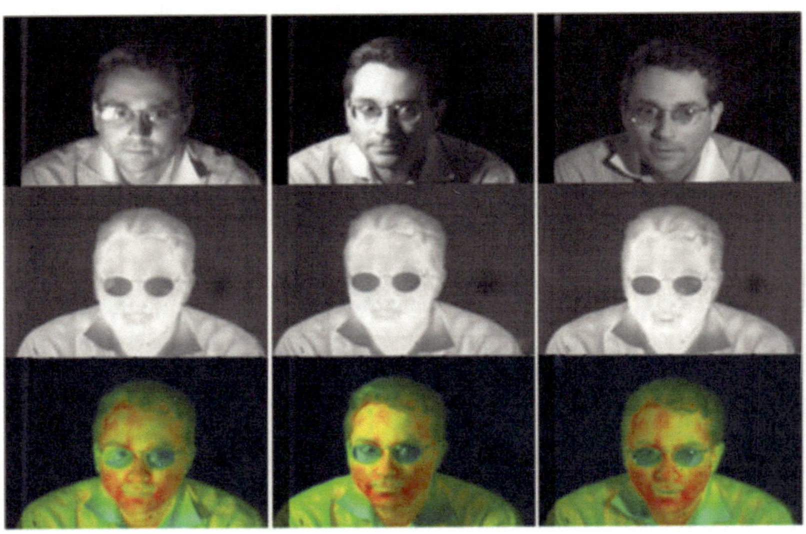

Figure 10. Thermal images taken from the Equinox database [121, 122].

Database	Participants	Elicitation	Primary 6	Neutral	Contempt	Embarrassment	Pain	Smile	Positive	Negative	Other	Additional information
Equinox [121, 122] 2002	340	Posed		X					X	X		Captured in SWIR, MWIR and LWIR
IRIS [123] 2007	4228	Posed		X					X	X		Some of the first thermal FE data-sets
NVIE [47] 2010	215	Posed and AVM[1]	X									Spontaneous expressions are not present for every subject
KTFE [125] 2014	26	Posed and AVM	X	X								

[1]Audiovisual media.

Table 8. Thermal databases.

Database	Participants	Elicitation	Primary 6	Neutral	Contempt	Embarrassment	Pain	Smile	Positive	Negative	Other	Additional information
Banse-Scherer [26] 1996	4	Posed	X		X	X					X	Vocally expressed emotions
Bank and Stock Service [126] 2004	350	Human-human interaction	✓	X							X	Collected from a call center and Capital Bank Service Center
ACC [127] 2005	1187	Human-computer interaction		X						X		Collected from automated call center applications

Table 9. Audio databases.

5. Conclusion

With the rapid increase of computing power and size of data, it has become more and more feasible to distinguish emotions, identify people, and verify honesty based on video, audio or image input, taking a large step forward not only in human-computer interaction, but also in mental illness detection, medical research, security and so forth. In this paper an overview of existing face databases in varying categories has been given. They have been organised into tables to give the reader an easy way to find necessary data. This paper should be a good starting point for anyone who considers training a model for emotion recognition.

Acknowledgements

This work has been partially supported by Estonian Research Council Grant PUT638, The Scientific and Technological Research Council of Turkey 1001 Project (116E097), The Spanish project TIN2016-74946-P (MINECO/FEDER, UE), CERCA Programme/Generalitat de Catalunya, the COST Action IC1307 iV&L Net (European Network on Integrating Vision and Language) supported by COST (European Cooperation in Science and Technology), and the Estonian Centre of Excellence in IT (EXCITE) funded by the European Regional Development Fund. We also gratefully acknowledge the support of the NVIDIA Corporation with the donation of the Titan X Pascal GPU.

Author details

Rain Eric Haamer[1], Eka Rusadze[1], Iiris Lüsi[1], Tauseef Ahmed[1], Sergio Escalera[2] and Gholamreza Anbarjafari[1,3]*

*Address all correspondence to: shb@icv.tuit.ut.ee

1 iCV Research Group, Institute of Technology, University of Tartu, Tartu, Estonia

2 The Computer Vision Center and University of Barcelona, Barcelona, Spain

3 Department of Electrical and Electronic Engineering, Hasan Kalyoncu University, Gaizantep, Turkey

References

[1] Dix A. Human-computer interaction. In Encyclopedia of database systems. US: Springer. 2009:1327-1331

[2] Noroozi F, Marjanovic M. Njegus A, Escalera S, Anbarjafari G. Audio-visual emotion recognition in video clips. IEEE Transactions on Affective Computing; 2017

[3] Toumi T, Zidani A. From human-computer interaction to human-robot social interaction. arXiv preprint arXiv:1412.1251; 2014

[4] Daneshmand M, Abels A, Anbarjafari G. Real-time, automatic digi-tailor mannequin robot adjustment based on human body classification through supervised learning. International Journal of Advanced Robotic Systems. 2017;**14**(3):1729881417707169

[5] Bolotnikova A, Demirel H, Anbarjafari G. Real-time ensemble based face recognition system for NAO humanoids using local binary pattern. Analog Integrated Circuits and Signal Processing. 2017;**92**(3):467-475

[6] Valstar MF, Schuller BW, Smith K, Eyben F, Jiang B, Bilakhia S, Schnieder S, Cowie R, Pantic M. AVEC 2013: The continuous audio/visual emotion and depression recognition challenge. In: AVEC-ACM Multimedia, Barcelona, Spain; 2013

[7] Gross R, Baker S, Matthews I, Kanade T. Handbook of face recognition. In: Li SZ, Jain AK, editors. Handbook of Face Recognition. 2005:193-216

[8] Jain AK, Li SZ. Handbook of Face Recognition. Springer; 2011

[9] Face databases. http://web.mit.edu/emeyers/ www.face_databases.html [Accessed 31 March 2017]

[10] 60 facial recognition databases. https://www.kairos.com/blog/60-facial-recognition-databases [Accessed 31 March 2017]

[11] Athanaselis T, Bakamidis S, Dologlou I, Cowie R, Douglas-Cowie E, Cox C. ASR for emotional speech: Clarifying the issues and enhancing performance. Neural Networks. 2005;**18**(4):437-444

[12] Valstar M, Schuller B, Smith K, Eyben F, Jiang B, Bilakhia S, Schnieder S, Cowie R, Pantic M. AVEC 2013: The continuous audio/visual emotion and depression recognition challenge. In: Proceedings of the 3rd ACM International Workshop on Audio/Visual Emotion Challenge; ACM; 2013. pp. 3-10

[13] Jaimes A, Sebe N. Multimodal human–computer interaction: A survey. Computer Vision and Image Understanding. 2007;**108**(1):116-134

[14] Savran A, Alyüz N, Dibeklioğlu H, Çeliktutan O, Gökberk B, Sankur B, Akarun L. Bosphorus database for 3D face analysis. In: European Workshop on Biometrics and Identity Management; Springer; 2008. pp. 47-56

[15] Yin L, Wei X, Sun Y, Wang J, Rosato MJ. A 3D facial expression database for facial behavior research. In: Automatic Face and Gesture Recognition, 2006. FGR 2006. 7th International Conference on; IEEE; 2006. pp. 211-216

[16] Yin L, Chen X, Sun Y, Worm T, Reale M. A high-resolution 3D dynamic facial expression database. In: 8th IEEE International Conference on Automatic Face and Gesture Recognition, 2008. FG08. ; IEEE; 2008. pp. 1-6

[17] Zhang X, Yin L, Cohn JF, Canavan S, Reale M, Horowitz A, Liu P, Girard JM. Bp4d-spontaneous: A high-resolution spontaneous 3D dynamic facial expression database. Image and Vision Computing. 2014;**32**(10):692-706

[18] NIST. Special database 18: Mugshot Identification Database (MID)

[19] Bruce V, Young A. Understanding face recognition. British Journal of Psychology. 1986;**77**(3): 305-327

[20] Richard G, Mengay Y, Guis I, Suaudeau N, Boudy J, Lockwood P, Fernandez C, Fernández F, Kotropoulos C, Tefas A, et al. Multi modal verification for teleservices and security applications (M2VTS). IEEE International Conference on Multimedia Computing and Systems, 1999; IEEE. 1999;**2**:1061-1064

[21] Grgic M, Delac K, Grgic S. Scface–surveillance cameras face database. Multimedia Tools and Applications. 2011;**51**(3):863-879

[22] Gunes H, Piccardi M. Bi-modal emotion recognition from expressive face and body gestures. Journal of Network and Computer Applications. 2007;**30**(4):1334-1345

[23] Batliner A, Hacker C, Steidl S, Nöth E, D'Arcy S, Russell MJ, Wong M. "You stupid tin box"-children interacting with the AIBO robot: A cross-linguistic emotional speech corpus. In: LREC, Lisbon, Portugal; 2004

[24] Wu C-H, Lin J-C, Wei W-L. Survey on audiovisual emotion recognition: Databases, features, and data fusion strategies. APSIPA Transactions on Signal and Information Processing. 2014;**3**:e12

[25] Sebe N, Cohen I, Gevers T, Huang TS. Multimodal approaches for emotion recognition: A survey. In: Electronic Imaging 2005; International Society for Optics and Photonics; 2005. pp. 56-67

[26] Banse R, Scherer KR. Acoustic profiles in vocal emotion expression. Journal of personality and social psychology. 1996;**70**(3):614

[27] Kanade T, Cohn JF, Tian Y. Comprehensive database for facial expression analysis. In: Proceedings of Fourth IEEE International Conference on Automatic Face and Gesture Recognition, 2000; IEEE; 2000. pp. 46-53

[28] Lawrence Shao-Hsien Chen. Joint processing of audio-visual information for the recognition of emotional expressions in human-computer interaction [PhD thesis]. Citeseer; 2000

[29] Ebner NC, Riediger M, Lindenberger U. Faces—A database of facial expressions in young, middle-aged, and older women and men: Development and validation. Behavior Research Methods. 2010;**42**(1):351-362

[30] Zeng Z, Pantic M, Roisman GI, Huang TS. A survey of affect recognition methods: Audio, visual, and spontaneous expressions. IEEE Transactions on Pattern Analysis and Machine Intelligence. 2009;**31**(1):39-58

[31] Bänziger T, Pirker H, Scherer K. Gemep-geneva multimodal emotion portrayals: A corpus for the study of multimodal emotional expressions. Proceedings of LREC. 2006;**6**:15-19

[32] Sebe N, Lew MS, Sun Y, Cohen I, Gevers T, Huang TS. Authentic facial expression analysis. Image and Vision Computing. 2007;**25**(12):1856-1863

[33] O'Toole AJ, Harms J, Snow SL, Hurst DR, Pappas MR, Ayyad JH, Abdi H. A video database of moving faces and people. IEEE Transactions on Pattern Analysis and Machine Intelligence. 2005;**27**(5):812-816

[34] Pfister T, Li X, Zhao G, Pietikäinen M. Recognising spontaneous facial micro-expressions. In: IEEE International Conference on Computer Vision (ICCV), 2011; IEEE; 2011. pp. 1449-1456

[35] Burger S, MacLaren V, Yu H. The ISL meeting corpus: The impact of meeting type on speech style. In: INTERSPEECH, Denver, Colorado, USA; 2002

[36] Roisman GI, Tsai JL, Chiang K-HS. The emotional integration of childhood experience: Physiological, facial expressive, and self-reported emotional response during the adult attachment interview. Developmental Psychology. 2004;**40**(5):776

[37] Hirschberg J, Benus S, Brenier JM, Enos F, Friedman S, Gilman S, Girand C, Graciarena M, Kathol A, Michaelis L, et al. Distinguishing deceptive from non-deceptive speech. In: Interspeech; 2005. pp. 1833-1836

[38] Kirouac G, Dore FY. Accuracy of the judgment of facial expression of emotions as a function of sex and level of education. Journal of Nonverbal Behavior. 1985;**9**(1):3-7

[39] Dhall A, Goecke R, Lucey S, Gedeon T. Acted facial expressions in the wild database. Australian National University, Canberra. Technical Report TR-CS-11, 2; 2011

[40] Dhall A, Lucey S, Joshi J, Gedeon T. Collecting Large, Richly Annotated Facial-Expression Databases from Movies, IEEE MultiMedia, 2012;**19**(3):34-41

[41] Rosas VP, Mihalcea R, Morency L-P. Multimodal sentiment analysis of Spanish online videos. IEEE Intelligent Systems. 2013;**28**(3):38-45

[42] Douglas-Cowie E, Campbell N, Cowie R, Roach P. Emotional speech: Towards a new generation of databases. Speech Communication. 2003;**40**(1):33-60

[43] Grimm M, Kroschel K, Narayanan S. The Vera am Mittag German audio-visual emotional speech database. In: IEEE International Conference on Multimedia and Expo, 2008; IEEE; 2008. pp. 865-868

[44] Lucey P, Cohn JF, Kanade T, Saragih J, Ambadar Z, Matthews I. The Extended Cohn-Kanade Dataset (CK+): A complete dataset for action unit and emotion-specified expression. In: IEEE Computer Society Conference on Computer Vision and Pattern Recognition Workshops (CVPRW), 2010; IEEE; 2010. pp. 94-101

[45] Pantic M, Patras I. Dynamics of facial expression: Recognition of facial actions and their temporal segments from face profile image sequences. IEEE Transactions on Systems, Man, and Cybernetics, Part B (Cybernetics). 2006;**36**(2):433-449

[46] Martin O, Kotsia I, Macq B, Pitas I. The enterface'05 audio-visual emotion database. In: . Proceedings of 22nd International Conference on Data Engineering Workshops, 2006; IEEE; 2006. p. 8

[47] Wang S, Liu Z, Lv S, Lv Y, Wu G, Peng P, Chen F, Wang X. A natural visible and infrared facial expression database for expression recognition and emotion inference. IEEE Transactions on Multimedia. 2010;**12**(7):682-691

[48] Ekman P, Friesen WV. Pictures of facial affect. Consulting Psychologists Press; 1975

[49] Ekman P. Facial expression and emotion. American Psychologist. 1993;**48**(4):384

[50] Cowie R, Douglas-Cowie E, Tsapatsoulis N, Votsis G, Kollias S, Fellenz W, Taylor JG. Emotion recognition in human-computer interaction. Signal Processing Magazine, IEEE. 2001;**18**(1):32-80

[51] Petridis S, Martinez B, Pantic M. The mahnob laughter database. Image and Vision Computing. 2013;**31**(2):186-202

[52] Gorbova J, Baró X, Escalera S, Demirel H, Allik J, Ozcinar C, Lüsi I, Jacques JCS, Anbarjafari G. Joint challenge on dominant and complementary emotion recognition using micro emotion features and head-pose estimation: Databases. IEEE; 2017

[53] Schuller B, Müeller R, Höernler B, Höethker A, Konosu H, Rigoll G. Audiovisual recognition of spontaneous interest within conversations. In: Proceedings of the 9th International Conference on Multimodal Interfaces; ACM; 2007. pp. 30-37

[54] Wang Y, Guan L. Recognizing human emotional state from audiovisual signals. IEEE Transactions on Multimedia. 2008;**10**(5):936-946

[55] Polikovsky S, Kameda Y, Ohta Y. Facial micro-expressions recognition using high speed camera and 3d-gradient descriptor. In:, 3rd International Conference on Crime Detection and Prevention (ICDP 2009); IET; 2009. pp. 1-6

[56] Loob C, Rasti P, Lüsi I, Jacques JCS, Baró X, Escalera S, Sapinski T, Kaminska D, Anbarjafari G. Dominant and complementary multi-emotional facial expression recognition using c-support vector classification. In: 12th IEEE International Conference on Automatic Face & Gesture Recognition (FG 2017); IEEE; 2017. pp. 833-838

[57] Ekman P, Friesen WV, Tomkins SS. Facial affect scoring technique: A first validity study. Semiotica. 1971;**3**(1):37-58

[58] Darwin C. The Expression of the Emotions in Man and Animals. New York: Oxford University Press; 1998

[59] Guillaume-Benjamin Duchenne. Mécanisme de la physionomie humaine: où, Analyse électro-physiologique de l'expression des passions. J.-B. Baillière, 1876.

[60] Hjortsjö C-H. Man's Face and Mimic Language. Lund: Studentlitteratur; 1969

[61] Ekman P, Friesen WV, Hager J. The facial action coding system (FACS): A technique for the measurement of facial action. Palo Alto: Consulting Psychologists Press, Inc.; 1983. Ekman P, Levenson RW, Friesen WV. Auto-nomic nervous system activity distinguishes among emotions. Science. 1978;**221**:1208-1212

[62] Mavadati SM, Mahoor MH, Bartlett K, Trinh P, Cohn JF. DISFA: A spontaneous facial action intensity database. IEEE Transactions on Affective Computing. 2013;**4**(2):151-160

[63] Pantic M, Valstar M, Rademaker R, Maat L. Web-based database for facial expression analysis. In: IEEE International Conference on Multimedia and Expo, 2005. ICME 2005; IEEE; 2005. p. 5

[64] Valstar M, Pantic M. Induced disgust, happiness and surprise: An addition to the MMI facial expression database. In: Proceedings of the 3rd International Workshop on EMOTION (Satellite of LREC): Corpora for Research on Emotion and Affect; 2010. p. 65

[65] Kleiner M, Wallraven C, Bülthoff HH. The MPI VideoLab-a system for high quality synchronous recording of video and audio from multiple viewpoints. Tübingen: MPI; 2004. p. 123

[66] Kaulard K, Cunningham DW, Bülthoff HH, Wallraven C. The MPI facial expression database—A validated database of emotional and conversational facial expressions. PloS One. 2012;**7**(3):e32321

[67] Cosker D, Krumhuber E, Hilton A. A FACS valid 3D dynamic action unit database with applications to 3D dynamic morphable facial modeling. In: Computer Vision (ICCV), 2011 IEEE International Conference on; IEEE; 2011. pp. 2296-2303

[68] Hager JC, Ekman P, Friesen WV. Facial action coding system. Salt Lake City: A Human Face. Technical Report. ISBN: 0-931835-01-1, 2002

[69] Cohn JF, Ambadar Z, Ekman P. Observer-based measurement of facial expression with the facial action coding system. In: The Handbook of Emotion Elicitation and Assessment; 2007. pp. 203-221

[70] Julle-Daniere E, Micheletta J, Whitehouse J, Joly M, Gass C, Burrows AM, Waller BM. Maqfacs (macaque facial action coding system) can be used to document facial movements in *Barbary macaques* (*Macaca sylvanus*). PeerJ. 2015;**3**:e1248

[71] Oster H. Baby FACS: Facial action coding system for infants andyoung children (Unpublished monograph and coding manual). New York: New York University; 2006

[72] Gross R, Matthews I, Cohn J, Kanade T, Baker S. Multi-PIE. Image and Vision Computing. 2010;**28**(5):807-813

[73] Ekman P, Freisen W. Pictures of Facial Affect. Palo Alto: Consulting Psychologists; 1976

[74] Michael Lyons, Shigeru Akamatsu, Miyuki Kamachi, and Jiro Gyoba. Coding facial expressions with Gabor wavelets. In: Proceedings of Third IEEE International Conference on Automatic Face and Gesture Recognition, 1998; IEEE; 1998. pp. 200-205

[75] Belhumeur PN, Kriegman DJ. The Yale face database. http://cvc.yale.edu/projects/yalefaces/yalefaces.html. 1997;**1**(2):4

[76] Matsumoto D, Ekman P. Japanese and Caucasian Facial Expressions of Emotion (JACFEE) and Neutral Faces (JACNeuF). 1995

[77] Samaria FS, Harter AC. Parameterisation of a stochastic model for human face identification. In: Applications of Computer Vision, 1994., Proceedings of the Second IEEE Workshop on; IEEE; 1994. pp. 138-142

[78] Cambridge AL. The Olivetti Research Ltd. database of faces

[79] Phillips PJ, Wechsler H, Huang J, Rauss PJ. The FERET database and evaluation procedure for face-recognition algorithms. Image and Vision Computing. 1998;**16**(5):295-306

[80] Karolinska Directed Emotional Faces (KDEF). http://www.emotionlab.se/resources/kdef [Accessed: 31 March 2017]

[81] Martinez AM. The AR face database. CVC Technical Report, 24, 1998

[82] Beaupré M, Cheung N, Hess U. La reconnaissance des expressions émotionnelles faciales par des décodeurs africains, asiatiques, et caucasiens. In: Poster presented at the annual meeting of the Société Québécoise pour la Recherche en Psychologie, Hull, Quebec; 2000

[83] Dailey M, Cottrell GW, Reilly J. California Facial Expressions (Cafe). Unpublished digital images, University of California, San Diego, Computer Science and Engineering Department; 2001

[84] Sim T, Baker S, Bsat M. The CMU pose, illumination, and expression (PIE) database. In: Proceedings of Fifth IEEE International Conference on Automatic Face and Gesture Recognition, 2002; IEEE; 2002. pp. 53-58

[85] Jain V, Mukherjee A. The Indian Face Database, 2002

[86] Nimstim Face Stimulus Set. http://www.macbrain.org/resources.htm [Accessed: 31 March 2017]

[87] Roh M-C, Lee S-W. Performance analysis of face recognition algorithms on Korean face database. International Journal of Pattern Recognition and Artificial Intelligence. 2007;**21**(06):1017-1033

[88] Minear M, Park DC. A lifespan database of adult facial stimuli. Behaviour Research Methods, Instruments, & Computers. 2004;**36**:630-633

[89] Chen L-F, Yen Y-S. Taiwanese Facial Expression Image Database. Brain Mapping Laboratory, Institute of Brain Science, National Yang-Ming University, Taipei, 2007

[90] Gao W, Cao B, Shan S, Chen X, Zhou D, Zhang X, Zhao D. The CAS-PEAL large-scale Chinese face database and baseline evaluations. IEEE Transactions on Systems, Man, and Cybernetics-Part A: Systems and Humans. 2008;**38**(1):149-161

[91] Kasinski A, Florek A, Schmidt A. The PUT face database. Image Processing and Communications. 2008;**13**(3-4):59-64

[92] Langner O, Dotsch R, Bijlstra G, Wigboldus DHJ, Hawk ST, van Knippenberg A. Presentation and validation of the Radboud Faces Database. Cognition and Emotion.2010;**24** (8):1377-1388

[93] Ekman P, Friesen WV. Nonverbal leakage and clues to deception. Psychiatry. 1969;**32** (1):88-106

[94] Shreve M, Godavarthy S, Goldgof D, Sarkar S. Macro-and micro-expression spotting in long videos using spatio-temporal strain. In: IEEE International Conference on Automatic Face & Gesture Recognition and Workshops (FG 2011); IEEE; 2011. pp. 51-56

[95] Warren G, Schertler E, Bull P. Detecting deception from emotional and unemotional cues. Journal of Nonverbal Behavior. 2009;**33**(1):59-69

[96] Yan W-J, Wu Q, Liu Y-J, Wang S-J, Fu X. CASME database: A dataset of spontaneous micro-expressions collected from neutralized faces. In: 10th IEEE International Conference and Workshops on Automatic Face and Gesture Recognition (FG), 2013; IEEE; 2013. pp. 1-7

[97] Black MJ, Yacoob Y. Recognizing facial expressions in image sequences using local parameterized models of image motion. International Journal of Computer Vision. 1997;**25**(1):23-48

[98] Battocchi A, Pianesi F. Dafex: Un database di espressioni facciali dinamiche. In: Proceedings of the SLI-GSCP Workshop; 2004. pp. 311-324

[99] Baron-Cohen S, Golan O, Wheelwright S, Hill JJ. Mind Reading: The Interactive Guide to Emotions. London: Jessica Kingsley; 2004

[100] Jiang P, Ma J, Minamoto Y, Tsuchiya S, Sumitomo R, Ren F. Orient video database for facial expression analysis. Age. 2007;**20**:40

[101] Busso C, Bulut M, Lee C-C, Kazemzadeh A, Mower E, Kim S, Chang JN, Lee S, Narayanan SS. IEMOCAP: Interactive emotional dyadic motion capture database. Language Resources and Evaluation. 2008;**42**(4):335

[102] Haq S, Jackson PJB, Edge J. Speaker-dependent audio-visual emotion recognition. In: AVSP; 2009. pp. 53-58

[103] Roy S, Roy C, Fortin I, Ethier-Majcher C, Belin P, Gosselin F. A dynamic facial expression database. Journal of Vision. 2007;**7**(9):944-944

[104] Wingenbach TSH, Ashwin C, Brosnan M. Validation of the Amsterdam dynamic facial expression set–bath intensity variations (ADFES-BIV): A set of videos expressing low, intermediate, and high intensity emotions. PLoS One. 2016;**11**(1):e0147112

[105] Lang PJ, Bradley MM, Cuthbert BN. International affective picture system (IAPS): Technical manual and affective ratings. In: NIMH Center for the Study of Emotion and Attention; 1997. pp. 39-58

[106] Face Place. http://wiki.cnbc.cmu.edu/Face_Place [Accessed: 31 March 2017]

[107] McDuff D, Kaliouby RE, Senechal T, Amr M, Cohn JF, Picard R Affectiva-MIT facial expression dataset (AM-FED): Naturalistic and spontaneous facial expressions collected "In-the-Wild". In: Proceedings of the 2013 IEEE Conference on Computer Vision and Pattern Recognition Workshops; 2013. pp. 881-888

[108] Corneanu CA, Escalera S, Baro X, Hyniewska S, Allik J, Anbarjafari G, Ofodile I, Kulkarni K. Automatic recognition of deceptive facial expressions of emotion. arXiv preprint arXiv:1707.04061, 2017

[109] Bartlett MS, Littlewort G, Frank M, Lainscsek C, Fasel I, Movellan J. Recognizing facial expression: machine learning and application to spontaneous behavior. In: Computer Vision and Pattern Recognition, 2005. CVPR 2005. IEEE Computer Society Conference on. Vol. 2; IEEE; 2005. pp. 568-573

[110] McKeown G, Valstar M, Cowie R, Pantic M, Schroder M. The SEMAINE database: Annotated multimodal records of emotionally colored conversations between a person and a limited agent. IEEE Transactions on Affective Computing. 2012;**3**(1):5-17

[111] McKeown G, Valstar MF, Cowie R, Pantic M. The SEMAINE corpus of emotionally coloured character interactions. In: Multimedia and Expo (ICME), 2010 IEEE International Conference on; IEEE; 2010. pp. 1079-1084

[112] Ringeval F, Sonderegger A, Sauer J, Lalanne D. Introducing the RECOLA multimodal corpus of remote collaborative and affective interactions. In: Automatic Face and Gesture Recognition (FG), 2013 10th IEEE International Conference and Workshops on; IEEE; 2013. pp. 1-8

[113] Henry SG, Fetters MD. Video elicitation interviews: A qualitative research method for investigating physician-patient interactions. The Annals of Family Medicine. 2012;**10** (2):118-125

[114] Douglas-Cowie E, Cowie R, Schroeder M. The description of naturally occurring emotional speech. In: Proceedings of 15th International Congress of Phonetic Sciences, Barcelona; 2003

[115] Goswami G, Vatsa M, Singh R. RGB-D face recognition with texture and attribute features. IEEE Transactions on Information Forensics and Security. 2014;**9**(10):1629-1640

[116] Hg RI, Jasek P, Rofidal C, Nasrollahi K, Moeslund TB, Tranchet G. An RGB-D database using Microsoft's Kinect for windows for face detection. In: Signal Image Technology and Internet Based Systems (SITIS), 2012 Eighth International Conference on; IEEE; 2012. pp. 42-46

[117] Min R, Kose N, Dugelay J-L. KinectFaceDB: A Kinect database for face recognition. IEEE Transactions on Systems, Man, and Cybernetics: Systems. 2014;**44**(11):1534-1548

[118] Lüsi I, Escarela S, Anbarjafari G. SASE: RGB-depth database for human head pose estimation. In: Computer Vision–ECCV 2016 Workshops; Springer; 2016. pp. 325-336

[119] Psychological image collection at Stirling (PICS). http://pics.psych.stir.ac.uk/ [Accessed: 31 March 2017]

[120] Microsoft, "Microsoft Kinect." http://www.xbox.com/en-US/xbox-one/accessories/kinect-for-xbox-one [Accessed: 28 March 2017]

[121] Wolff LB, Socolinsky DA, Eveland CK. Quantitative measurement of illumination invariance for face recognition using thermal infrared imagery. In Proceedings of SPIE. 2002;**4820**:140-151

[122] Equinox Corporation. "Equinox face database". 2002

[123] Akhloufi M, Bendada A, Batsale J-C. State of the art in infrared face recognition. Quantitative InfraRed Thermography Journal. 2008;**5**(1):3-26

[124] Corneanu CA, Simón MO, Cohn JF, Guerrero SE. Survey on RGB, 3D, thermal, and multimodal approaches for facial expression recognition: History, trends, and affect-related

applications. IEEE Transactions on Pattern Analysis and Machine Intelligence. 2016;**38**(8): 1548-1568

[125] Nguyen H, Kotani K, Chen F, Le B. A thermal facial emotion database and its analysis. In: Pacific-Rim Symposium on Image and Video Technology; Springer; 2013. pp. 397-408

[126] Devillers L, Vasilescu I. Reliability of lexical and prosodic cues in two real-life spoken dialog corpora. In: LREC; 2004

[127] Lee CM, Narayanan SS. Toward detecting emotions in spoken dialogs. IEEE Transactions on Speech and Audio Processing. 2005;**13**(2):293-303

[128] Robert Ladd D, Scherer K, Silverman K. An integrated approach to studying intonation and attitude. Intonation in Discourse. London/Sidney: Crom Helm. 1986;**125**:138

[129] Cauldwell RT. Where did the anger go? The role of context in interpreting emotion in speech. In: ISCA Tutorial and Research Workshop (ITRW) on Speech and Emotion; 2000

[130] Song M, You M, Li N, Chen C. A robust multimodal approach for emotion recognition. Neurocomputing. 2008;**71**(10):1913-1920

[131] Zeng Z, Jilin T, Pianfetti BM, Huang TS. Audio–visual affective expression recognition through multistream fused HMM. IEEE Transactions on Multimedia. 2008;**10**(4):570-577

[132] Wan J, Escalera S, Anbarjafari G, Escalante HJ, Baró X, Guyon I, Madadi M, Allik J, Gorbova J, Chi L, Yiliang X. Results and analysis of ChaLearn LAP multi-modal isolated and continuous gesture recognition, and real versus fake expressed emotions challenges. In ChaLearn LaP, Action, Gesture, and Emotion Recognition Workshop and Competitions: Large Scale Multimodal Gesture Recognition and Real Versus Fake Expressed Emotions, ICCV; 2017;**4**(6)

[133] Lu K, Jia Y. Audio-visual emotion recognition with boosted coupled HMMM. In: 21st International Conference on Pattern Recognition (ICPR), 2012; IEEE; 2012. pp. 1148-1151

Chapter 4

Mental Task Recognition by EEG Signals: A Novel Approach with ROC Analysis

Takashi Kuremoto, Masanao Obayashi,
Shingo Mabu and Kunikazu Kobayashi

Additional information is available at the end of the chapter

http://dx.doi.org/10.5772/intechopen.71743

Abstract

Electroencephalogram or electroencephalography (EEG) has been widely used in medical fields and recently in cognitive science and brain-computer interface (BCI) research. To distinguish metal tasks such as reading, calculation, motor imagery, etc., it is generally to extract features of EEG signals by dimensionality reduction methods such as principle component analysis (PCA), linear determinant analysis (LDA), common spatial pattern (CSP), and so on for classifiers, for example, k-nearest neighbor method (kNN), kernel support vector machine (SVM), and artificial neural networks (ANN). In this chapter, a novel approach of feature extraction of EEG signals with receiver operating characteristic (ROC) analysis is introduced.

Keywords: brain-computer interface (BCI), electroencephalogram or electroencephalography (EEG), artificial neural networks (ANN), support vector machine (SVM), receiver operating characteristic (ROC), Fourier transformation (FT)

1. Introduction

The electrical activity of the brain can be measured by electrodes placed on the scalp and the observed signal is called electroencephalogram or electroencephalography (EEG). EEG is also called "brain wave" and it has been widely used in clinical diagnose of brain disease since the early time of last century [1].

Different mental tasks yield EEG signals in different patterns in the different observation values. For example, in the case of human brain, the resting state (relax state), the most prominent power spectra are 8–15 Hz EEG signals (so-called "alpha-wave") observed in posterior sites,

IntechOpen

© 2018 The Author(s). Licensee IntechOpen. This chapter is distributed under the terms of the Creative Commons Attribution License (http://creativecommons.org/licenses/by/3.0), which permits unrestricted use, distribution, and reproduction in any medium, provided the original work is properly cited. (cc) BY

meanwhile, 16–31 Hz signals (beta-wave) appears in the mental tasks such as active thinking, high alert, anxious, etc. Gamma-wave, EEG with higher than 32 Hz, displays during cross-modal sensory processing such as combining the stimuli of visual and auditory. On the other hand, the location of electrodes on scalp records different EEG signals spatially, and they are called EEG signals in different "channels". The allocation of electrodes is usually with the international 10–20 system. The name of 10–20 system comes from those adjacent electrodes that are allocated in distances of 10 or 20% of the total front-back or right-left of skull. More channels, more spatial features, may result in higher recognition rate of mental tasks. On the other hand, few channels give lower computational cost in the EEG classification systems.

In last decades, EEG has been utilized in the field of the brain-computer interface (BCI) for its ability of the mental task recognition [2–6]. Mental tasks indicate the state of activity of the brain with some specific tasks. For example, imagining writing a letter, counting, calculating, or raising a hand, a leg, etc. There are many classifiers for EEG recognition that have been proposed such as linear discriminant analysis (LDA), support vector machine (SVM), artificial neural networks (ANN), fuzzy inference systems, Bayesian graphical network (BGN), and so on. However, for the reasons of the complex nature of EEG signals, for example, noise and outliers, nonstationarity, high dimensionality, individual difference, etc., the pattern recognition (classification) problem of EEG signals is still a high hurdle for BCI realization.

To normalize the raw EEG signals, Nakayama and Inagaki proposed to reduce the number of the time series data of power spectrum of frequency given by fast Fourier transformation (FFT) with average values and normalize the FFT by a nonlinear normalization function [4]. To extract discriminant features of EEG signals for mental task recognition, Li and Zhang proposed a regularized tensor discriminative feature space, which includes multichannels, power spectrum of frequency, and those data in time series: channel × frequency × time [5]. Obayashi et al. applied Nakayama and Inagaki's pre-processing method to their practical EEG recognition system with single channel information in [6]. In [7], Jrad and Congedo used spatially weighted SVM (*sw*SVM) to build a spatial filter for each temple feature. In the previous works of authors [8], discriminant temporal frequency data were utilized to reduce the flattening of different EEG patterns adopting the pre-processing method of [4], temporal spatial frequency concept, and average moving processing of [7] were adopted to obtain higher rate of mental task recognition.

Recently, we proposed to find the discriminant feature of temporal frequency by receiver operating characteristic (ROC) analysis in [9]. The discriminant feature of temporal frequency indicates the power spectra of FFT in an interval of time series of EEG data, which are higher relative to a mental task comparing with other intervals (windows). ROC analysis has been widely utilized in medical & diagnostic science [10, 11], microarray classification [12], and recently in EEG classification [13]. It is a stochastic criterion to classify two kinds of probability distributions and the details will be described in the next section.

In this chapter, discriminative feature extraction methods of EEG signals, which play an important role for classifiers, are discussed. Specially, an advanced temporal–spatial spectrum feature extraction method is introduced [9].

2. Discriminant feature extraction using ROC analysis

2.1. ROC analysis

Receiver operating characteristic (ROC) analysis was first used in radar signal detection in 1940s. The classification results of data in two kinds of distributions can be divided into four categories: true positive (TP), false positive (FP), true negative (TN), and false negative (FN). A curve is plotted by the rate of TP against the rate of FP and it can be a measure of classification accuracy.

Now, let the TP of class A be in the shadow area α, and FP in area $1-\beta$, where β is the TP of class B (See **Figure 1**). When the dividing line between A and B is slid along x axis, a ROC curve is plotted indexing the divisibility of the two probability density functions (See **Figure 2**). If two distributions completely overlapped, $\alpha = 1-\beta$.

In **Figure 2**, the area below the ROC curve is called "area under the curve" (AUC). This value takes from 0.0 to 1.0, and it is an indicator of the divisibility of the two distributions. If the value of AUC becomes 0.5, two distributions are completely overlapped. Conversely, when the value of AUC reaches 1.0 (or 0.0), it means that the two distributions are completely separated.

In the practice procedure of ROC analysis, the area of α, that is, the rate of TP, and $1-\beta$, the rate of TN, can be calculated by the number of training samples, which are labeled data belonging to different classes.

2.2. Discriminant feature extraction of EEG signals

In [8], power spectrums of an interval of frequencies given by EEG signals FFT, which has a distinguish value to neighbors were used as discriminant features as the input vectors of classifiers. The flow chart of this method is depicted in **Figure 3**. **Algorithm I** shows the method in detail.

Algorithm I.

Step 1. Dividing (windowing) the original EEG signals into several intervals;

Step 2. Executing discrete Fourier transformation (DFT) in different intervals and normalizing the transformation results;

Step 3. Calculating the average power spectrum of banded (limited) frequencies in each phases;

Step 4. Finding a special (feature) interval, in which average power spectrum is the most different one from its neighborhoods;

Step 5. The power spectrum of FFT in the windowed frequencies and their average values are used as the feature data for classifiers.

A sample of the first processing (Step 1) is shown in **Figure 4**. In **Figure 4**, an EEG signal, which is a time series data (the potential of an electrode) of one channel, is divided into five intervals. DFT is executed in each interval at Step 2, and as a sample, the result of the second intervals (at time 30–60) is shown in **Figure 5**.

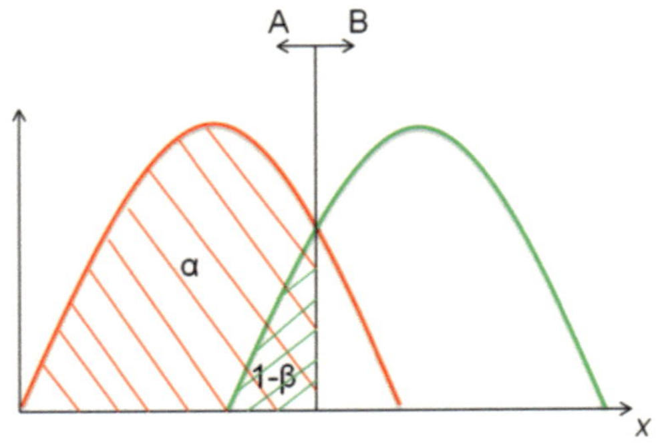

Figure 1. Overlapping of the probabilities of two classes of data.

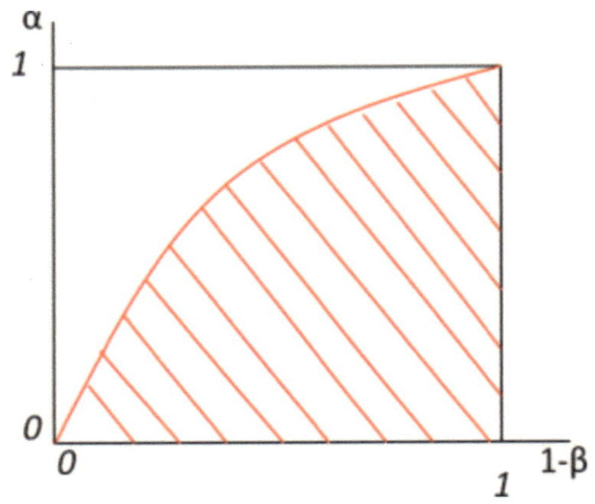

Figure 2. AUC of ROC curve.

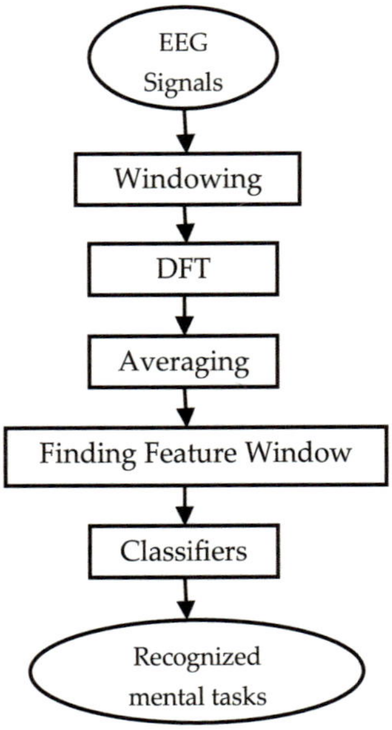

Figure 3. Flow chart of EEG signal recognition in [8].

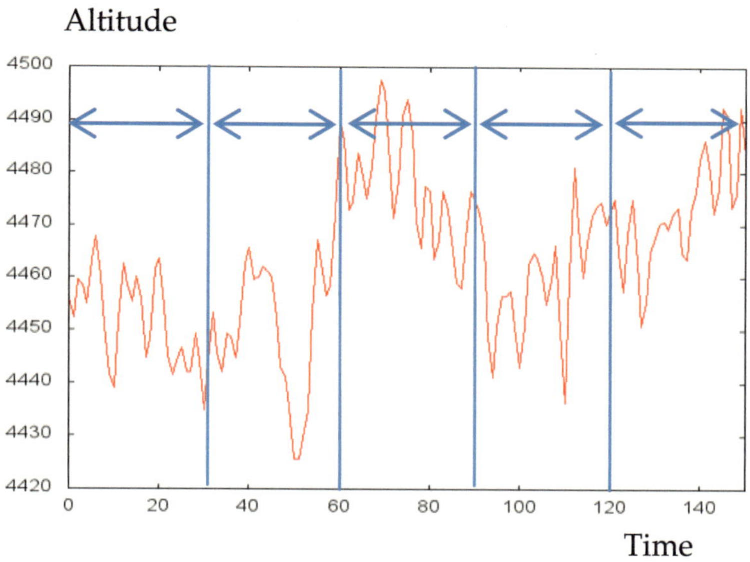

Figure 4. A sample of Step 1 processing: dividing EEG signals into several intervals.

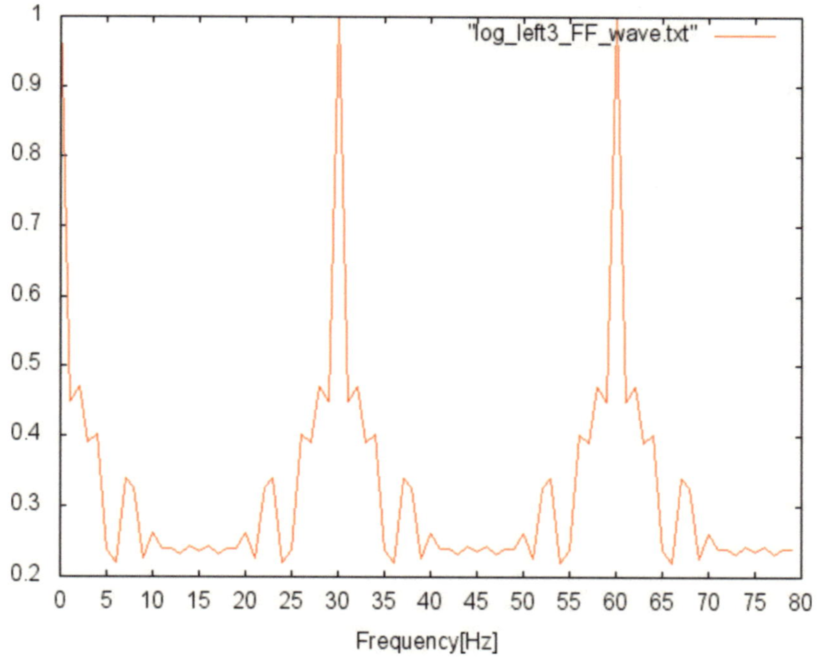

Figure 5. A sample of Step 2 processing: DFT and normalizing results of an interval of EEG time series data.

The normalization of DFT results is given by a nonlinear function [4].

$$x(n) = \frac{\log(x(n) - \max(x(n)) + 1)}{\log(\max(x(n)) - \min(x(n)) + 1)} \tag{1}$$

where $x(n)$ is the original DFT power spectrum of frequency n.

This nonlinear normalization reduces the vibration of time series of DFT results, avoiding the overfitting when classifiers are designed.

A frequency interval, which has distinguished power spectra for a certain mental task is chosen by Eq. (2).

$$\arg\max_{p} L(p) = \sum_{h=h_{low}}^{h=h_{up}} | F_{(p+1)h} - F_{ph} | \tag{2}$$

where $p = 1, 2, \ldots, P$ is the number of intervals, F_{ph} is the power spectrum on the frequency, $h = h_{low,}\ h_{low+1}, \ldots, h_{up}$ is the frequency, h_{low} and h_{up} are bands of feature frequencies of mental tasks and they were 4 and 45 Hz, respectively in our experiments.

For ROC analysis, it gives a measure of the difference between two probability distributions, it is validly used to find the discriminant features for EEG signal classification. In [13], Nguyen et al. utilized the AUC of ROC curve to select the elite wavelet coefficients, and in [9], we adopted an algorithm that using high AUC values to select metal task-related frequencies of EEG signals in different channels, respectively, and using the power spectrum of these frequencies as discriminant features for various classifiers such as SVM, ANN [including multi-layer perceptron (MLP), and deep neural networks (DNN)], k-nearest neighbor, decision tree (DT), and so on. The discriminant feature extraction method using ROC analysis is given by **Algorithm II**.

Algorithm II.

Let the input signals be $x_{kc,m,n}$ ($c = 1$ or 2, $k = 1, 2, \ldots, K$), where k indicates the kth EEG signal of a set of EEG data, and c indicates the class of mental task, m indicates the channel number, and n is the time of signal.

Step 1. Perform FFT to all the EEG signals $x_{kc,m,n}$ and let the result be power spectrum $E_{m,p}$ ($p = 1, 2, \ldots, P$) corresponding to frequency $F_{kc,m,p,}$ where p indicates the order number of frequencies.

Step 2. Obtain $P_{k1,m,p}$ and $P_{k2,m,p}$, which are two probability density functions of $F_{kc,m,p}$ at p frequency, where class c = 1 and 2 of K signals of channel m.

Step 3. Calculate the ROC curve and its AUC $A_{m,p}$ of $P_{k1,m,p}$ and $P_{k2,m,p}$.

Step 4. Repeat Step 2 and Step 3 on all channels, a set $AUC_{m,n}$ of frequency p in channel m is obtained.

Step 5. Find P points of frequencies, in which $A_{m,p}$ is high.

Step 6. Power spectrum $E_{m,p}$(p = 1, 2, …, P) of the unknown EEG signal are used as input feature vector of a classifier.

The main difference between **Algorithm I** and **II** is that the power spectra in a special interval of frequencies, which is mostly related to an event of brain activity, are chosen in the former, meanwhile the power spectra of special frequencies chosen by high AUC of ROC are chosen as discriminant features in the later algorithm. The flow chart of EEG signal classification using ROC analysis is depicted in **Figure 6**.

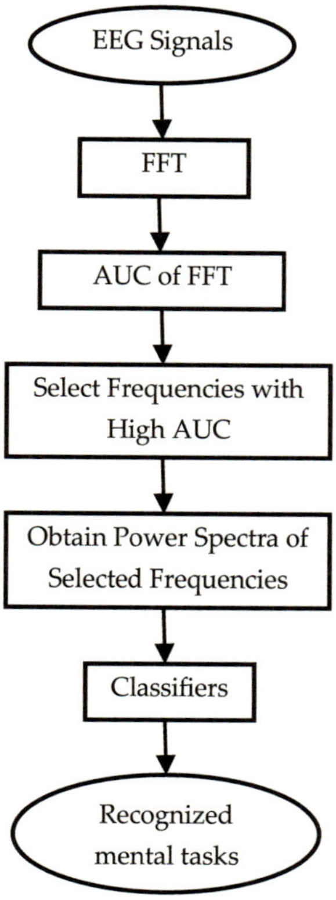

Figure 6. Flow chart of the EEG signal classification using ROC analysis.

Figures 7–9 showed a sample of the processing. In **Figure 7**, a raw EEG signal and its FFT result are shown. Note that the number of horizontal axis indicates the order of frequencies, and the value of vertical axis is the power spectrum. In **Figure 8**, the distribution of the power

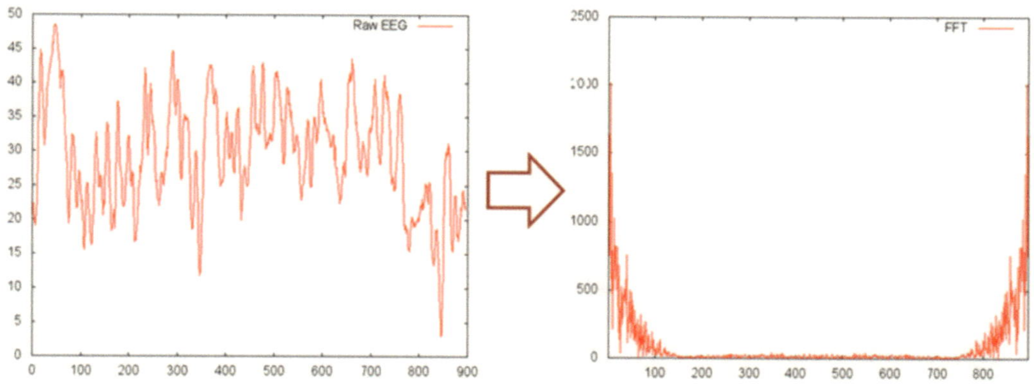

Figure 7. A raw EEG signal (left) and its FFT results (right).

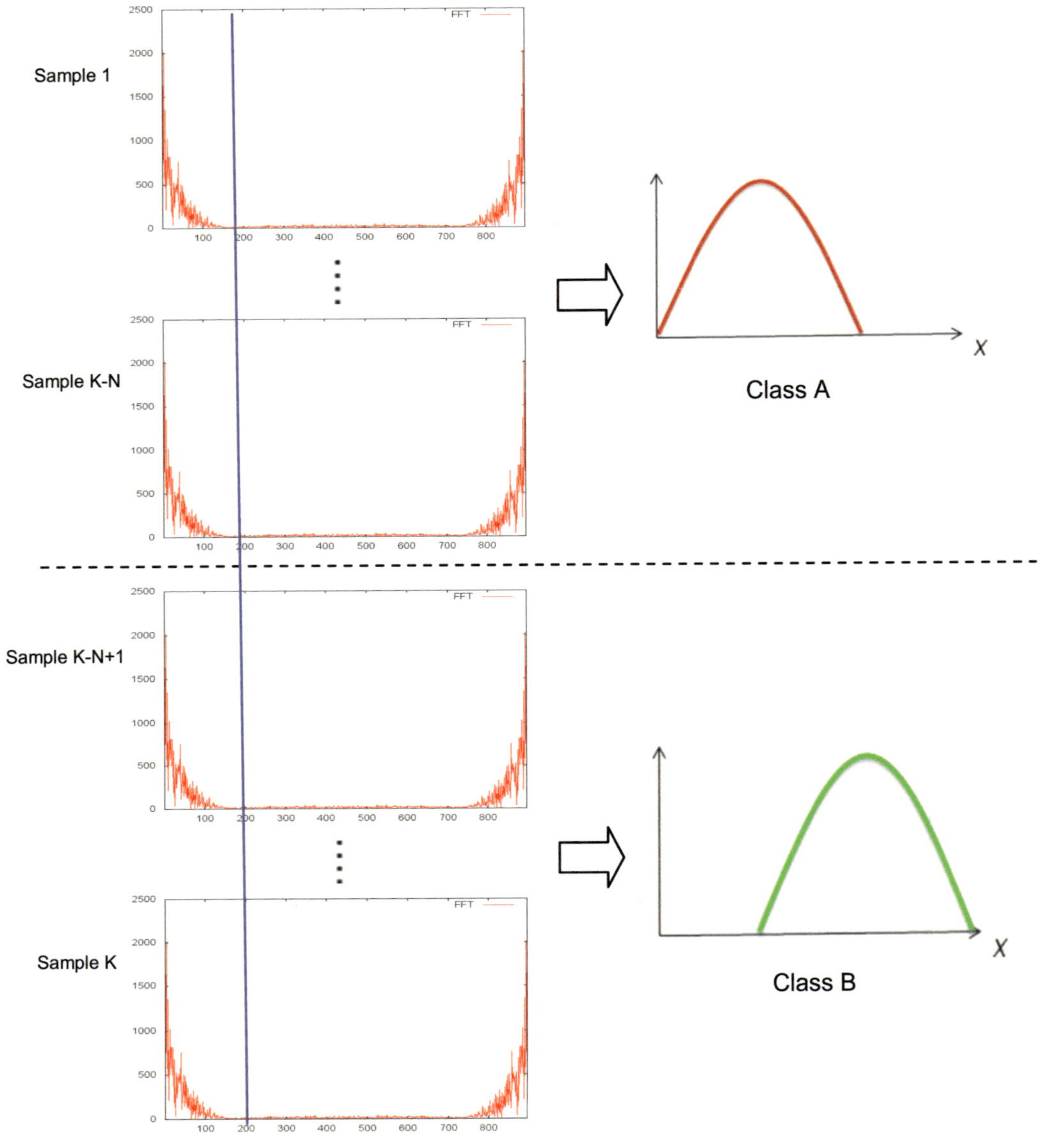

Figure 8. Calculation of the power spectra distribution (histogram) of each frequency of two classes of EEG signals. Frequency 200 (series number) is illustrated as a sample here.

spectrum of each frequency is calculated using the labeled samples. For example, there are K samples including N samples of class A and K–N samples of class B as shown in **Figure 8**. AUC of the power spectra on each frequency is shown in **Figure 9**. Additionally, frequencies with high AUC extracted by a threshold line are used as criteria of discriminant feature selection. For example, in the case of three input dimensions for a classifier, the input vector is the power spectra with high AUC of frequencies as shown in **Table 1**.

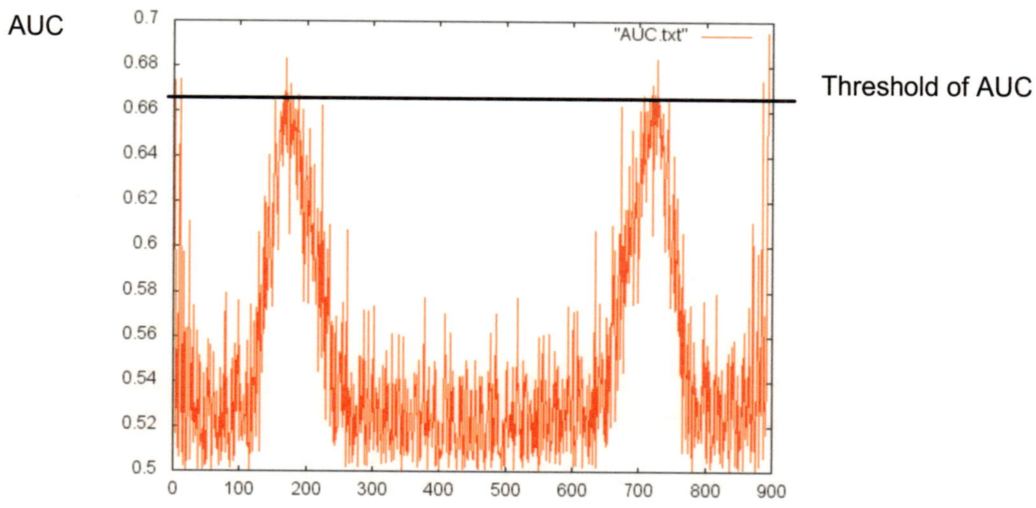

Figure 9. AUC of the power spectra on each frequency of two classes of EEG signals.

Ordered AUC	Number of freq.	Power spectrum (input of classifiers)
0.695	896	1545.186
0.691	158	10.093
0.688	726	9.535

Table 1. A sample of discriminant features extracted by ROC analysis.

3. Experiments

To compare the performance of different feature extract methods for EEG signal classification, experiments with two kinds of EEG data were performed [9]. One was a benchmark data set given by Brain-Computer Interfaces Laboratory, Colorado State University [14, 15], and another was from BCI competition II [16]. Classifiers used in the comparison experiments for different feature extraction methods were kernel SVM, MLP, kNN, deep neural network (DNN), and DT, in which source coded are in a software package R [17] as shown in **Table 2**.

The evaluation of the performance of different feature extraction methods uses the accuracy of classification, which is given by Eq. (3).

$$Accuracy = \frac{TP + TN}{TP + TN + FP + FN} \tag{3}$$

Name	Function
ROCR	ROC analysis/AUC calculation
Kernlab	Support vector machine (kernel SVM)
nnet	Neural network (MLP)
class	k-nearest neighbor (kNN)
h2o(+JavaVM)	deep neural network (DNN)
rpart	decision tree (DT)

Table 2. Software R [17] and its function used in the experiment.

4. Benchmark data and experiment results

Open access free website of BCI laboratory of Colorado State University [14, 15] provides Benchmark EEG data with five kinds of mental tasks as shown in **Table 3**. The data were measured by six channels with EEG sensors (See **Figure 10**) and one channel data of an EOG sensor (to measure the movement of an eye). The sampling rate is 250 Hz, and EEG data are recorded in 10 seconds, that is, 2500 time series data obtained by one trial. EEG signals of each mental task are recorded in 10 trials of five subjects. For the ROC analysis classifies two classes data, "Baseline" (relaxing state) and "Multiplication" (Multiplication calculation mentally) data, were used in our experiment. Additionally, training samples and testing samples used EEG data of the same subject, which were chosen randomly with a ratio of 15:5.

The classification accuracies of **Algorithm I** [8], and **Algorithm II** [9] by different classifiers are shown in **Table 4**. In **Table 4**, it is also shown that different dimensionalities of the input vector influenced the classification accuracy. Feature extraction method using **Algorithm II**. (FFT and ROC analysis) had a prior performance especially in the case of 140-dimension input vector. The highest classification accuracy 97.5% was given by kernel SVM classifier, and DNN stood the second position with 95.37% using **Algorithm II** feature extraction method, respectively.

4.1. BCI competition II data and experiment results

BCI competition II data [16] were also used in the performance comparison of different feature extraction methods. There are two-class data named "Ia" and "Ib," which are EEG data obtained

Mental task	Contents
Baseline	Relaxing as much as possible
Multiplication	Calculating multiplication mentally.
Letter-composing	Considering the contents of a letter
Rotation	Imagining rotation of a 3-D object
Counting	Imagining writing a number in order

Table 3. Mental tasks in a benchmark database [14, 15].

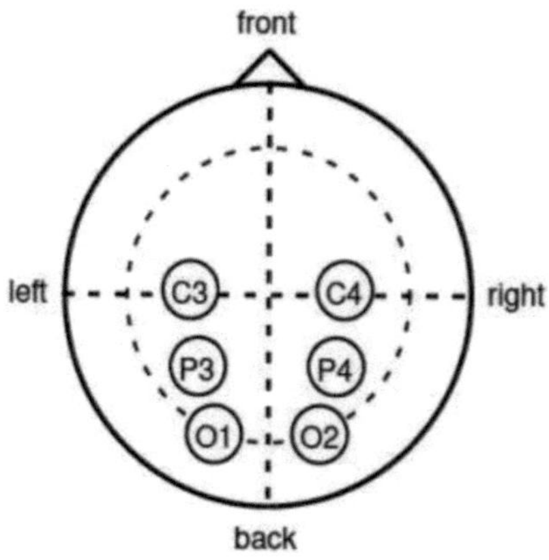

Figure 10. Positions of EEG sensors with six channels [8].

Classifier	Feature extraction method			
	Algorithm I (Temporal FFT)		Algorithm II (FFT and ROC analysis)	
	140-D	1120-D	140-D	1120-D
Kernel SVM	59.58	70	**97.5**	75
MLP	49.58	38.33	**55.0**	52.92
k-Nearest neighbor	55.92	66.67	**73.33**	66.03
Deep neural network	61.67	71.67	**95.37**	94.58
Decision tree	34.5	35.5	**50.0**	**50.0**

Unit: %.

The bold values indicate the best recognition result between different feature extraction algorithms for one classifier in the case of benchmark data.

Table 4. Classification results of benchmark data [14, 15].

by a healthy subject and an amyotrophic lateral sclerosis (ALS) patient. In each data set, two kinds of mental tasks were required, respectively. One was to move a cursor up (class A) and another was to move the cursor down (class B). Details of these EEG data descriptions are shown in **Table 5**. Additionally, training samples and testing samples were chosen randomly with a ratio of 240:28 for Ia and 180:20 for Ib.

The accuracies of classification of Ia and Ib by different feature extraction methods and classifiers are shown in **Tables 6** and **7**, respectively. **Algorithm II** (FFT and ROC analysis) showed the highest classifications for all classifiers. The highest accuracy for data Ia was 91.23%, given by

Data set	Mental tasks	Trials	Channels	Samples/Ch.	Sampling freq.
Ia	2	135/133	6	896	256
Ib	2	100/100	7	1152	256

Table 5. Description of EEG data of BCI competition II [16].

Classifier	Feature extraction method			
	Algorithm I (Temporal FFT)		Algorithm II (FFT and ROC analysis)	
	140-D	**1120-D**	**140-D**	**1120-D**
Kernel SVM	61.10	58.98	87.04	**91.23**
MLP	49.09	49.95	68.06	**70.86**
k-Nearest neighbor	50.55	55.46	**79.17**	55.76
Deep neural network	57.72	62.08	83.48	**86.10**
Decision tree	41.79	43.15	67.5	**73.22**

Unit: %.
The bold values indicate the best recognition result between different feature extraction algorithms for one classifier in the case of data Ia.

Table 6. Classification results of BCI competition II data Ia [16].

Classifier	Feature extraction method			
	Algorithm I (Temporal FFT)		Algorithm II (FFT and ROC analysis)	
	140-D	**1120-D**	**140-D**	**1120-D**
Kernel SVM	52.99	53.91	76.16	**77.65**
MLP	46.40	53.36	**58.15**	49.09
k-Nearest neighbor	45.90	48.25	**60.04**	57.81
Deep neural network	43.90	49.25	69.93	**75.25**
Decision tree	28.43	47.99	45.44	**55.55**

Unit: %.
The bold values indicate the best recognition result between different feature extraction algorithms for one classifier in the case of data Ib.

Table 7. Classification results of BCI competition II data Ib [16].

kernel SVM using 1120 dimensions of input vector, which were discriminant features extracted by **Algorithm II**, and the same methods yielded the highest classification rate 77.65% for data Ib. These accuracies are higher than the best classification rates 90.10 and 56.67%, which are the results of a state-of-the-art method of EEG signal recognition [13]. The future work of the improvement of **Algorithm II** is to find the optimal dimensionality of the discriminant feature space. It is hard to consider higher dimensionality results higher classification accuracy as shown in these experiments. It was better to choose 140-D in the case of benchmark data (**Table 4**), and oppositely, 1120-D was more suitable for BCI competition II data (**Tables 6** and **7**).

5. Conclusion

To recognize the mental tasks by EEG signals, two kinds of temporal-spatial frequency–based feature extraction methods were introduced in this chapter. In **Algorithm I**, event-related intervals of the raw EEG time series data (temporal information) was extracted at first, and the averaged power spectra of frequencies given by FFT within the interval (frequency information) were used as the discriminant features. In **Algorithm II**, event-related frequencies of EEG's FFT were extracted by ROC analysis with high AUCs. The input space for classifiers was composed by all features extracted by two algorithms from multiple channels, so the spatial information was also included in these feature extraction methods.

Pattern recognition of EEG signals has been studied for decades, and it plays an important role in the field of human robot interaction (HRI). So, we expect that the feature extraction methods introduced in this chapter can be adopted in the real HRI systems in the near future.

Acknowledgements

We would like to thank dear Editors for their appropriate advices during the revision of this paper. This work was supported by Grant-in-Aid for Scientific Research (JSPS No. 26330254 & No. 25330287).

Author details

Takashi Kuremoto[1]*, Masanao Obayashi[1], Shingo Mabu[1] and Kunikazu Kobayashi[2]

*Address all correspondence to: wu@yamaguchi-u.ac.jp

1 Yamaguchi University, Japan

2 Aichi Prefectural University, Japan

References

[1] Malmivuo J, Plonsey R. Bioelectromagnetism: Principles and Applications of Bioelectric and Biomagnetic Fields. Oxford University Press, Oxford; 1995. http://www.bem.fi/book/

[2] Lotte F, Congedo M, Lecuyer A, Lamarche F, Arnaldi B. A review of classification algorithms for EEG-based brain-computer interfaces. Journal of Neural Engineering. 2007;**4**: 24-48

[3] Cheng SY, Hsu HT. Mental Fatigue Measurement Using EEG, Risk Management Trends. In: Nota G, editor. InTech, Rijeka, Croatia; 2011. pp. 203-228

[4] NakayamaK, Inagaki K. A brain computer interface based on neural network with efficient pre-processing. In: Proceedings of 2006 International Symposium on Intelligent Signal Processing and Communication Systems (ISPACS 2006). 2006. pp. 673-676

[5] Li J, Zhang L. Regularized tensor discriminant analysis for single trial EEG classification in BCI. Pattern Recognition Letters. 2010;**31**:619-628

[6] Obayashi M, Watanabe K, Kuremoto T, Kobayashi K. Development of a brain computer interface using inexpensive commercial EEG sensor with one-channel. In: Proceedings of the 17th International Symposium on Artificial Life and Robotics (ISAROB). 2012. pp. 714-717

[7] Jrad N, Conedo M. Identification of spatial and temporal features of EEG. Neurocomputing. 2012;**90**:66-71

[8] Kuremoto T, Baba Y, Obayashi M, Mabu S, Kobayashi K. To extraction the feature of EEG signals for mental task recognition. In: Proceedings of 54th Annual Conference of the SICE. 2015. pp. 353-358

[9] Kuremoto T, Baba Y, Obayashi M, Mabu S, Kobayashi K. A method of feature extraction for EEG signals recognition using ROC curve. In: Proceedings of 2017 International Conference on Artificial Life and Robotics. 2017. pp. 654-657

[10] Hanley JA, Mcneil BJ. The meaning and use of the area under a receiver operating characteristic (ROC) curve. Radiology. 1982;**143**:29-36

[11] Mamitsuka H. Selecting features in microarray classification using ROC curves. Pattern Recognition. 2006;**39**(12):2393-2404

[12] Pereira P. Evaluation of rapid diagnostic test performance. In: Saxena SK, editor. Chapter 8. Proof and Concepts in Rapid Diagnostic Tests and Technologies. InTech, Rijeka, Croatia; 2016

[13] Nguyen T, Khosravi A, Creighton D, Nahavandi S. EEG signal classification for BCI applications by wavelets and interval type-2 fuzzy logic systems. Expert Systems with Applications. 2015;**42**:4370-4380

[14] Benchmark EEG Data: Brain-Computer Interfaces Laboratory, Colorado State University: http://www.cs.colostate.edu/eeg/main/data/1989_Keirn_and_Aunon

[15] Anderson CW, Sijercic Z. Classification of EEG signals from four subjects during five mental tasks. In: IEEE Proceeding on Engineering Application in Neural Network. 1997. pp. 407-414

[16] BCI Competition II: http://www.bbci.de/competition/ii/#datasets

[17] The R Project for Statistical Computing: https://www.r-project.org/

Section 2

Robot Navigation

Chapter 5

Person Identification Using Multimodal Biometrics under Different Challenges

Önsen Toygar, Esraa Alqaralleh and Ayman Afaneh

Additional information is available at the end of the chapter

http://dx.doi.org/10.5772/intechopen.71667

Abstract

The main aims of this chapter are to show the importance and role of human identification and recognition in the field of human-robot interaction, discuss the methods of person identification systems, namely traditional and biometrics systems, and compare the most commonly used biometric traits that are used in recognition systems such as face, ear, palmprint, iris, and speech. Then, by showing and comparing the requirements, advantages, disadvantages, recognition algorithms, challenges, and experimental results for each trait, the most suitable and efficient biometric trait for human-robot interaction will be discussed. The cases of human-robot interaction that require to use the unimodal biometric system and why the multimodal biometric system is also required will be discussed. Finally, two fusion methods for the multimodal biometric system will be presented and compared.

Keywords: person identification, biometrics, multimodal biometrics, face recognition, iris recognition, palmprint recognition, ear recognition, speech recognition

1. Introduction

Human identification is one of the oldest behaviors that were done by people to distinguish each other. In the old ages, it was unusual to wrongly identify a person because the number of people was not much in each community. Consequently, memorizing all the persons that you deal within that time was possible. Additionally, it was enough to see the face of any person or to hear his voice to recognize him; therefore, human identification was not considered as a hard issue. The increase of the number of people and the occurrence of commercial and financial transactions forced people to find new reliable methods for human identification in order to prevent the unauthorized person to access authorized information. The new methods of

IntechOpen

© 2018 The Author(s). Licensee IntechOpen. This chapter is distributed under the terms of the Creative Commons Attribution License (http://creativecommons.org/licenses/by/3.0), which permits unrestricted use, distribution, and reproduction in any medium, provided the original work is properly cited. (cc) BY

human identification were classified into two main approaches as traditional and biometrics approaches. Matching process of these methods is conducted not only by humans but also by automated systems, which speed up the matching process in addition to the capability of the large size of memory.

2. Person identification approaches (traditional vs. biometrics)

The traditional human identification approaches depend on changeable parameters such as passwords or magnetic/ID cards. These parameters can be easily used by illegal persons, if they know the password or have the card. Losing, forgetting, or stealing are common disadvantages for all the traditional identification methods which make it unreliable and inaccurate especially in the high precise system such as forensics, financial, bank, and border ports systems. The need for more robust systems of person identification in addition to the development of the sensors and automated systems was incentive to construct the systems that depend on the unique features of each person. These features are extracted from a human trait such as fingerprint, face, and speech. Human recognition using features that are extracted from inherent physical or behavioral traits of the individuals is defined as biometrics. In addition to the enhancement of the efficiency and capability of recognition systems, biometrics facilitates identifying, and claiming process, where it is not required to memorize any passwords or to carry any ID cards such as passports or driving license.

Biometrics is the science of establishing the identity of an individual based on a vector of features derived from a behavioral characteristics or specific physical attribute that the person holds. The behavioral characteristic includes how the person interacts and moves, such as their speaking style, hand gestures, signature, etc. The physiological category includes the physical human traits such as fingerprints, iris, face, veins, eyes, hand shape, palmprint, and many more. Evaluating these traits assists the recognition process using the biometric systems [1].

A biometric system includes two main phases as enrollment and recognition. Biometric data (image, video, or speech) are captured and stored in a database in enrollment phase. The recognition phase mainly includes extraction of the salient features and generation of the matching scores in order to compare query features against the stored templates. The biometric system will report an identity at the end of the decision process after performing matching, and this will be the identity of the most resembling person in the database.

3. Common biometric traits

In this section, a brief overview, requirements, advantages, and disadvantages of the most commonly used unimodal biometric traits are presented and explained.

3.1. Face

Face recognition is one of the most important abilities that we use in our daily lives. Face recognition has been an active research area over the last 40 years, and the first automated face recognition system was developed by Takeo Kanade in 1973 [2]. The increasing interest in the face recognition research is caused by the satisfactory performance in many widely used applications such as the public security, commercial, and multimedia data management applications that use face as biometric trait. Face recognition has several advantages over other biometrics such as fingerprint and iris besides being natural and nonintrusive. First, the most important advantage of face is that it can be captured at a distance and in covert manner. Second, in addition to the identity, the face can also show the expression and emotion of the individual such as sadness, wonder, or scaring. Moreover, it provides a biographic data such as gender and age. Third, large databases of face images are already available, where the users should provide their face image in order to acquire driver's license or ID card. Finally, people are generally more willing to share their face images in the public domain as evinced by the increasing interest in social media applications (e.g., Facebook) with functionalities like face tagging.

A face recognition system generally consists of four modules namely face detection, preprocessing, feature extraction, and matching as shown in **Figure 1**. An original face image and its preprocessed variant are also shown in **Figure 2**.

3.2. Iris

Iris recognition is one of the most reliable methods for personal identification. The use of iris texture analysis for biometric identification is clearly well established with the advantages of uniqueness and stability. Iris recognition has been successfully applied in access control systems managing large databases. The United Arab Emirates has been using iris biometrics for border control and expellees tracking purposes for the past decade [3].

Iris is one of the most valuable traits for automatic identification of human being. A number of reasons justify this interest. First of all, the iris is a protected internal organ of the eye that is visible from the exterior. The iris is an annular structure and planar shape that turns easily, and it has a rich texture. Furthermore, iris texture is predominantly a phenotypic with limited genetic penetrance. The appearance is stable over lifetime, which holds tremendous promise

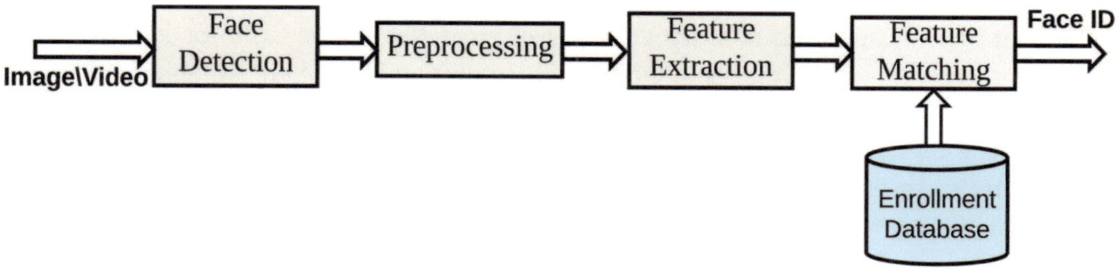

Figure 1. Block diagram of a face recognition system.

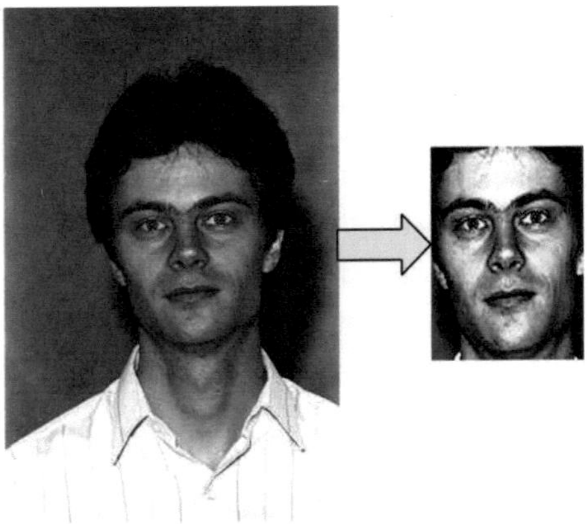

Figure 2. An original and a preprocessed face image.

for leveraging iris recognition in diverse application scenarios such as border control, forensic investigations, and cryptosystems.

There are also some drawbacks with it. It needs much user cooperation for data acquisition, and it is often sensitive to occlusion. Iris data acquisition needs a controlled environment. Additionally, data acquisition devices are quite costly. Iris recognition cannot be used in a covert situation.

A typical iris recognition system has four different modules such as acquisition, segmentation, normalization, and matching. These modules are shown in **Figure 3** for a general iris recognition system.

3.3. Palmprint

The palmprint recognition system is considered as one of the most successful biometric systems that are reliable and effective. This system identifies the person based on the principal lines, wrinkles, and ridges on the surface of the palm. Studies and research over 10 years have proven that the interesting feature of palmprint is fixed and invariant, and a palmprint acquired from any person is unique, so it can be reliable as a biometric trait.

Some of the advantages of the palmprint recognition compared with other biometric trait systems are invariant line structure, low intrusiveness, and the low cost of capturing device. Palmprint identification requires either high (refers to 400 dpi or more) or low (refers to 150 dpi or less) resolution images in which high-resolution images are suitable for forensic applications such as criminal detection [4] and low-resolution images are more suitable for civil and commercial applications such as access control. High-resolution and low-resolution palmprint images are demonstrated in **Figure 4**. Additionally, the area of palmprint is larger than fingerprint; consequently, there is a possibility of capturing more distinctive features in it.

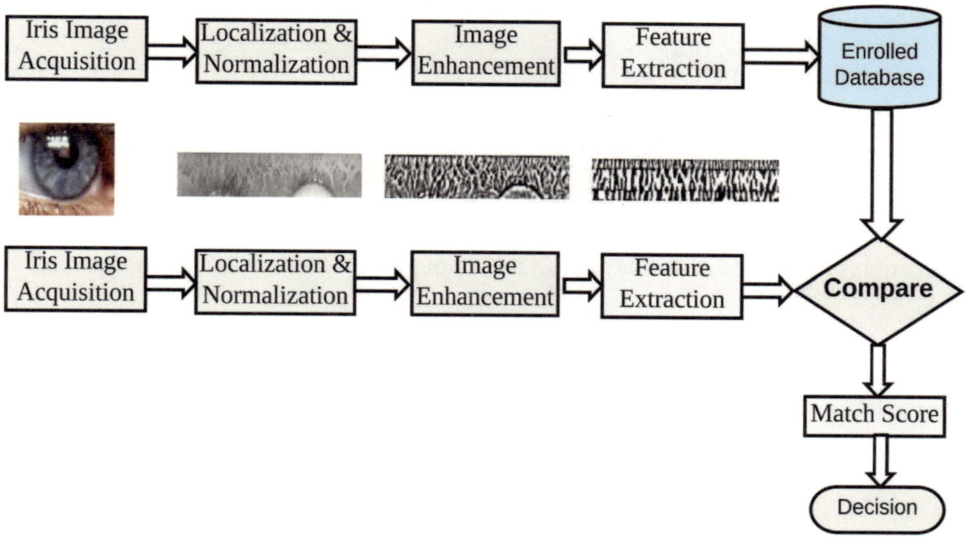

Figure 3. Block diagram of an iris recognition system [1].

Due to its low cost, user friendly system, high speed, and high accuracy of palmprint recognition, it can be considered as one of the most reliable and suitable biometric recognition system. A lot of work has already been done about palmprint recognition, since it is a very interesting research area. However, more research is needed to obtain efficient palmprint system [4].

There are three groups of marks which are used in palmprint identification [5] as geometric features, line features (e.g., principle lines, wrinkles), and point features (e.g., minutiae points). A typical palmprint recognition system consists of palmprint acquisition, preprocessing, feature extraction, and matching phases [6].

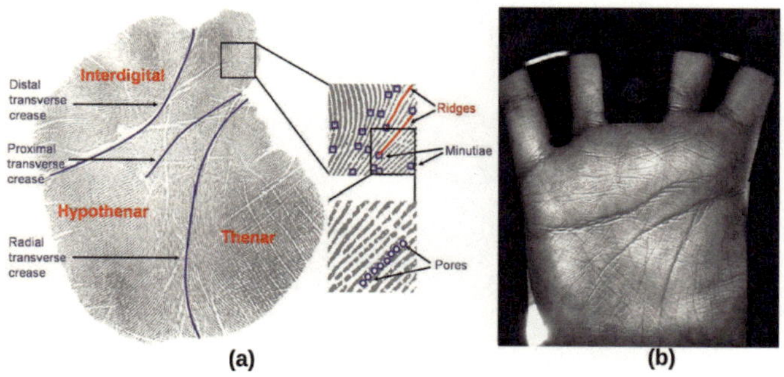

Figure 4. Palmprint features (a) a high-resolution image and (b) a low-resolution image.

3.4. Fingerprint

The modern history of fingerprint identification begins in the 19th century with the development of identification bureaus charged with keeping accurate records about indexed individuals. The acquisition of fingerprint was performed firstly by using ink technique [7].

The main application of fingerprint identification is forensic investigation of crimes. John Maloy performed a forensic identification in the late 1850s [8] by designing a high-security identification system that has always been the main goal in the security business.

The main reasons for the popularity of fingerprint recognition are as follows:

- The pattern of fingerprint is unique to each individual and immutable throughout life from infancy to old age and the patterns of no two hands resemble each other,
- Its success in various applications in the forensics, government, and civilian domains,
- The fact that criminals often leave their fingerprints at crime scenes,
- The existence of large legacy databases such as National Institute of Standards and Technology (NIST), Fingerprint Verification Competition (FVC) evaluation databases from 2000, 2002, and 2004.
- The availability of compact and relatively inexpensive fingerprint readers.

A typical fingerprint feature called minutiae is extracted from fingerprint images, as shown in **Figure 5**, and used for matching process for a fingerprint recognition system.

3.5. Ear

Recognizing people by their ear has recently received significant attention in the literature. There are many factors that made ear a widely used biometrics. First, the shape of the ear and the structure of cartilaginous tissue of the pinna are very discriminate. It is formed by the outer helix, the antihelix, the lobe, the tragus, the antitragus, and the concha. The ear recognition approaches are based on matching the distance of salient points on the pinna from a landmark location. Second, ear has a structure which does not vary with facial expressions or time, and it is very stable for the end of life. It has been shown

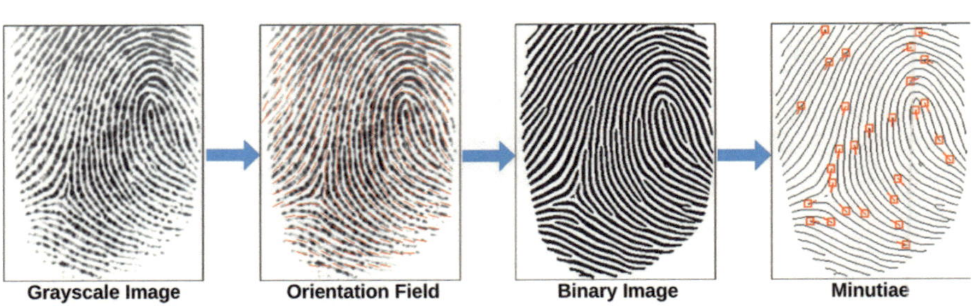

Figure 5. A typical minutiae feature extraction algorithm [9].

that the recognition rate is not affected by aging [10]. Third, ear biometric is convenient as its acquisition is easy because the size of the ear is larger than fingerprint, iris, and retina and smaller than face. Ear data can also be captured even without the knowledge or cooperation of the user from far distance [11]; therefore, it can be used in passive environment. This makes ear recognition especially interesting for smart surveillance tasks and for forensic image analysis, because ear images can typically be extracted from profile head shots or video footage.

The main drawback of ear biometric is occlusion, where the ear can be partially or fully covered by hair or by other items such as head dress, hearing aids, jewelry, or headphone. In an active identification system, it is not a critical point as the subject can pull his or her hair back, but in a passive identification, it is a problem as there will be nobody informing the subject. Other challenges on ears are different poses (angles), left and right rotation, and different lighting conditions.

3.6. Speech

The activities of automatic speaker verification and identification have a long history going back to the early 1960s [12]. Dragon systems were the early applications that were used as speech recognizer [13], which focused on the ability of recognition system to provide acoustic knowledge about speaker. Baum-Welch HMM procedures were employed by these systems to train models.

Speech or voice is one of the behavioral traits that can be used in biometric systems to identify the user based on the stored voice in the enrollment phase, where the voice characteristics such as pronunciation style and voice texture are unique and distinctive for each person. On the other hand, voice can also be considered physiological in addition to behavioral feature based on the shape of the vocal track.

3.6.1. Advantages and disadvantages of voice recognition

Generally, voice recognition is nonintrusive, and people are willing to accept a speech-based biometric system with as little inconvenience as possible. It also offers a cheap recognition technology, because general purpose voice recorders can be used to acquire the data. However, a person's voice can be easily recorded and can be used for authorized access, and the noise can be canceled by specific software. As a result, these make speech recognition to be used in many applications such as financial applications, security, retail, crime investigation, entertainment, etc.

Speech-based features are sensitive to a number of factors such as background noise, room reverberation, the channel through which the speech is acquired (such as cellular, land-line, and VoIP), overlapping speech, and Lombard or hyper-articulated speech. Additionally, the emotional and physical state of the speaker are important. An illness such as flu can change a person's voice, and it makes voice recognition difficult. Speech-based authentication is currently restricted to low-security applications because of high variability in an individual's voice and poor accuracy performance of a typical speech-based authentication system. Existing techniques are able to reduce variability caused by additive noise or linear distortions, as well as compensating slowly varying linear channels [14].

3.6.2. Speech recognition

Speech recognition process starts by acquiring the sound from a user using microphone, and then, the series of acoustic signals are converted to a set of identifying words. The speech recognition depends on many factors such as language model, vocabulary size, speaking style, speaker enrollment, and transducer [15]. Speech recognition system is classified to "speaker dependent system," if the user should train the system before using it, and to "speaker independent system," if the system can recognize any speaker's speech without the need to train phase. Speech recognition systems can also be divided into "isolated word speech" or "continuous speech" based on the number of the used vocabularies for identification process.

Speaker models [16, 17] enable us to generate the scores from which we will make decisions. As in any pattern recognition problem, the choices are numerous, and the most popular and dominated technique in last two decade is Hidden Markov Models. There are also other techniques used for speech recognition systems such as Artificial Neural Networks (ANN), Back Propagation Algorithm (BPA), Fast Fourier Transform (FFT), Learn Vector Quantization (LVQ), and Neural Networks (NN). A typical speech recognition system is shown in **Figure 6**.

3.7. Performance evaluation of biometrics systems

Different measurements can be used to evaluate the performance of biometric systems. The most famous measurement is the recognition rate, which is defined as the percentage of the samples that are correctly matched samples to the total tested samples. Another popular measurement is False Reject Rate (FRR) versus False Accept Rate (FAR) at various threshold values, where FRR refers to the expected probability for two mate samples which

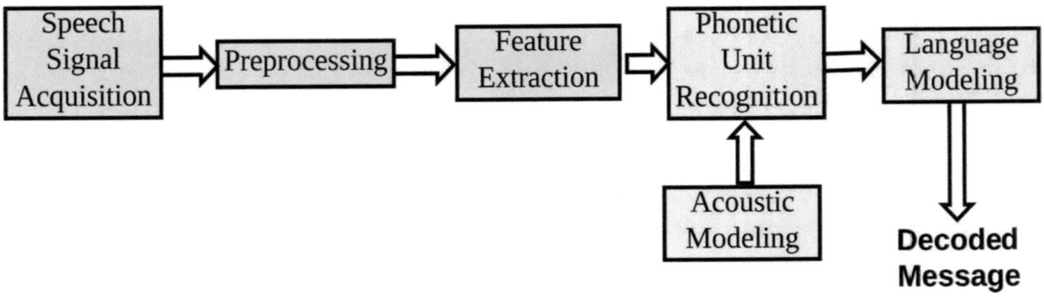

Figure 6. Block diagram of a speech recognition system.

are wrongly mismatched and FAR refers to the expected probability that two non-mate samples are incorrectly matched.

Single-valued measure "Equal Error Rate (EER)," that is threshold independent, can also be used to evaluate the performance of recognition systems. EER is the value, where FRR and FAR are equal.

Detection Error Trade-off (DET) or Receiver Operating Characteristic (ROC) curves are also used to compare the performance of biometric systems in which both curves plot FRR against FAR in the normal deviate and linear scale, respectively.

4. Biometric challenges

There are several challenges and key factors that can significantly affect the recognition performance as well as degrading the extraction of robust and discriminant features. Some of these challenges such as pose, illumination, aging, facial expression variations, and occlusions are briefly described below, and these challenges are illustrated in **Figure 7**.

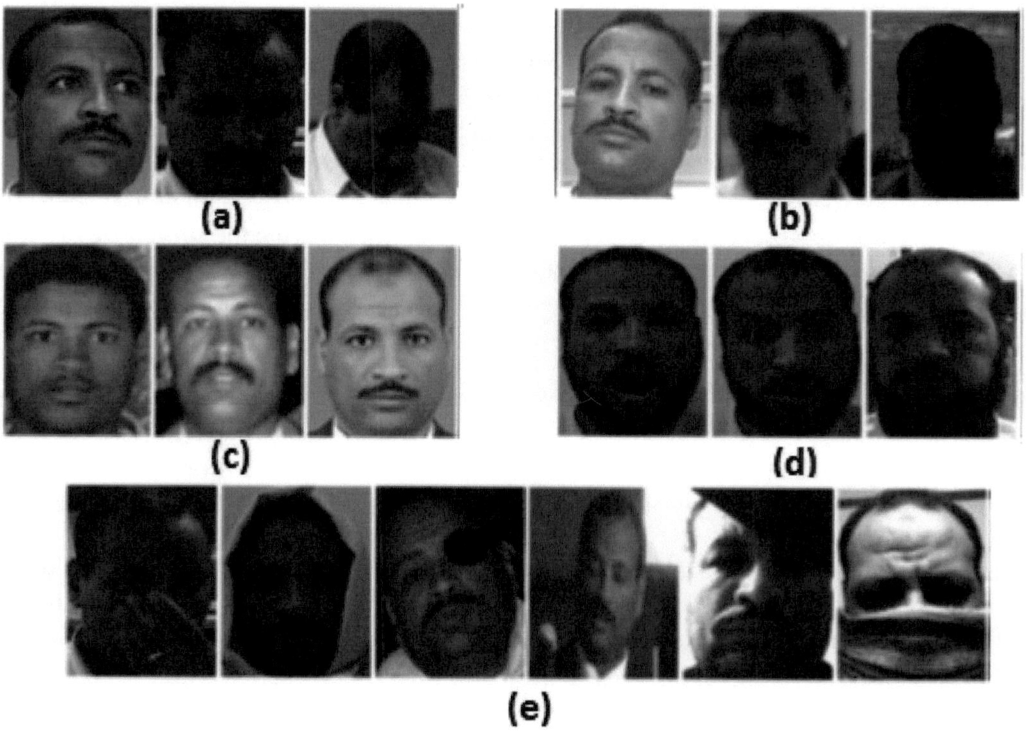

Figure 7. The challenges in the context of face recognition: (a) pose variations, (b) illumination variations, (c) aging variations, (d) facial expressions, (e) occlusions.

1. Pose variation: the images of a face or ear vary because of the camera pose (different viewpoints) as shown in **Figure 7a**. In this condition, some facial parts such as the eyes or nose may become partially or fully occluded. Pose variation has more influence on recognition process because of introducing projective deformations and self-occlusion. Thus, it is possible that images of the same person taken from two different poses may appear more different (intra-user variation) than images of two different people taken with the same poses (inter-user variation). There are many studies that deal with pose variation challenges in [18–20].

2. Illumination variation: when the image is captured, it may be affected by many factors to some degree. The appearance of the human face or ear is affected by factors such as lighting that includes spectra, source distribution, and intensity and also camera characteristics such as sensor response and lenses. Illumination variations can also have an effect on the appearance because of skin reflectance properties and the internal camera control [21]. The problem of illumination variation is considered to be one of the main technical challenges in biometric systems especially for face and ear traits, where the face of a person can appear dramatically different as shown in **Figure 7b**. In order to handle variations in lighting conditions or pose, an image relighting technique based on pose-robust albedo estimation [22] can be used to generate multiple frontal images of the same person with variable lighting.

3. Aging: aging can be a natural cause of age progression and an artificial cause of using make-up tools. Facial appearance changes more drastically at younger ages less than 18 years due to the change in subject's weight or stiffness of skin. All aging related variations such as wrinkles, speckles, skin tone, and shape degrade face recognition performance. One of the main reasons for the small number of studies concerning face recognition in the context of age factor was the absence of a public domain database for studying the effect of aging [23], since it was very difficult to collect a dataset for face images that contains images for the same subject taken at different ages along his/her life. An example set of images for different ages of the same person is presented in **Figure 7c**.

4. Occlusion: faces may be partially occluded by other objects such as scarf, hat, spectacles, beard, and mustache as shown in **Figure 7e**. This makes the face detection process a difficult task and the recognition itself might be difficult because of some hidden facial parts making features hard to be recognized. For these reasons, in surveillance and commercial applications, face recognition engines reject the images when some part of it is not detected. In the literature, local-feature based methods have been proposed to overcome these occlusion problems [24]. On the other hand, the iris could potentially be occluded due to the eyelashes, eyelids, shadows, or specular reflections, and these occlusions can lead to higher false non-match rates.

5. Facial expression: the appearance of faces is directly affected by a person's facial expression such as anger, surprise, and disgust as shown in **Figure 7d**. Additionally, facial hair such as beard and mustache can change facial appearance specifically near the mouth and

chin regions. Moreover, facial expression causes large intra-class variations. In order to handle these facial expression problems, local-feature-based approaches and 3D-model-based approaches are designed [25].

5. Human robot interaction (HRI)

Human-robot interaction (HRI) is the study of how people can interact with robots and to what extent robots are exploited and used for successful interaction with human beings. It could also be defined as a field of study dedicated to understanding, designing, and evaluating robotic systems for use by or with humans. In general, the interaction is based on the communication with or reaction to each other, either people or things as shown in **Figure 8**.

5.1. The importance and the role of person identification in human-robot interaction

Person identification is a very important function for robots, which work with humans in the real world [26]. Human identification by robot may enhance the extent of interaction and

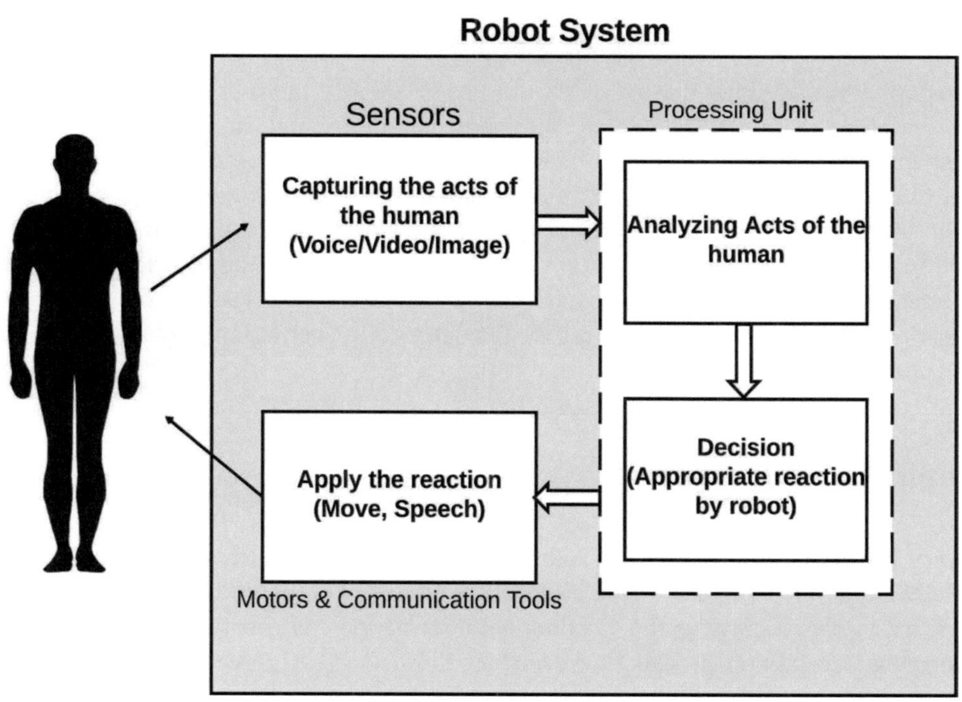

Figure 8. Block diagram of a human-robot interaction system.

communication with each other, where identifying the user does not only require ID but also many other information such as age, gender, interests/hobbies, and language of each user. Knowing the age of the user will help the robot to choose the tone of voice, where child may prefer childish voice tone instead of the manly voice and vice versa. Calling "Mr, Ms, Sir, Madam" when communicating with a person is based on gender, which is also important. Additionally, identifying the interest/hobby of the user will highly enhance the interaction, since it is not acceptable to discuss boxing with a person whose interest is ballet. In addition, communicating with a person using his/her original language ensures promotion of the interaction.

5.2. The most appropriate biometric traits of a person that can easily be identified by robot

Interaction depends on the extent of communication between robots and humans. Human and a robot can construct a communication between each other using several forms. Proximity to each other is the main factor that impacts the communication forms between human and robot. Thus, communication and interaction can be classified into two general categories [27]:

- Remote interaction: the human and the robot are not at the same place and are separated spatially or even temporally (different rooms, countries, or planets)
- Proximate interaction: the humans and the robots are collocated (same room)

Choosing biometric traits that robot should use to identify the user should be compatible with the aforementioned interaction categories. For the remote interaction, the biometric traits whose raw features are images such as face, ear, and iris are not convenient choices, since the majority of remote interaction is conducted by voice communication. Therefore, speech recognition may be the best choice, since it is suitable for direct (different room) and mobile calling. For proximate interaction (face-to-face interaction) and in order to create more real interaction, identification process should use a biometric trait that does not require direct contact with the user in order to capture the biometric traits such as face, ear, and voice, which are captured from a far distance.

6. Multibiometric systems

Some of the limitations imposed by unimodal biometric systems (that is, biometric systems that rely on the evidence of a single biometric trait) can be overcome by using multiple biometric modalities. Increasing the discriminant information and constraints leads to decrease the error in recognition process. More information can be acquired when using different sources of information simultaneously, and the sources of information may be on several types such as multiple biometric traits, algorithms, instances, samples, and sensors. Various scenarios in a multimodal biometric system are demonstrated on **Figure 9**.

http://dx.doi.org/10.5772/intechopen.71667

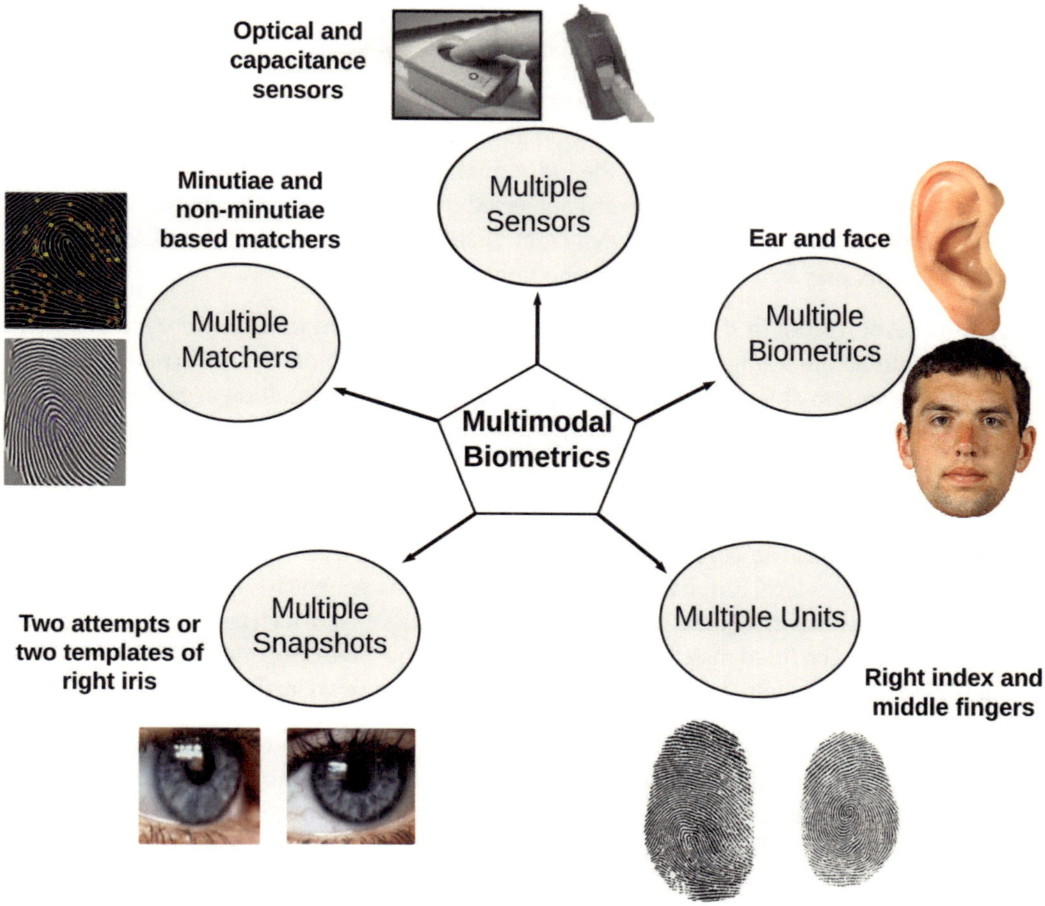

Figure 9. Various scenarios in a multimodal biometric system.

Consolidating multiple features that are acquired from different biometric sources in order to construct a person recognition system is defined as multibiometric systems. For example, fingerprint and palmprint traits, or right and left iris of an individual, or two different samples of the same ear trait may be fused together to recognize the person more accurate and reliable than unimodal biometric systems. Due to the use of more than one biometric source, many of the limitations of unimodal systems can be overcome by the multimodal biometric systems [28].

Multibiometric systems are able to compensate a shortage of any source using the other source of information. In addition, the difficulty of circumvention of multiple biometric sources simultaneously creates more reliable systems than unimodal systems. On the other hand, the unimodal biometric systems are low cost and require less enrollment and recognition time compared to multimodal systems. Hence, it is essential to carefully analyze the tradeoff between the added cost and the benefits earned when making a business case for the use of multibiometrics in a specific application such as commercial, forensics, and the biometric systems that include large population.

The information used in recognition process can be fused in five different levels [29]:

1. Sensor level fusion: information of the individual is captured by multiple sensors in order to generate new data that is afterward subjected to feature extraction phase. For instance, in the case of iris biometrics, samples from "Panasonic BM-ET 330" and "LG IrisAccess 4000" sensors may be fused to obtain one sample.
2. Feature level fusion: in this level, the extracted features from multiple biometric sources are fused to obtain a single feature vector that contains rich biometric information about a client. Integration at feature level is expected to offer good recognition accuracy because it detects the correlated feature values generated by different biometric algorithms, thereby identifying a set of distinguished features.
3. Score level fusion: it is the most commonly used fusion technique due to the ease of performing a fusion of the match scores in multibiometric systems. Match scores of multiple classifiers are integrated in score-level fusion to produce a single match score, which is used to get a final decision. Score level fusion requires performing score normalization, which converts the scores into common scale. The fused match score is then calculated by three categories, namely likelyhood ratio–based score fusion, transformation-based score fusion, and classifier-based score fusion.
4. Rank level fusion: it is defined as consolidating associated ranks of multiple classifiers in order to derive consensus rank of each identity to establish the final decision. Rank-level fusion provides less information compared to score level fusion, and it is relevant in identification mode. The final decision of rank-level fusion is obtained by three well-known methods namely Highest Rank, Borda Count, and Logistic Regression methods.
5. Decision level fusion: the outputs (decisions) of different matchers may be fused to obtain a single/final decision (genuine or imposter in a verification system or the identity of the client in an identification system). A single class label can be obtained by employing techniques like majority voting, behavior knowledge space, etc.

Among the aforementioned fusion techniques, the most popular ones are score-level fusion and feature-level fusion. Most of the person identification systems use these fusion techniques because of their simplicity and high performance. These systems are compared in **Table 1** by demonstrating many details of the state-of-the-art multibiometric systems.

The results shown in **Table 1** prove that consolidation of different unimodal biometric systems construct a recognition system that is robust against many challenges such as occlusion, pose, and nonuniform illumination. Additionally, the studies presented in **Table 1** demonstrate that score-level fusion of more than one biometric trait overcomes the limitations of unimodal biometric systems, and in most of the studies, score-level fusion results outperform feature-level fusion results for person identification.

Identification approach	Biometric traits	Databases and challenges	Fusion strategy	Recognition rate (%)
Toygar et al. [30]	Face Voice	*XM2VTS:* (P) *BANCA:* (P, I, E, O, N)	Score-level fusion	*XM2VTS:* Voice: 78.01 Face: 86.53 Face + Voice: 94.24 *BANCA:* Voice: 91.54 Face: 92.07 Face + Voice: 97.43
Eskandari and Toygar [31]	Iris Face	*CASIA-Iris_Distance:* (I, O, N, D) *FERET, ORL, BANCA (used for weight optimization):* (P, I, E, O, N) *UBIRIS (used for weight optimization):* (I, O, N)	Feature-level and Score-level fusion	*CASIA-Iris_Distance:* Face: 92.77 Iris: 77.65 Face + Iris: 98.66
Farmanbar and Toygar [32]	Palmprint Face	*FERET:* (P, I, E) *PolyU:* (P)	Feature-level and Score-level fusion	*FERET ± PolyU:* Palmprint: 94.30 Face: 83.21 Palmprint + Face: 99.17
Hezil and Boukrouche [33]	Ear Palmprint	*IITDelhi-2 Ear* *IITDelhi Palmprint*	Feature-Level Fusion	*IITDelhi-2 Ear ± IITDelhi Palmprint* Palmprint: 97.73 Ear: 98.9 Palmprint + Ear: 100
Ghoualmi et al. [34]	Iris Ear	*CASIA IrisV1* *USTB 2* (P,I)	Feature-Level Fusion	*CASIA IrisV1 ± USTB-2* Iris: 95.8 Ear: 91.36 Iris + Ear: 99.67
Telgad et al. [35]	Face Fingerprint	*FVC 2004*	Score-level fusion	*FVC 2004:* Face-PCA: 92.4 Fingerprint-Minutiae: 93.05 Fingerprint-Gabor Filter: 95 Face + Fingerprint: 97.5
Patil and Bhalke [36]	Fingerprint Palmprint Iris	*FVC* *IITD* *CASIA*	Score-level fusion	*FVC ± IITD ± CASIA* Fingerprint: 72.73 Plamprint: 65.57 Iris: 80 Fingerprint + Palmprint + Iris = 95.23

P, pose; I, illumination; E, expression; O, occlusion; N, noise; D, distance.

Table 1. Comparison of person identification approaches using multimodal biometric traits under different challenges.

7. Fusion of face and speech traits

Based on the purpose of the robot, a unimodal or a multimodal recognition system could be selected to be used for human-robot interaction. For example, a military purpose robot should be more accurate than home purpose robot. As mentioned in Section 5.2, the common trait that can be used for human identification by robot in both remote and proximate interaction is voice biometric trait. On the other hand, the face is the most realistic biometric trait in case of proximate interaction.

It will be appropriate to fuse face and voice in human-robot interaction, since both of these traits are noncontacted and the user is unaware that recognition is being performed. Many studies proved that the fusion of face and speech is appropriate for many purposes [37–39], where face and speech are the best choices since both of them do not need physical or direct contact with sensors [40, 41]. Another advantage of speech over face is that speech can be recognized even when a human and robot are not found in the same physical place. This is useful for voice recognition purposes by mobile phone or when a user and robot are in two different rooms in the same place. Consequently, a realistic human-robot interaction system is achieved, either HRI is conducted by face-to-face, blind, or invisible interaction.

8. Conclusion

Multimodal biometrics in the context of human-robot interaction is discussed under different challenges. The most commonly used biometric traits namely face, iris, fingerprint, ear, palmprint, and voice are discussed in this chapter. Various challenges such as pose, illumination, expression, aging variations, and occlusion are explained, and many state-of-the-art biometric systems involving these challenges are presented and compared. The comparison of these systems shows that multimodal biometrics overcomes the limitations of unimodal systems and achieves better person identification performance. Additionally, score-level fusion technique applied on more than one biometric trait obtains higher recognition rates for person identification. On the other hand, fusion of face and speech is an appropriate choice for human-robot interaction, since the enrollment phase of face and speech biometric systems does not require physical or direct contact with sensors. The face image or speech of a person can be captured by a robot, even if the person is far away from the robot.

Author details

Önsen Toygar*, Esraa Alqaralleh and Ayman Afaneh

*Address all correspondence to: onsen.toygar@emu.edu.tr

Computer Engineering Department, Faculty of Engineering, Eastern Mediterranean University, Famagusta, North Cyprus, via Mersin, Turkey

References

[1] Jain AK, Ross AA, Nandakumar K. Introduction to Biometrics. Springer; 2011. 312 p. DOI: 10.1007/978-0-387-773261

[2] Takeo K. Picture Processing by Computer Complex and Recognition of Human Faces [Thesis]. Kyoto, Japan: Dept. of Science, Kyoto University; 1974. 143 p . DOI: 10.14989/doctor.k1486Available from: http://hdl.handle.net/2433/162079

[3] Bowyer KW, Hollingsworth K, Flynn PJ. Image understanding for iris biometrics: A survey. Computer Vision and Image Understanding. 2008;**110**(2):281-307. DOI: 10.1016/j.cviu.2007.08.005

[4] Zhang D, Kong WK, You J, Wong M. Online palmprint identification. IEEE Transactions on Pattern Analysis and Machine Intelligence. 2003;**25**(9):1041-1050. DOI: 10.1109/TPAMI.2003.1227981

[5] Raut SD, Humbe VT. Biometric palm prints feature matching for person identification. International Journal of Modern Education and Computer Science. 2012;**4**(11):61. DOI: 10.5815/ijmecs.2012.11.06

[6] Kong A, Zhang D, Kamel M. A survey of palmprint recognition. Pattern Recognition. 2009;**42**(7):1408-1418. DOI: 10.1016/j.patcog.2009.01.018

[7] Berry JS, David A. The history and development of fingerprinting. In: Lee HC, Ramotowski R, Gaensslen RE, editors. Advances in fingerprint Technology. 2nd ed. CRC press; 2001:13-52. DOI: 10.1201/9781420041347.ch1

[8] Cole S, Col A. Suspect Identities: A History of Fingerprinting and Criminal Identification. Cambridge, Mass /London: Harvard University Press; 30-10-2009.38 p. DOI: 10.1023/B:MESC.0000005857.89878.a9

[9] Jain AK, Prabhakar S, Hong L, Pankanti S. Filterbank-based fingerprint matching. IEEE Transactions on Image Processing. 2000;**9**(5):846-859. DOI: 10.1109/83.841531

[10] Mina I. Mark N. Sasan M. The effect of time on ear biometrics. In: International Joint Conference on Biometrics (IJCB), 2011; Washington, DC, USA. IEEE; 2011. p. 1-6. DOI: 10.1109/IJCB.2011.6117584

[11] Pflug A, Busch C. Ear biometrics: A survey of detection, feature extraction and recognition methods. IET Biometrics. 2012;**1**(2):114-129. DOI: 10.1049/iet-bmt.2011.0003

[12] Pruzansky S, Mathews MV. Talker-recognition procedure based on analysis of variance. The Journal of the Acoustical Society of America. 1964;**36**(11):2041-2047. DOI: 10.1121/1.1795335. PACS

[13] Peskin B et al. Topic and speaker identification via large vocabulary continuous speech recognition. In: Proceedings of the workshop on Human Language Technology. Association

for Computational Linguistics: Stroudsburg, PA, USA; 1993. p. 119-124. DOI: 10.3115/1075671.1075697

[14] Yu D, Deng L, Droppo J, Wu J, Gong Y, Acero A. Robust speech recognition using a cepstral minimum-mean-square-error-motivated noise suppressor. IEEE Transactions on Audio, Speech and Language Processing. 2008;**16**(5):1061-1070. DOI: 10.1109/TASL.2008.921761

[15] Varile GB, Zampolli A. Survey of the State of the Art in Human Language Technology. Linguistica Computazionale. Cambridge University Press; 1997. 413 p. DOI: 10.1.1.366.9300

[16] Cowling M, Sitte R. Comparison of techniques for environmental sound recognition. Pattern Recognition Letters. 2003;**24**(15):2895-2907. DOI: 10.1016/S0167-8655(03)00147-8

[17] Furui S. Recent advances in speaker recognition. Pattern Recognition Letters. 1997;**18**(9):859-872. DOI: 10.1016/S0167-8655(97)00073-1

[18] Blanz V, Grother P, Phillips PJ, Vetter T. Face recognition based on frontal views generated from non-frontal images. In: IEEE Computer Society Conference on Computer Vision and Pattern Recognition, 2005. CVPR; 2005. p. 454-461

[19] Prince SJ, Elder JH, Warrell J, Felisberti FM. Tied factor analysis for face recognition across large pose differences. IEEE Transactions on Pattern Analysis and Machine Intelligence. 2008;**30**(6):970-984. DOI: 10.1109/TPAMI.2008.48

[20] Asthana A, Marks TK, Jones MJ, Tieu KH, Rohith MV. Fully automatic pose-invariant face recognition via 3D pose normalization. In: IEEE International Conference on Computer Vision (ICCV), 2011; Barcelona, Spain. IEEE; 2011. p. 937-944. DOI: 10.1109/ICCV.2011.6126336

[21] Liu DH, Lam KM, Shen LS. Illumination invariant face recognition. Pattern Recognition. 2005;**38**(10):1705-1716. DOI: https://doi.org/10.1016/j.patcog.2005.03.009

[22] Patel VM, Wu T, Biswas S, Phillips PJ, Chellappa R. Dictionary-based face recognition under variable lighting and pose. IEEE Transactions on Information Forensics and Security. 2012;**7**(3):954-965. DOI: 10.1109/TIFS.2012.2189205

[23] Park U, Tong Y, Jain AK. Age-invariant face recognition. IEEE Transactions on Pattern Analysis and Machine Intelligence. 2010;**32**(5):947-954. DOI: 10.1109/TPAMI.2010.14

[24] Tan X, Chen S, Zhou ZH, Liu J. Face recognition under occlusions and variant expressions with partial similarity. IEEE Transactions on Information Forensics and Security. 2009;**4**(2):217-230. DOI: 10.1109/TIFS.2009.2020772

[25] Levine MD, Yu Y. Face recognition subject to variations in facial expression, illumination and pose using correlation filters. Computer Vision and Image Understanding. 2006;**104**(1):1-15. DOI: 10.1016/j.cviu.2006.06.004

[26] Fukui K, Yamaguchi O. Face recognition using multi-viewpoint patterns for robot vision. Robotics Research. 2005;**15**:192-201. DOI: 10.1.1.474.7008

[27] Goodrich MA, Schultz AC. Human-robot interaction: A survey. Foundations and trends (r) in human-computer interaction. 2007;**1**(3):203-275. DOI: 10.1561/1100000005

[28] Jain AK, Ross A. Multibiometric systems. Communications of the ACM. 2004;**47**(1):34-40. DOI: 10.1145/962081.962102

[29] Ross A, Govindarajan R. Feature level fusion using hand and face biometrics. In: Jain AK, Ratha NK, editors. Proceedings of SPIE Conference on Biometric Technology for Human Identification II. Orlando, USA; 2005. p. 196-204. DOI: org/10.1117/12.606093

[30] Toygar Ö, Ergün C, Altinçay H. Using local features based face experts in multimodal biometric identification systems. In: Fifth International Conference on Soft Computing, Computing with Words and Perceptions in System Analysis, Decision and Control, 2009. ICSCCW 2009. 2009. p. 1-4

[31] Eskandari M, Toygar Ö. Selection of optimized features and weights on face-iris fusion using distance images. Computer Vision and Image Understanding. 2015;**137**:63-75. DOI: 10.1016/j.cviu.2015.02.011

[32] Farmanbar M, Toygar Ö. Feature selection for the fusion of face and palmprint biometrics. Signal, Image and Video Processing. 2016;**10**(5):951-958. DOI: 10.1007/s11760-015-0845-6

[33] Hezil N, Boukrouche A. Multimodal biometric recognition using human ear and palmprint. IET Biometrics. 2017:9. DOI: 10.1049/iet-bmt.2016.0072

[34] Ghoualmi L, Chikhi S, Draa A. A SIFT-based feature level fusion of iris and ear biometrics. In: Schwenker F, Scherer S, Morency LP, editors. Multimodal Pattern Recognition of Social Signals in Human-Computer-Interaction. MPRSS 2014. Lecture Notes in Computer Science, vol 8869. Springer, Cham; 2014:102-112. DOI: 10.1007/978-3-319-14899-1_10

[35] Telgad RL, Deshmukh PD, Siddiqui AM. Combination approach to score level fusion for Multimodal Biometric system by using face and fingerprint. In IEEE: International Conference on Recent Advances and Innovations in Engineering (ICRAIE), 9-11 May 2014; Jaipur, India. IEEE; p. 1-8. DOI: 10.1109/ICRAIE.2014.6909320

[36] Patil AP, Bhalke DG. Fusion of fingerprint, palmprint and iris for person identification. In IEEE: Automatic Control and Dynamic Optimization Techniques (ICACDOT), International Conference on; 9-10 Sep 2016; Pune, India. IEEE; p. 960-963. DOI: 10.1109/ICACDOT.2016.7877730

[37] Soltane M, Doghmane N, Guersi N. Face and speech based multi-modal biometric authentication. International Journal of Advanced Science and Technology. 2010;**21**(6):41-56

[38] Ben-Yacoub S, Abdeljaoued Y, Mayoraz E. Fusion of face and speech data for person identity verification. IEEE Transactions on Neural Networks. 1999;**10**(5):1065-1074. DOI: 10.1109/72.788647

[39] Jain AK, Hong L, Kulkarni Y. A multimodal biometric system using fingerprint, face and speech. In: Proceedings of 2nd Int'l Conference on Audio- and Video-Based Biometric Person Authentication, Washington DC. 1999. p. 182-187

[40] Demirel H, Anbarjafari G. Probability Distribution Functions Based Face Recognition System Using Discrete Wavelet Subbands. In: Olkkonen JT, editor. Discrete Wavelet Transforms-Theory and Applications. ISBN: 978-953-307-185-5, InTech, Available from: http://www.intechopen.com/books/discrete-wavelet-transforms-theory-and-applications/probability-distribution-functions-based-face-recognition-system-using-discrete-wavelet-subbands; 2011

[41] Maucec MS, Zgank A. Speech recognition system of Slovenian broadcast news. In: Ipsic I, editor. Speech Technologies. InTech, DOI: 10.5772/17161. Available from: https://www.intechopen.com/books/speech-technologies/speech-recognition-system-of-slovenian-broadcast-news; 2011

Chapter 6

Active Collaboration of Classifiers for Visual Tracking

Kourosh Meshgi and Shigeyuki Oba

Additional information is available at the end of the chapter

http://dx.doi.org/10.5772/intechopen.74199

Abstract

Recently, discriminative visual trackers obtain state-of-the-art performance, yet they suffer in the presence of different real-world challenges such as target motion and appearance changes. In a discriminative tracker, one or more classifiers are employed to obtain the target/nontarget label for the samples, which in turn determine the target's location. To cope with variations of the target shape and appearance, the classifier(s) are updated online with different samples of the target and the background. Sample selection, labeling, and updating the classifier are prone to various sources of errors that drift the tracker. In this study, we motivate, conceptualize, realize, and formalize a novel active co-tracking framework, step by step to demonstrate the challenges and generic solutions for them. In this framework, not only classifiers cooperate in labeling the samples but also exchange their information to robustify the labeling, improve the sampling, and realize efficient yet effective updating. The proposed framework is evaluated against state-of-the-art trackers on public dataset and showed promising results.

Keywords: visual tracking, active learning, active co-tracking, uncertainty sampling

1. Introduction

Visual tracking is one of the building blocks of human-robot interaction. Implicit or explicit, this task is embedded in many high-level complicated tasks of the robot: automating industrial workcells [1], attending the speaker in a multimodal spoken dialog system [2], following the target [3] and vision-based robot navigation [4], aerial visual servoing [5], imitating the behavior of a human [6], extracting tacit information of an interaction [7], sign-language interpretation [8], and autonomous driving as well as simpler tasks such as human-robot cooperation [9], obstacle avoidance [10], first-person view action recognition, [11] and human-computer interfaces [12].

IntechOpen

© 2018 The Author(s). Licensee IntechOpen. This chapter is distributed under the terms of the Creative Commons Attribution License (http://creativecommons.org/licenses/by/3.0), which permits unrestricted use, distribution, and reproduction in any medium, provided the original work is properly cited.

The most general type of tracking is single-object model-free online tracking, in which the object is annotated in the first frame and tracked in the subsequent frames with no prior knowledge about the target's appearance, its motions, the background, the configurations of the camera, and other conditions of the scene. Visual tracking is still considered as a challenging problem despite numerous efforts made to address abrupt appearance changes of the target [13], complex transformations [14] and deformations [15, 16], background clutter [17], occlusion [18], and motion artifacts [19].

Generative trackers attempt to construct a robust object appearance model or to learn it on the fly using advanced machine learning techniques such as subspace learning [20], hash learning [21], dictionary learning [22], and sparse code learning [13]. General object tracking is the task of tracking arbitrary objects through one-shot learning, typically with no *a priori* knowledge about the target's geometry, category, or appearance. Called model-free tracking, the task is to learn the target appearance and update it by adjusting to target's changes on the fly. To this end, discriminative models focus on target/background separation using correlation filters [23–25] or dedicated classifiers [26], which assist them to dominate the visual tracking benchmarks [27–29]. Using tracking-by-detection approaches is a popular trend in recent years, due to significant breakthroughs in object detection domain (deep residual neural networks [30], for instance), yielding strong discriminating power with offline training. Adopted for visual tracking, many of such trackers are adjusted for online training and accumulate knowledge about a target with each successful detection (e.g., [26, 31–33]).

Tracking-by-detection methods primarily treat tracking as a detection problem to avoid having model object dynamics especially in the case of sudden motion changes, extreme deformations, and occlusions [34, 35]. However, there is a multitude of drawbacks in the tracking-by-detection setting:

1. *Label noise*: inaccurate labels confuse the classifier [15] and degrade the classification accuracy [34]. The labeler is typically built upon heuristics and intuitions, rather than using the accumulated knowledge about the target.

2. *Self-learning loop*: the classifier is retrained by their own output from earlier frames, thus accumulating error over time [35].

3. *Uniform treatment of samples*: equal weight for all samples in evaluating the target [36] and training the classifier [37], despite the uneven contextual information in different samples. The classifier is trained using all the examples with equal weights, meaning that negative examples which overlap very little with the target bounding box are treated equally as those negative examples with significant overlaps.

4. *Stationarity assumption*: assuming a stationary distribution of the target appearance does not hold for most of the real-world scenarios with drastic target appearance changes [35]. In the context of visual tracking, the non-stationarity means that the appearance of an object may change so significantly that a negative sample in the current frame looks more similar to a positive example in the previous frames.

5. *Model update difficulties*: adaptive trackers inherently suffer from the drifting problem. Noisy model update [38] and the mismatch between model update frequency and target

	T0	T1	T2	T3	T4	T5	T6
Online update		✓	✓	✓	✓	✓	✓
Co-tracking				✓	✓	✓	✓
Active learning					✓	✓	✓
Dual memory						✓	✓
Ensemble							✓

Table 1. Trackers introduced in this chapter: **T0**, a part-based tracker without model update; **T1**, the part-based tracker with model update; **T2**, a KNN-based tracker with color and HOG features; **T3**, co-tracking of KNN-based classifier T2 and part-based detector T1; **T4**, active co-tracking of T1 and T2 with online update; **T5**, active asymmetric co-tracking of short-memory T1 and long-memory T2 (modified from [40]); and **T6**, active ensemble co-tracking of bagging-induced ensemble and long-memory T2 (modified from [41]).

evolution rate [39] are two major challenges of the model update. If the update rate is small, the changes of the target are not reflected into target's template, whereas rapid update of the tracker renders it vulnerable to data noise and small target localization errors. This phenomenon is also known as *stability plasticity dilemma*.

In this study we motivate, conceptualize, realize, and formalize a novel co-tracking framework. First, the importance of such system is demonstrated by a recent and comprehensive literature review. Then a discriminative tracking framework is formalized to be evolved to a co-tracking by explaining all the steps, mathematically and intuitively. We then construct various instances of the proposed co-tracking framework (**Table 1**), to demonstrate how different topologies of the system can be realized, how the information exchange is optimized, and how different challenges of tracking (e.g., abrupt motions, deformations, clutter) can be handled in the proposed framework. Active learning will be explored in the context of labeling and information exchange of this co-tracking framework to speed up the tracker's convergence while updating the tracker's classifiers effectively. Dual memory is also proposed in the co-tracking framework to handle various tracking scenarios ranging from camera motions to temporal appearance changes of the target and occlusions.

It should be noted that preliminary results of this research were published in [40, 41]; however, the results presented here are slightly different because of using different feature-based auxiliary classifier, different target estimations, and ROI-detection scheme (that was omitted here to conserve the flow of the progressive system design).

2. Tracking by detection

Typically tracking-by-detection method consists of five major steps: **SAMPLING, CLASSIFYING, LABELING, ESTIMATING, UPDATING**.

SAMPLING: To obtain the positive sample(s) and negative samples (the target and the background, respectively), dense or sparse (stochastic) sampling is performed either around last known target position (using Gaussian distributions, particle filters, or various motion models) or around the saliencies or key points in the current frame [21]. Adaptive weights for the samples based on their appearance similarity to the target [42], occlusion state [18], and spatial distance to previous target location [43] have been considered; especially in the context of tracking by detection, boosting [44] has been extensively investigated [45–47].

CLASSIFYING: The classification module of tracking-by-detection schemes utilizes offline-trained classifiers or online supervised learning methods to classify the target from its background (e.g., [48]). To robustify this module especially against label noise, supervised learning with robust loss functions [46, 49] and semi-supervised [39, 50] and multi-instance [47, 51, 52] learning approaches are considered. Efficient sparse sampling [53], leveraging context information [17, 54], considering sample information content for the classifier [55], and landmark-based label propagation [43] are among other proposed approaches to address this issue. Another interesting approach is to reformulate to couple the labeling and updating process to bridge the gap between the objectives of these two steps, as labeling aims for predicting binary sample labels, whereas updating typically tries to estimate object location [15]. The label noise problem amplifies when the tracker does not have a forgetting mechanism or a way to obtain external scaffolds (i.e., self-learning loop). This inspired the use of co-tracking [34], ensemble tracking [56, 57], or label verification schemes [58] to break the self-learning loop using auxiliary classifiers.

LABELING: The result of classification process provides the target/background label for each sample, a process which can be enhanced by employing an ensemble of classifiers [56, 57], exchanging information between collaborative classifiers [34], and verifying labels by auxiliary classifiers [58] or landmarks [43].

ESTIMATING: The state of the target, i.e., the location and scale of the target usually described with a bounding box, is then determined by selecting the sample with the highest classification score [15], calculating the expectation of target state [41], or performing an estimated bounding box regression [59].

UPDATING: Updating the classifier is another challenge of the tracking-by-detection schemes. Updating the classifier, with the data labeled by itself previously in a closed-loop (known as self-learning loop), is susceptible to drift from the original data distribution because a tiny error or a small noise can be amplified. Therefore along with many types of research to revalidate the data labels (such as [58]), the importance of having a "teacher" to guide the classifier during training is discussed in literature [39]. Cooperative classifiers in frameworks such as ensembles of homogeneous or heterogeneous classifiers [60], co-learning [34], and hybrids of generative and discriminative models [61] are some of the approaches to provide this guidance through cooperation. Furthermore, feature selection based on its discrimination ability [45], replacing the weakest classifier of an ensemble [45] or the oldest one [60], or applying a budget on the sample pool (hence, keeping only some prototypical samples) [15, 43] is proposed to improve the performance of such solutions.

On top of that, the frequency of update is another important role player in tracker's performance [39]. Higher update rates capture the rapid target changes but is prone to occlusions, whereas slower update paces provide a long memory for the tracker to handle temporal target variations but lack the flexibility to accommodate permanent target changes. To this end, researchers try to combine long- and short-term memories [62] and role-back improper updates [57] or utilize different temporal snapshots of the classifier to overcome non-stationary distribution of the target's appearance [63]. This pipeline, however, was altered in some studies to introduce desired properties, e.g., to avoid label noise by merging sampling and labeling steps [15].

2.1. Formalization

Online visual tracking is the task to update the state vector $\mathbf{p}_t$ involving location, size, and shape of the bounding box, at each observation of video frame $t = 1, \ldots, T$. The update process is sometimes written with transformation $\mathbf{y}_t$ that transforms the previous state vector $\mathbf{p}_{t-1}$ to the current state $\mathbf{p}_t = \mathbf{p}_{t-1} \circ \mathbf{y}_t$.

In tracking-by-discrimination framework, we utilize a classifier θ_t that discriminates an image patch $\mathbf{x}$ into either target or background, where the classifier is denoted as a real valued discriminant function $h(\mathbf{x}|\theta_t) \in \mathbb{R}$ and the function value $s = h(\mathbf{x}|\theta_t)$ is called a discrimination score or, in short, score. The patch $\mathbf{x}$ (i.e., the area of the image bounded by the bounding box $\mathbf{p}_t$) is labeled as target if $s > \tau$ with a threshold τ and as background if $x < \tau$. A typical procedure of the tracking-by-discrimination is written as follows.

SAMPLING: The samples are defined using these transformations, and their corresponding image patches $\mathbf{x}_t^j \in \mathcal{X}_t$ are selected from image. We obtain N samples of state $p_t^j, j = 1, \ldots, N$ by drawing random transformations $\mathbf{y}_t^j \in \mathcal{Y}_t$ using dense or sparse sampling strategy, transforming the previous state p_{t-1} with a transformations $\mathbf{y}_t^j$ as $\mathbf{p}_t^j = \mathbf{p}_{t-1} \circ \mathbf{y}_t^j \in \mathcal{P}_t$.

CLASSIFYING: We calculate the score s_t^j of the image patches $\mathbf{x}_t^{\mathbf{p}_t^j}$ corresponding to all samples, or bounding boxes, using the current classifier θ_t ($h : \mathcal{X} \to \mathbb{R}$):

$$s_t^j = h\left(\mathbf{x}_t^{\mathbf{p}_{t-1} \circ \mathbf{y}_t^j} | \theta_t\right) \tag{1}$$

LABELING: We determine label l_t^j of each sample j using the score of the sample. If the score is above a threshold τ, the sample is likely to be target match:

$$l_t^j = \text{sign}\left(s_t^j - \tau\right) \tag{2}$$

ESTIMATING: We determine the next target state $\mathbf{p}_t$ typically by selecting the best $\mathbf{p}_t^j$ that corresponds to the maximum score s_t^j, $\mathbf{p}_t = \mathbf{p}_{t-1} \circ \mathbf{y}_t^{j^*}$ s.t. $j^* = \text{argmax}_{j \in \{1,\ldots,N\}} s_t^j$.

UPDATING: Finally, we update the classifier by its own labeled data:

$$\theta_{t+1} = u(\theta_t, \mathcal{X}_t, \mathcal{L}_t) \tag{3}$$

in which $u(l)$ is the update function (e.g., budgeted SVM update [15]) and $\mathcal{X}_t$, $\mathcal{L}_t$ are the set of input patches and output labels used as the training set of the discriminator.

2.2. Baseline system implementation

To develop a baseline tracking-by-detection algorithm for this study, we use a robust part-based detector for the **CLASSIFYING** process. This detector employs strong low-level features based on histograms of oriented gradients (HOG) and uses a latent SVM to perform efficient matching for deformable part-based models (pictorial structures) [64]. From each frame, we draw N samples from a Gaussian distribution whose mean is the target's bounding box in the last frame (including its location and size). The selected detector then outputs the classification score for each sample, which is thresholded to obtain the sample's label. The highest classification score is considered as the current target location (**Figure 1**).

In the first frame, we generate $\alpha_1 N$-positive samples by perturbing the first annotated target patch by few pixels in location and size, select $\alpha_2 N$-negative samples from local neighborhood of the target, and select $\alpha_3 N$-negative samples from global background of the object in a regular grid ($\alpha_1 + \alpha_2 + \alpha_3 = 1$). These samples are used to train the SVM detector in the first frame. From the next frames, the labels are obtained by the detector itself, and the classifier is batch-trained with all of the samples collected so far.

There are several parameters in the system such as the parameters of sampling step (number of samples N, effective search radius Σ_{search}). These parameters were tuned using a simulated annealing optimization on a cross validation set. The part-base detector dictionary, and the thresholds τ_l, τ_u, and the rest of abovementioned parameters have been adjusted using cross validation. With $N = 1000$, $\tau = 0.34$ T1 achieved the speed of 47.29 fps on a Pentium IV PC @ 3.5 GHz and a Matlab/C++ implementation on a CPU.

2.3. Method of evaluation

The experiments are conducted on 100 challenging video sequences, OTB-100 [65], which involves many visual tracking challenges such as target appearance, pose and geometry changes, environment lighting and camera position changes, target movement artifacts such

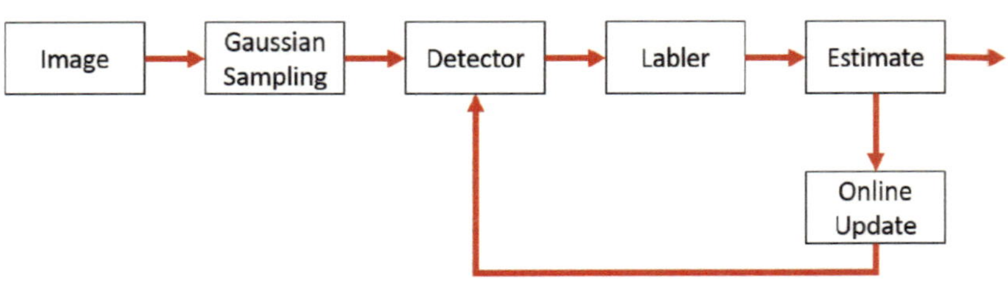

Figure 1. A simple tracking-by-detection pipeline. After gathering some samples from the current frame, the tracker employs its detector to label the samples as positive (target) or negative (background). The target position is estimated using these labeled samples. The labels, in turn, are used to update the classifier for the next frame.

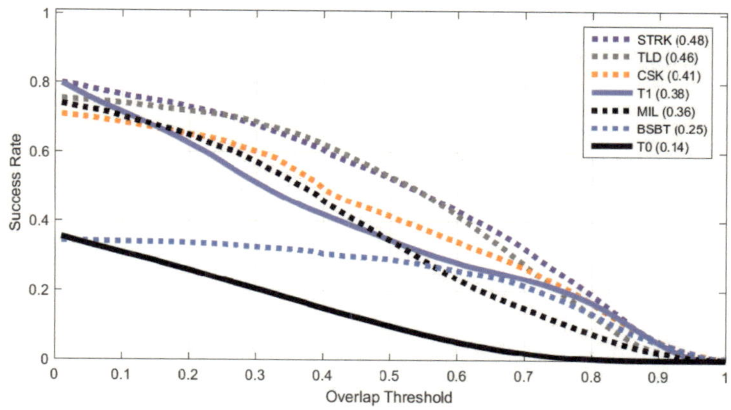

Figure 2. Quantitative performance comparison of the baseline tracker (T1), its variant without model update (T0), and the state-of-the-art trackers using success plot.

as blur and trajectory variations, and low imaging resolution and noise and background objects which may cause occlusions, clutter, or target identity confusion. The performance of the trackers is compared with the area under the curve of success plots and precision plots, on all of the sequences, or a subset of them with the given attribute.

Success plot indicates the reliability of the tracker and its overall performance, while precision plot reflects the accuracy of the localization. The area under the surface of this plot (*AUC*) counts the number of successes of tracker over time $t \in \{1, \ldots, T\}$, i.e., when the overlap of the tracker target estimation $\mathbf{p}_t$ with the ground truth $\mathbf{p}_t^*$ exceeds the threshold τ_{ov}. Success plot graphs the success of the tracker against different values of the threshold τ_{ov}, and its *AUC* is calculated as

$$AUC = \frac{1}{T}\int_0^1 \sum_{t=1}^{T} 1\left(\frac{|\mathbf{p}_t \cap \mathbf{p}_t^*|}{|\mathbf{p}_t \cup \mathbf{p}_t^*|} > \tau_{ov}\right) d_{\tau_{ov}}, \tag{4}$$

where T is the length of sequence; $|.|$ denotes the area of the region; $\cap$ and $\cup$ stand for intersection and union of the regions, respectively; and $1(.)$ denotes the step function that returns 1 iff its argument is positive and 0 otherwise. This plot provides an overall performance of the tracker, reflecting target loss, scale mismatches, and localization accuracy.

To establish a fair comparison with the state of the art of tracking-by-detection algorithms, TLD [58] and STRUCK [15] are selected based on the results of [27], BSBT [66] and MIL [47] are selected based on popularity, and CSK [36] was selected as one of the latest algorithms in the category. Since our trackers contain random elements (in sampling and resampling), the results reported here are the average of five independent runs.

2.4. Results

Figure 2 presents the success and precision plots of T1 along with other competitive trackers for all sequences. We also included a fixed version of T1 tracker (a detector without model update) as T0 to emphasize the role of updating. The figure demonstrates that without the model update, the detector cannot reflect the changes in target appearance and lose the target rapidly in most of the scenarios (comparing T0 and T1). However, it is also evident that having a single tracker is not robust against all of the target's variations (in line with [60]) and the performance of T1 is still low.

3. Co-tracking

A single detector may have difficulties in distinguishing the target from the background in certain scenarios. In those cases, it is beneficial to consult another detector with higher robustness. These second detector may have complimentary characteristics to the first one or simply may be a more sophisticated detector that trades computational complexity with speed.

Collaborative discriminative trackers utilize classifiers that exchange their information, to achieve more robust tracking. These information exchanges are in the form of queries that one classifier sends to another. The purpose of this information exchange is to bridge across long-term and short-term memories [62]; accommodate multi-memory dictionaries [67], mixture of deep and shallow models [68]; facilitate multi-view on the data [34]; and enable learning from mistakes [58].

3.1. Formalization

Built on co-training principle [69], collaborative tracking (co-tracking) provides a framework in which two classifiers exchange their information to promote tracking results and break self-learning loop (**Figure 3**). In this two-classifier framework [34], the challenging samples for one classifier are labeled by the other one, i.e., if a classifier finds a sample difficult to label, it relies on the other classifier to label it for this frame and similar samples in the future. In this case, we calculate the discrimination score s_t^j as a weighted sum of the two discriminant functions, $s_t^j = \sum_{c=1}^{2} \alpha_t^{(c)} h\left(\mathbf{x}_t^j | \theta_t^{(c)}\right)$ where $\alpha_t^{(c)}$ denotes the weight of each discriminator $\theta_t^{(c)}$, $c = 1, 2$. At the **CLASSIFYING** step, the corresponding sample $\mathbf{x}_t^j$ is considered as a challenging sample for the cth discriminator when $\tau_l < h\left(\mathbf{x}_t^j | \theta_t^{(c)}\right) < \tau_u$ holds because it locates close to the corresponding discrimination boundary. When one of the two discriminators answered it challenging, the score of the sample is calculated with using the other score:

$$s_t^j = \begin{cases} \alpha_t^{(2)} h\left(\mathbf{x}_t^j | \theta_t^{(2)}\right) & , h\left(\mathbf{x}_t^j | \theta_t^{(1)}\right) \in (\tau_l, \tau_u) \text{ and } h\left(\mathbf{x}_t^j | \theta_t^{(2)}\right) \notin (\tau_l, \tau_u) \\ \alpha_t^{(1)} h\left(\mathbf{x}_t^j | \theta_t^{(1)}\right) & , h\left(\mathbf{x}_t^j | \theta_t^{(2)}\right) \in (\tau_l, \tau_u) \text{ and } h\left(\mathbf{x}_t^j | \theta_t^{(1)}\right) \notin (\tau_l, \tau_u) \\ \sum_{c=1}^{2} \alpha_t^{(c)} h\left(\mathbf{x}_t^j | \theta_t^{(c)}\right) & , \text{otherwise} \end{cases} \tag{5}$$

At the **UPDATING** step, the weight $\alpha_t^{(c)}$ of the discriminator c is adjusted according to the degree of contradiction to the provisional answers that are determined at the **ESTIMATION**

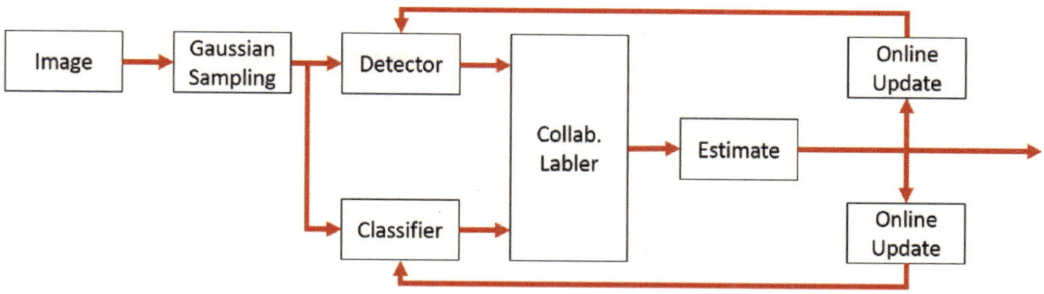

Figure 3. Collaborative tracking. A detector and an auxiliary classifier trust each other to handle the sample difficult for them to classify.

step by an integration of all the information. Finally, the classifiers are updated using only the samples that they successfully labeled in the previous frame to reflect the latest target changes.

3.2. Evaluation

For this experiment, we selected a naive classifier with complementary properties to the main classifier in the previous section. This classifier is a KNN classifier using HOC and HOG features, trained on the samples trained from the first frame and updated with all the labeled samples by the collaboration of the classifiers. Not being pre-trained, the performance of this auxiliary classifier is poor in the beginning but gradually gets better. The quick classification of the KNN (owning to its kd-tree implementations and lightweight features) and lack of pre-training grant it high speed and generalization which is in contrast to the main detector. However, it should be noted that without being supervised by the main SVM-based detector, this classifier cannot perform well in isolation for tracking task. **Figure 5** presents the performance of this auxiliary tracker as T2. As observed in the figure, the performance of the obtained co-tracker (T3) is better than the main detector (T1) and the auxiliary classifier (T2) as a result of co-labeling, data exchange, and co-learning.

4. Active co-tracking

The co-tracking framework provides a means for classifiers to exchange information. This framework utilizes a utility measure (e.g., the classification confidence in [34]) to select the data for which one of the collaborators fails to classify with high confidence and then trains the other classifier on those data. This approach has two main shortcomings: (1) the redundant labeling of all samples for both classifiers and (2) training the collaborator with "all" of the uncertain samples. While the former increases the complexity of the system, the latter is not the optimal solution for tracking a target with non-stationary appearance distributions [35].

In this view, a principled ordering of samples for training [70] and selecting a subset of them based on criteria [37] can reduce the cost of labeling leading to faster performance increase as a function of the amount of data available. It is found that detectors trained with an effective, noise-free, and outlier-free subset of the training data may achieve higher performance than those trained with the full set [71, 72].

Robust learning algorithms provide an alternative way of differentially treating training examples, by assigning different weights to different training examples or by learning to ignore outliers [73]. Learning first from easy examples [74], pruning adversarial examples[1] [75], and sorting the samples based on their training value [37] are some of the approaches explored in the literature. However, the most common setting is active learning, whereby most of the data is unlabeled and an algorithm selects which training examples to label at each step, for the highest gains in performance. Thus, some active learning approaches focus on learning the hardest examples first (those closest to the decision boundary). Some approaches focus on learning the hardest examples first (e.g., those closest to the decision boundary), whereas some others gauge the information contained in the sample and select the most informative ones first. For example, Lewis and Gale [76] utilized the uncertainty of the classifier for a sample as an index of its usefulness for training.

4.1. The idea

Active learning has been used in visual tracking to consider the uncertainty caused by bags of samples [55], to reduce the number of necessary labeled samples [77], to unify sample learning and feature selection procedure [78], and to reduce the sampling bias by controlling the variance [79].

In this study, we utilized the sampling uncertainty that can bind the active learning and co-tracking. As mentioned earlier, the baseline classifier, despite being accurate, has low generalization on new samples, slow classification speed, and computationally expensive retraining. On the other hand, the auxiliary classifier is agile and learns rapidly, with negligible retraining time. To combine the merits of these two classifiers, to cancel out their demerits with one another, and to address the aforementioned issues of co-tracking (redundant labeling and excessive samples), we incorporate an active learning module to select the most informative data, i.e., those for which the naive classifier is most uncertain, and query their labels from the part-based detector. This architecture (**Figure 4**, here called T4) mainly uses naive classifier for labeling the data and only asks the label of hard samples from the slower detector and, therefore, limits the redundancy and unleashes the speed of the agile classifier. In addition, by training the naive classifier only on hard samples, the generalization of this classifier is preserved while increasing its accuracy.

To further increase the accuracy of the tracker and make it more robust against occlusions and drastic temporal changes of the target, it is possible to update the detector less frequently. This asymmetric version of the active co-tracker (T5), by introducing long-term memory to the tracker, benefits from combining the long- and short-term collaboration (as in [62]) and reduces the frequency of the expensive updates of the tracker (Algorithm 1).

[1] Images with tiny, imperceptible perturbations that fool a classifier into predicting the wrong labels with high confidence

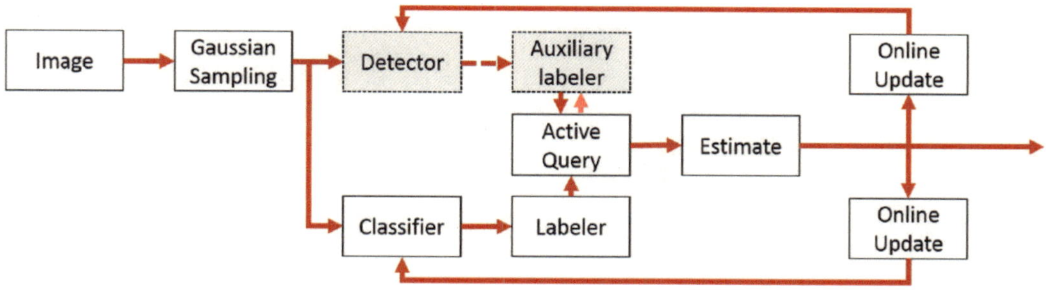

Figure 4. Active co-tracker, a collaborative tracker that utilizes an active query mechanism to query the most informative samples from the main detector and feeds them to the lightweight classifier to learn.

Algorithm 1: Active co-tracking (ACT)

Input: Target position in last frame $\mathbf{p}_{t-1}$

Output: Target position in current frame $\mathbf{p}_t$

for $j \leftarrow 1$ **to** n **do**

Generate a sample $\mathbf{p}_t^j \sim \mathcal{N}(\mathbf{p}_{t-1}, \Sigma_{search})$

Calculate $s_t^j \leftarrow h\left(\mathbf{x}_t^{\mathbf{p}_t^j} | \theta_t^{(1)}\right)$ (Eq.(6))

Determine uncertain samples $\mathcal{U}_t$ (Eq.(7))

if $\mathbf{p}_t^j \in \mathcal{U}_t$ **then** $\theta_t^{(1)}$ is uncertain

Query $\theta_t^{(2)}: l_t^j \leftarrow Sign\left(h\left(\mathbf{x}_t^{\mathbf{p}_t^j} | \theta_t^{(2)}\right)\right)$

else

Label using $\theta_t^{(1)}: l_t^j \leftarrow Sign\left(s_t^j\right)$

$\mathcal{D}_t \leftarrow \mathcal{D}_t \cup \left\langle \mathbf{x}_t^{\mathbf{p}_t^j}, l_t^j \right\rangle$

Update $\theta_t^{(2)}$ *with* $\mathcal{D}_{t-\Delta,..,t}$ *every* Δ *frames* ($\Delta = 1$ for T4)

if $\sum_{j=1}^n 1\left(l_t^j > 0\right) > \tau_p$ *and* $\sum_{j=1}^n \pi_t^j > \tau_a$ **then**

Approximate target state $\widehat{\mathbf{p}}_t$ (Eq.(9))

Update $\theta_t^{(1)}$ *with* $\mathcal{U}_t$

else target occluded

$\widehat{\mathbf{p}}_t \leftarrow \mathbf{p}_{t-1}$

4.2. Formalization

In the proposed active co-tracking framework, a main classifier attempts to label the sample, and it queries the label from the other classifier if the main classifier emits uncertain results. This is in contrast with using a linear combination of both classifiers based on their classification accuracy as adopted in T3. At the **CLASSIFYING** step, the proposed tracker can score each sample based on the classifier confidence, i.e., for sample $\mathbf{p}_t^j$ we calculate score s_t^j:

$$s_t^j = h\left(\mathbf{x}_t^{\mathbf{p}_t^j} | \theta_t^{(1)}\right). \tag{6}$$

Based on uncertainty sampling [76], the samples for which the classification score is more uncertain (i.e., $s_t^j \to 0$) contain more information for the classifier if they are labeled by the other classifier. Therefore, the scores of all samples are sorted, and m samples with the closest values to 0 are selected to be queried from $\theta_t^{(2)}$. To handle the situations for which the number of highly uncertain samples are more than m, a range of scores are determined by lower and higher thresholds (τ_l and τ_u), and all the samples in this range are considered highly uncertain:

$$\mathcal{U}_t = \left\{\mathbf{p}_t^i | \tau_l < s_t^i < \tau_u \quad \text{or} \quad \left|\left\{\exists j \neq i | s_t^j \leq s_t^i\right\}\right| < m\right\} \tag{7}$$

in which $\mathcal{U}_t$ is the list of uncertain samples. The label of the samples $l_t^j \in \mathcal{L}_t, j = 1, \ldots, N$ is then determined by

$$l_t^j = \begin{cases} \text{sign}\left(h\left(\mathbf{x}_t^{\mathbf{p}_t^j} | \theta_t^{(1)}\right)\right) & , \mathbf{p}_t^j \in \mathcal{U}_t \\ \text{sign}\left(h\left(\mathbf{x}_t^{\mathbf{p}_t^j} | \theta_t^{(2)}\right)\right) & , \mathbf{p}_t^j \notin \mathcal{U}_t \end{cases} \tag{8}$$

and all image patches $\mathbf{x}_t^{\mathbf{p}_t^j}$ and labels l_t^j are stored in $\mathcal{D}_t$.

At the **ESTIMATION** step, we follow the importance sampling mechanism originally employed by particle filter trackers:

$$\widehat{\mathbf{p}}_t = \frac{\sum_{j=1}^{n} \pi_t^j \mathbf{p}_t^j}{\sum_{j=1}^{1} \pi_t^j}. \tag{9}$$

where $\pi_t^j = s_t^j 1\left(l_t^j > 0\right)$ and $1(.)$ are the indicator function, 1 if true, zero otherwise. This mechanism approximates the state of the target, based on the effect of positive samples, in which samples with higher scores gravitate the final results more toward themselves. Upon the events such as massive occlusion or target loss, this sampling mechanism degenerates [13]. In such cases, the number of positive samples and their corresponding weights shrinks significantly, and the importance sampling is prone to outliers, distractors, and occluded patches. To

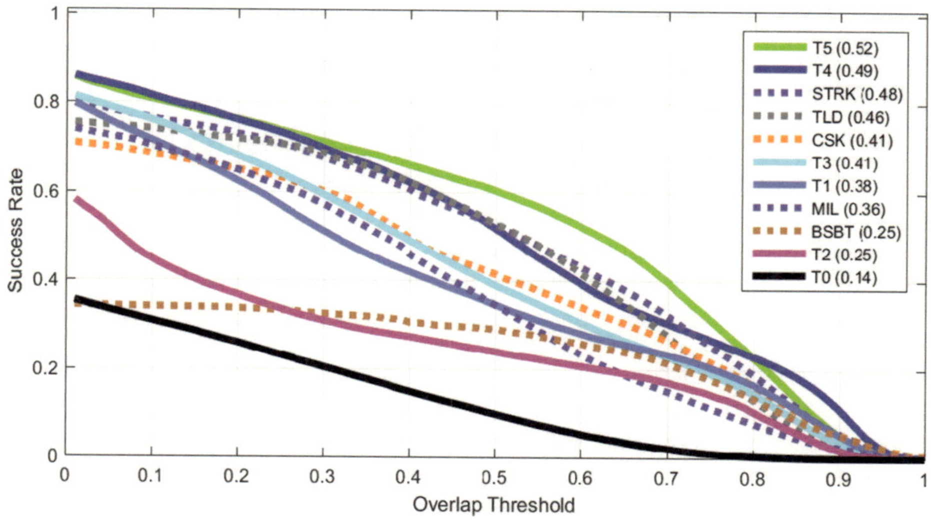

Figure 5. Quantitative performance comparison of the asymmetric active co-tracker (T5), active co-tracker (T4), the ordinary co-tracker (T3), and their individual trackers (T1 and T2).

address this issue, if the number of positive samples is less than τ_p, and their score average is less than τ_a, the target is deemed occluded to avoid tracker degeneracy.

4.3. Evaluation

Figure 5 illustrates the effectiveness of the proposed trackers against their baselines. The active query mechanism in T4 improves the efficiency and effectiveness of co-tracking (T3). Especially in the asymmetric co-tracker (T5), the mixture of long-term and short-term memory classifiers using this method is to key to automatically balance the stability-plasticity equilibrium. It is also prudent for the tracker to adapt to the temporal distribution of the target appearance, before its redistribution by illumination changes, etc.

In summary, the advantages of the proposed trackers especially the asymmetric ones (T5) compared to the conventional co-tracking (T3) are as follows: (1) the classifiers do not exchange all the data they have problems in labeling; instead, the most informative samples are selected by uncertainty sampling and exchanged; (2) the update rate of classifiers is different to realize a short- and long-term memory mixture; (3) the samples that are labeled for the target localization can be reused for training, and the need for an extra round of sampling and labeling is revoked; and (4) since in the proposed asymmetric co-tracking, one of the classifiers scaffolds the other one instead of participating in every labeling process, a more sophisticated classifier with higher computational complexity can be used.

5. Active ensemble co-tracking

Ensemble discriminative tracking utilizes a committee of classifiers, to label data samples, which are in turn used for retraining the tracker to localize the target using the collective knowledge of the committee. In such frameworks the labeling process is performed by leveraging a group of classifiers with different views [45, 56, 80], subsets of training data [57, 81], or memories [57, 82].

In ensemble tracking [45, 47, 56, 57, 60, 83–85], the self-learning loop is broken, and the labeling process is performed by eliciting the belief of a group of classifiers. However, this framework typically does not address some of the demands of tracking-by-detection approaches like a proper model update to avoid model drift or non-stationary of the target sample distribution. Besides, ensemble classifiers do not exchange information, and collaborative classifiers entirely trust the other classifier to label the challenging samples for them and are susceptible to label noise.

Traditionally, ensemble trackers were used to providing a multi-view classification of the target, realized by using different features to construct weak classifiers. In this view, different classifiers represent different hypotheses in the version space, to accurately model the target appearance. Such hypotheses are highly overlapping; therefore an ensemble of them overfits the target. The desired committee, however, consists of competing hypotheses, all consistent with the training data, but each of the specialized in certain aspect. In this view, the most informative data samples are those about which the hypotheses disagree the most, and by labeling them, the version space is minimized leading to quick convergence yet accurate classification [86]. Motivated by this, we proposed a tracker that employs a randomized ensemble of classifiers and selects the most informative data samples to be labeled.

5.1. The idea

To create ensembles of classifiers, researchers typically make different classifiers by altering the features [45], using a pool of appearance and dynamics models [87], utilizing different memory horizons [82], and employing previous snapshots of a classifier in different times [57], but creating a collaborative mechanism in the ensemble, where classifiers exchange information is hardly addressed in the visual tracking literature. This data exchange can be in the form of query passing between ensemble members, in which the queries can be the samples for which a classifier is uncertain or even the ensemble is most uncertain.

Selecting such queries is addressed in different machine learning domains such as curriculum learning [74] and active learning. Query-by-Committee (QBC) algorithm [86, 88] is an active learning approach for ensembles that selects the most informative query to pass within a committee of models which are all trained on the current labeled set but represent competing hypotheses. The label of the queried sample is then decided by the vote of the ensemble members, and the samples for which the ensemble has more diverse ideas are selected as the next query to ask from the teacher (here, the auxiliary classifier). In this case, where the task is a binary classification, the most disputed sample (i.e., with close positive and negative votes) is the most informative since learning its label would maximally train the ensemble. Training with the external label for this sample, shrinks the version space (i.e., the space of all consistent hypotheses with the training data) such that it remains consistent with the hypotheses of all classifiers, but rejects more potential incorrect ones.

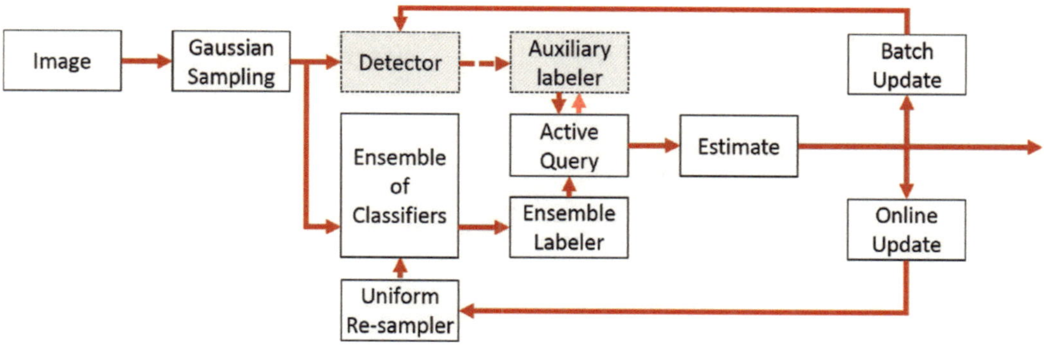

Figure 6. Active ensemble co-tracker. The bagging-induced ensemble labels the input samples and only queries the most disputed ones from the slow part-based classifier.

QBC was originally designed to work with stochastic learning algorithms, which pose limitations to use it with non-probabilistic or deterministic models. To alleviate this problem, Abe and Mamitsuka [89] enable deterministic classifiers to work with random subsets of training data to create different variations of the same learning model. By creating temporary ensemble using this "bagging" procedure [90], they realized Query-by-Bagging (QBag) to enhance the learning speed and generalization of the base learning algorithm.

We propose the adjustment of the QBag algorithm for online training to solve the label noise problem in T6. Similar to T5, the drift problem is handled using dual-memory strategy: the committee rapidly adapts to target changes, whereas the main classifier possesses a longer memory to promote the stability of the target template (**Figure 6**).

5.2. Formalization

An ensemble discriminative tracker employs a set of classifiers instead of one. These classifiers, hereafter called *committee*, are represented by $\mathcal{C} = \left\{\theta_t^{(1)}, \ldots, \theta_t^{(C)}\right\}$ and are typically homogeneous and independent (e.g., [56, 85]). Popular ensemble trackers utilize the majority voting of the committee as their utility function:

$$\mathbf{s}_t^j = \sum_{c=1}^{C} \text{sign}\left(h\left(\mathbf{x}_t^{\mathbf{p}_{t-1} \circ \mathbf{y}_t^j} | \theta_t^{(c)}\right)\right). \tag{10}$$

And Eq. (8) is used to label the samples. Finally, the model is updated for each classifier independently, meaning that each of the committee members is trained with a random subset of the uncertain set. $\theta_{t+1}^{(c)} = u\left(\theta_t^{(c)}, \Gamma_t^{(c)} \sim \mathcal{U}_t\right)$ where $u(\theta, \mathcal{X})$ is the updating the model θ with samples $\mathcal{X}$. The uncertain set $\mathcal{U}_t$ contains all of the samples for which the ensemble disagrees and was sent to the auxiliary classifier for labeling. The detector $\theta_t^{(o)}$ is also updated with all recent data $\mathcal{D}_{t-\Delta,..,t}$ every Δ frames.

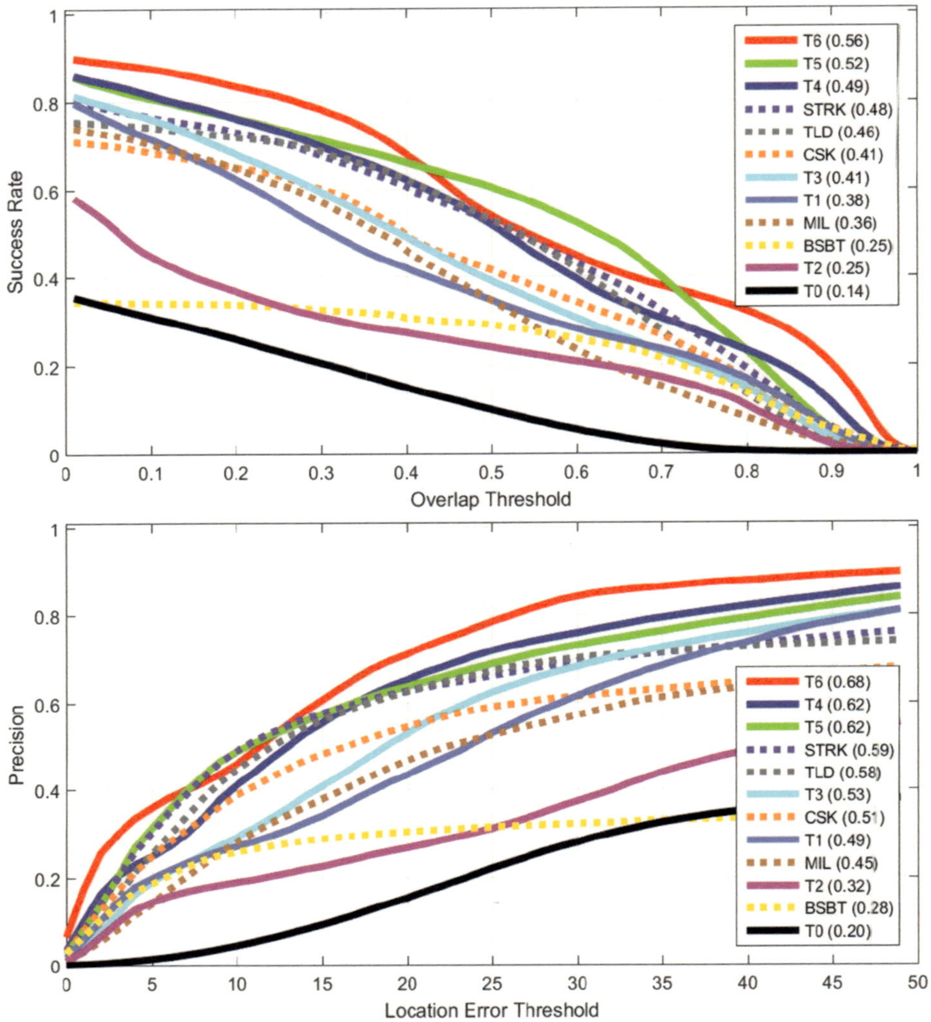

Figure 7. Quantitative performance comparison of the active ensemble co-tracker (T6) with its predecessors.

5.3. Evaluation

Figure 7 depicts the overall performance of the proposed tracker against other benchmarked algorithms on all sequences of the dataset. The plots show that T6 has a superior performance over T5 and its predecessors. The steep slope between $0.9 \geq \tau_{ov} > 1$ indicates the high quality of the predictions (i.e., more predictions have higher overlap with the ground truth, rather than being partially correct), and the other slope around $\tau_{ov} \approx 0.4$ along with high success rate near $\tau_{ov} \rightarrow 0$ indicates that the algorithm was successful in continue tracking, despite all the tracking challenges.

6. Discussion

The instances of the proposed framework are evaluated against state-of-the-art trackers on public sequences that become the de facto standards of benchmarking the trackers. The trackers are compared with popular metrics such as success plot and precision plot to establish a fair benchmark. In addition, the performance of the proposed trackers is investigated for videos with a distinguished tracking challenge, and the results are compared with state of the art and discussed. Additionally, the effect of the information exchanged will be examined thoroughly to illustrate the dynamics of the system. The preliminary results of the proposed framework demonstrate a superior performance for the proposed trackers when applied on all the sequences and most of the subsets of the test dataset with distinguished challenges. Finally, the future research direction is discussed, and the opened research avenues are introduced to the field.

As **Figure 7** and **Table 2** demonstrate, T6 has the best overall performance among investigated trackers on this dataset. While this algorithm has a clear edge in handling many challenges, its performance is comparable with T5 in the case of occlusions and z-rotations. It is also evident that T6 is troubled with fast deformations since neither of the ensemble members is specialized in handling a specific type of deformations and the collective decision of the ensemble may involve mistakes with high confidence. On the other hand, T5 utilizes a dual-memory scheme, and a single classifier can handle extreme temporal deformations better than the ensemble in

	IV	DEF	OCC	SV	IPR	OPR	OV	LR	BC	FM	MB	ALL
T0	12	12	13	12	13	13	14	5	12	15	18	14
T1	37	29	3	36	42	39	43	30	33	39	36	38
T2	23	19	23	23	28	25	25	22	23	24	20	25
T3	41	32	39	40	44	42	43	30	36	43	39	41
T4	50	39	47	48	53	49	48	37	44	50	45	49
T5	52	47	53	51	59	56	52	38	41	53	46	52
T6	57	40	51	53	61	55	63	46	53	60	58	56
TLD	49	32	42	44	50	43	45	37	40	45	42	46
STRK	46	41	44	43	51	48	44	39	39	52	48	48
CSK	40	36	36	34	43	39	32	29	42	39	32	41
MIL	35	35	38	35	41	39	40	32	31	35	28	36
BSBT	23	18	23	21	27	24	32	23	23	26	24	25

The first, second, and third best methods are shown in color. The challenges are illumination variation (IV), scale variation (SV), occlusions (OCC), deformations (DEF), motion blur (MB), fast motion (FM), in-plane rotation (IPR), out-of-play rotation (OPR), out-of-view problem (OV), background clutter (BC), and low resolution (LR)

Table 2. Quantitative evaluation of state of the art under different visual tracking challenges using AUC of success plot (%).

Figure 8. Qualitative results of T6 in red against other trackers (T0–T5 in blue and TLD, STRK, CSK, MIL, and BSBT in gray) on challenging video scenarios of OTB-100 [65]. The sequences are (from top to bottom, left to right) FaceOcc2 and Walking2 with severe occlusion, Deer and Skating1 with abrupt motions, Firl and Ironman with drastic rotations, Singer1 and CarDark and Shaking with poor lighting, Jumping and Basketball with nonrigid deformations, and Shaking,Soccer with drastic lighting, pose, and noise level changes and Board with intensive background clutter. The ground truth is illustrated with yellow dashed box. The results are available in http://ishiilab.jp/member/meshgi-k/act.html.

T6. Interestingly, it is observed that in most of the subcategories that T6 is clearly better than the other trackers, the success plot of T6 starts with a plateau and later has a sharp drop around $\tau_{ov} = 0.8$. This means that T6 provides high-quality localization (i.e., bigger overlaps with the ground truth). Similarly, from precision plot, it is evident that T6 shows a graceful degradation in different scenarios, and although it does not provide a good scale adaptation for targets, it is able to localize them better than the competing trackers (**Figure 8**).

7. Conclusions and future works

This chapter provides a step-by-step tutorial for creating an accurate and high-performance tracking-by-detection algorithm out of ordinary detectors, by eliciting an effective collaboration among them. The use of active learning in junction with co-learning enables the creation of a battery of tracker that strives to minimize the uncertainty of one classifier by the help of another. The progressive design leads to use a committee of classifiers that use online bagging to keep up with the latest target appearance changes while improving the accuracy and generalization of the base tracker (a feature-based KNN). Inspired by the query-by-bagging algorithm, this algorithm selects the most informative samples to learn from the long-term memory auxiliary detector, which realizes a gradually decreasing dependence on this slow and likely overfit detector yet robust against fluctuations in target appearance and occlusions. Furthermore, using an expectation of the bounding boxes compensates for overreliance of the tracker on the classifiers' confidence function. The balance in stability-plasticity equilibrium is achieved by the combination of several short-term classifiers with a long-term classifier and managing their interaction with an active learning mechanism.

The trail of proposed trackers led to T6, which incorporates ensemble tracking, active learning, and co-learning in a discriminative tracking framework and outperform state-of-the-art discriminative and generative trackers on a large video dataset with various types of challenges such as appearance changes and occlusions.

The future direction of this study involves other detectors to care for context, to have accurate physical models for known categories, to use deep features to improve discrimination, and to examine different methods of building the ensemble and detecting most informative samples or exchanging.

Acknowledgements

This article is based on results obtained from a project commissioned by the Japan NEDO and was supported by Post-K application development for exploratory challenges from the Japan MEXT.

Author details

Kourosh Meshgi* and Shigeyuki Oba

*Address all correspondence to: meshgi-k@sys.i.kyoto-u.ac.jp

Graduate School of Informatics, Kyoto University, Kyoto, Japan

References

[1] Borangiu T. "Visual conveyor tracking in high-speed robotics tasks," in Industrial Robotics: Theory, Modelling and Control. InTech, Rijeka, Croatia 2006

[2] Cech J, Mittal R, Deleforge A, Horaud R. Active-speaker detection and localization with mic and cameras embedded into a robotic head. In: Humanoids'13; 2013

[3] Cosgun A, Florencio DA, Christensen HI. Autonomous person following for telepresence robots. In: ICRA'13; IEEE; 2013. pp. 4335-4342

[4] Andersen NA, Andersen JC, Bayramoglu E, Ravn O. Visual navigation for mobile robots. In: Robot Vision. Rijeka, Croatia: InTech; 2010

[5] Campoy P, Mondragón IF, Olivares-Méndez MA, Martínez C. Visual servoing for UAVs. In: Visual Servoing. Rijeka, Croatia: InTech; 2010

[6] Moeslund TB, Hilton A, Krüger V. A survey of advances in vision-based human motion capture and analysis. CVIU. 2006;**104**(2):90-126

[7] Störring M, Moeslund TB, Liu Y, Granum E. Computer vision-based gesture recognition for an augmented reality interface. In: VIIP'04. Vol. 3; 2004. pp. 766-771

[8] Koller O, Zargaran O, Ney H, Bowden R. Deep sign: Hybrid CNN-HMM for continuous sign language recognition. In: BMVC'16; 2016

[9] Wang L, Schmidt B, Nee AY. Vision-guided active collision avoidance for human-robot collaborations. Manufacturing Letters. 2013;**1**(1):5-8

[10] Ess A, Leibe B, Schindler K, Van Gool L. Moving obstacle detection in highly dynamic scenes. In: ICRA'09; IEEE; 2009. pp. 56-63

[11] Xia L, Gori I, Aggarwal JK, Ryoo MS. Robot-centric activity recognition from first-person RGB-D videos. In: WACV'15; IEEE; 2015. pp. 357-364

[12] Rautaray SS, Agrawal A. Vision based hand gesture recognition for human computer interaction: A survey. AI Review. 2015;**43**(1):1-54

[13] Bao C, Wu Y, Ling H, Ji H. Real time robust l1 tracker using accelerated proximal gradient approach. In: CVPR'12; 2012

[14] Kwon J, Lee KM. Tracking by sampling trackers. In: ICCV'11; IEEE; 2011. pp. 1195-1202

[15] Hare S, Saffari A, Torr PH. Struck: Structured output tracking with kernels. In: ICCV'11; 2011

[16] Hilsmann A, Schneider DC, Eisert P. Image-based tracking of deformable surfaces. In: Object Tracking. Rijeka, Croatia: InTech; 2011

[17] Dinh TB, Vo N, Medioni G. Context tracker: Exploring supporters and distracters in unconstrained environments. In: CVPR'11; 2011

[18] Meshgi K, Maeda S-I, Oba S, Ishii S. Data-driven probabilistic occlusion mask to promote visual tracking. In: CRV'16; IEEE; 2016. pp. 178-185

[19] Wu Y, Ling H, Yu J, Li F, Mei X, Cheng E. Blurred target tracking by blur-driven tracker. In: ICCV'2011; 2011

[20] Ross DA, Lim J, Lin R-S, Yang M-H. Incremental Learning for Robust Visual Tracking. International Journal of Computer Vision. Springer; 2008;**77**(1-3):125-141

[21] Fang J, Xu H, Wang Q, Wu T. Online Hash Tracking with Spatio-Temporal Saliency Auxiliary. Computer Vision and Image Understanding. Elsevier; 2017;**160**:57-72

[22] Taalimi A, Qi H, Khorsandi R. Online multi-modal task-driven dictionary learning and robust joint sparse representation for visual tracking. In: AVSS'15; 2015

[23] Kiani H, Sim T, Lucey S. Correlation filters with limited boundaries. In: CVPR'15; 2015

[24] Danelljan M, Hager G, Shahbaz Khan F, Felsberg M. Learning spatially regularized correlation filters for visual tracking. In: ICCV'15; 2015. pp. 4310-4318

[25] Danelljan M, Robinson A, Khan FS, Felsberg M. Beyond correlation filters: Learning continuous convolution operators for visual tracking. In: ECCV'16; 2016

[26] Nam H, Han B. Learning multi-domain convolutional neural networks for visual tracking. In: CVPR'16; 2016

[27] Wu Y, Lim J, Yang M-H. Online object tracking: A benchmark. In: CVPR'13; IEEE; 2013. pp. 2411-2418

[28] Kristan M, Matas J, Leonardis A, Felsberg M. The visual object tracking vot2015 challenge results. In: ICCVw'15; 2015

[29] Li A, Lin M, Wu Y, Yang M-H, Yan S. NUS-PRO: A new visual tracking challenge. IEEE Transactions on Pattern Analysis and Machine Intelligence. IEEE; 2016;**38**(2):335-349

[30] He K, Zhang X, Ren S, Sun J. Deep residual learning for image recognition. In: CVPR'16; 2016. pp. 770-778

[31] Wang N, Yeung D-Y. Learning a deep compact image representation for visual tracking. In: NIPS'13; 2013. pp. 809-817

[32] Li H, Li Y, Porikli F, et al. Deeptrack: Learning discriminative feature representations by convolutional neural networks for visual tracking. In: BMVC. Vol. 2014; 2014

[33] Hong S, You T, Kwak S, Han B. Online tracking by learning discriminative saliency map with convolutional neural network. In: ICML'15; 2015. pp. 597-606

[34] Tang F, Brennan S, Zhao Q, Tao H. Co-tracking using semi-supervised support vector machines. In: ICCV'07; 2007

[35] Bai Q, Wu Z, Sclaroff S, Betke M, Monnier C. Randomized ensemble tracking. In: ICCV'13; 2013

[36] Henriques JF, Caseiro R, Martins P, Batista J. Exploiting the circulant structure of tracking-by-detection with kernels. In: ECCV'12; Springer; 2012. pp. 702-715

[37] Lapedriza A, Pirsiavash H, Bylinskii Z, Torralba A. Are all Training Examples Equally Valuable? arXiv. 2013

[38] Matthews I, Ishikawa T, Baker S. The template update problem. IEEE Transactions on Pattern Analysis and Machine Intelligence. IEEE; 2004;**26**(6):810-815

[39] Grabner H, Leistner C, Bischof H. Semi-supervised on-line boosting for robust tracking. In: ECCV'08; 2008

[40] Meshgi K, Mirzaei MS, Oba S, Ishii S. Efficient asymmetric co-tracking using uncertainty sampling. In: ICSIPA'17; 2017

[41] Meshgi K, Oba S, Ishii S. Robust discriminative tracking via query-by-committee. In: AVSS'16; 2016

[42] Pérez P, Hue C, Vermaak J, Gangnet M. Color-based probabilistic tracking. In: ECCV'02; 2002

[43] Wu Y, Pei M, Yang M, Jia Y. Robust Discriminative Tracking Via Landmark-Based Label Propagation. IEEE Transactions on Image Processing. IEEE; 2015;**24**(5):1510-1523

[44] Oza NC, Russell S. Online ensemble learning. In: AAAI'00, 2000

[45] Grabner H, Grabner M, Bischof H. Real-time tracking via on-line boosting. In: BMVC'06; 2006

[46] Leistner C, Saffari A, Roth P, Bischof H. On robustness of on-line boosting: a competitive study. In: ICCVw'09; 2009

[47] Babenko B, Yang M-H, Belongie S. Visual tracking with online multiple instance learning. In: CVPR'09; 2009

[48] Avidan S. Support vector tracking. PAMI. 2004;**26**(8):1064-1072

[49] Masnadi-Shirazi H, Mahadevan V, Vasconcelos N. On the design of robust classifiers for computer vision. In: CVPR'10; 2010

[50] Leistner C, Saffari A, Santner J, Bischof H. Semi-supervised random forests. In: ICCV'09; 2009

[51] Zeisl B, Leistner C, Saffari A, Bischof H. On-line semi-supervised multipleinstance boosting. In: CVPR'10; 2010

[52] Zhang K, Song H. Real-Time Visual Tracking via Online Weighted Multiple Instance Learning. Pattern Recognition. Elsevier; 2013;**46**(1):397-411

[53] Henriques JF, Caseiro R, Martins P, Batista J. High-speed tracking with kernelized correlation filters. PAMI. 2015;**37**(3):583-596

[54] Grabner H, Matas J, Van Gool L, Cattin P. Tracking the invisible: Learning where the object might be. In: CVPR'10; 2010

[55] Zhang K, Zhang L, Yang M-H, Hu Q. Robust Object Tracking via Active Feature Selection. IEEE Transactions on Circuits and Systems for Video Technology. IEEE; 2013;**23**(11): 1957-1967

[56] Saffari A, Leistner C, Santner J, Godec M, Bischof H. On-line random forests. In: ICCVw'09; 2009

[57] Zhang J, Ma S, Sclaroff S. MEEM: Robust tracking via multiple experts using entropy minimization. In: ECCV'14; 2014

[58] Kalal Z, Mikolajczyk K, Matas J. Tracking-learning-detection. PAMI. 2012;**34**(7):1409-1422

[59] Girshick R, Donahue J, Darrell T, Malik J. Rich feature hierarchies for accurate object detection and semantic segmentation. In: CVPR'14; 2014. pp. 580-587

[60] Avidan S. Ensemble tracking. IEEE Transactions on Pattern Analysis and Machine Intelligence. IEEE; 2007;**29**(2):261-271

[61] Woodley T, Stenger B, Cipolla R. Tracking using online feature selection and a local generative model. In: BMVC'07; 2007

[62] Hong Z, Chen Z, Wang C, Prokhorov D, Tao D. Multi-store tracker (muster): A cognitive psychology inspired approach to object tracking. In: CVPR'15; 2015

[63] Li J, Hong Z, Zhao B. Robust visual tracking by exploiting the historical tracker snapshots. In: ICCVW'15; 2015. pp. 41-49

[64] Felzenszwalb PF, Girshick RB, McAllester D, Ramanan D. Object detection with discriminatively trained part-based models. PAMI. 2010;**32**(9):1627-1645

[65] Wu Y, Lim J, Yang M-H. Object tracking benchmark. IEEE Transactions on Pattern Analysis and Machine Intelligence. IEEE Transactions on Pattern Analysis and Machine Intelligence. IEEE; 2015;**37**(9):1834-1848

[66] Stalder S, Grabner H, Van Gool L. Beyond semi-supervised tracking: Tracking should be as simple as detection, but not simpler than recognition. In: ICCVw'09; 2009

[67] Xing J, Gao J, Li B, Hu W, Yan S. Robust object tracking with online multi-lifespan dictionary learning. In: ICCV'13; 2013. pp. 665-672

[68] Zhuang B, Wang L, Lu H. Visual tracking via shallow and deep collaborative model. Neurocomputing. 2016;**218**:61-71

[69] Blum A, Mitchell T. Combining labeled and unlabeled data with co-training. In: COLT'98; 1998

[70] Vijayanarasimhan S, Grauman K. Cost-Sensitive Active Visual Category Learning. International Journal of Computer Vision. Springer; 2011;**91**(1):24-44

[71] Razavi N, Gall J, Kohli P, Van Gool L. Latent Hough transform for object detection. In: ECCV'12; 2012

[72] Zhu X, Vondrick C, Ramanan D, Fowlkes CC. Do we need more training data or better models for object detection? In: BMVC'12; 2012

[73] De la Torre F, Black MJ. Robust principal component analysis for computer vision. In: ICCV'01; 2001

[74] Bengio Y, Louradour J, Collobert R, Weston J. Curriculum learning. In: ICML'09; 2009

[75] Lu J, Issaranon T, Forsyth D. Safetynet: Detecting and Rejecting Adversarial Examples Robustly. arXiv. 2017

[76] Lewis DD, Gale WA. A sequential algorithm for training text classifiers. In: ACM SIGIR'94; 1994. pp. 3-12

[77] Lampert CH, Peters J. Active structured learning for high-speed object detection. In: PR; Springer; 2009. pp. 221-231

[78] Li C, Wang X, Dong W, Yan J, Liu Q, Zha H. Active sample learning and feature selection: A unified approach. arXiv. 2015

[79] Beygelzimer A, Dasgupta S, Langford J. Importance weighted active learning. In: ICML'09; ACM; 2009. pp. 49-56

[80] Han B, Sim J, Adam H. Branchout: Regularization for online ensemble tracking with convolutional neural networks. In: ICCV'17; 2017. pp. 2217-2224

[81] Meshgi K, Oba S, Ishii S. Efficient version-space reduction for visual tracking. In: CRV'17; 2017

[82] Meshgi K, Oba S, Ishii S. Active discriminative tracking using collective memory. In: MVA'17; 2017

[83] Oza NC. Online bagging and boosting. In: SMC'05; 2005

[84] Saffari A, Leistner C, Godec M, Bischof H. Robust multi-view boosting with priors. In: ECCV'10; 2010

[85] Leistner C, Saffari A, Bischof H. Miforests: Multiple-instance learning with randomized trees. In: ECCV'10; 2010

[86] Seung S, Opper M, Sompolinsky H. Query by committee. In: COLT'92; 1992

[87] Kwon J, Lee KM. Visual tracking decomposition. In: CVPR'10; 2010

[88] Settles B. Active Learning. Morgan & Claypool Publishers; 2012

[89] Abe N, Mamitsuka H. Query learning strategies using boosting and bagging. In: ICML'98; 1998

[90] Breiman L. Bagging predictors. Machine Learning. Springer; 1996;**24**(2):123-140

Chapter 7

Autonomous Robots and Behavior Initiators

Oscar Chang

Additional information is available at the end of the chapter

http://dx.doi.org/10.5772/intechopen.71958

Abstract

We use an autonomous neural controller (ANC) that handles the mechanical behavior of virtual, multi-joint robots, with many moving parts and sensors distributed through the robot's body, satisfying basic Newtonian laws. As in living creatures, activities inside the robot include behavior initiators: self-activating networks that burn energy and function without external stimulus. Autonomy is achieved by mimicking the dynamics of biological brains, in resting situations, a default state network (DSN), specialized set of energy burning neurons, assumes control and keeps the robot in a safe condition, where other behaviors can be brought to use. Our ANC contains several kinds of neural nets trained with gradient descent to perform specialized jobs. The first group generates moving wave activities in the robot muscles, the second yields basic position/presence prediction information about sensors, the third acts as timing masters, empowering sequential tasks. We add a fourth category of self-activating networks that push behavior from the inside. Through evolutive methods, the composed network share clue information along a few connecting weights, producing self-motivated robots, capable of achieving noticeable self-level of competence. We show that this spirited robot interacts with humans and, through appropriate interfaces, learn complex behaviors that satisfy unknown, subjacent human expectative.

Keywords: autonomous robot, behavior initiators, deep learning

1. Introduction

To reach the degree of complexity required in human-robot interaction, artificial neural networks (ANNs) seem to be good nominees. The new powerful training algorithms known globally as deep learning have made possible massively trained ANN capable of recognizing a specific human face in a blink. However, these powerful neural processors lack a key component of life: self-motivation. What internal force moves a fruit fly? Important research [1, 2]

IntechOpen

© 2018 The Author(s). Licensee IntechOpen. This chapter is distributed under the terms of the Creative Commons Attribution License (http://creativecommons.org/licenses/by/3.0), which permits unrestricted use, distribution, and reproduction in any medium, provided the original work is properly cited.

has found that in ultimate navigating lifesaving situations, the decisions in the fly's brain, with about 250,000 neurons, are taken by a reduced set of neurons that consume energy and originate an inner noisy output that in turn fires a massive body response (change in flying direction, for instance). So, at this scale, by using its own onboard neural processor, a self-motivated behavior initiator situation occurs inside the fly, causing noticeable changes in the activity of the individual.

As a significant consequence, this internal capacity converts the fly into a free-running autonomous living creature. One of our objectives in the chapter is thus to develop design methods that bring this genuine spontaneity and autonomy to our robots.

At the bigger scale of human brains with about eighty billion of neurons, the function of autonomous behaviors initiator is a much more elaborated matter, well documented by Raichel and its research team by using modern functional magnetic resonance imaging (fMRI) [3, 4]. From these studies, one noticeable finding is that the human brain never really rests but stays always in constant activity, burning a substantial amount of energy that seems to go nowhere. Raichel called this phenomenon "the brain dark energy," and his discovery changes every previous concept about brain functioning. This energy-burning attitude seems to be the common way of living brains, and signs of constant burning energy have been reported in bees [5] and submillimeter worms [6].

1.1. Previous works

The use of artificial neural nets to control robots represents a promising activity, and recent research has been published. In [7], the authors develop an autonomous robot with the application of neural network and apply it for monitoring and rescue activities in case of natural or man-made disaster. In [8], the use of an artificial neural network to improve the estimation of the position of a mobile node in indoor environment using wireless networks is studied. In [9], the author focuses on deep convolutional neural networks, capable of differentiating between thousands of objects by self-learning from millions of images. In [10], the authors study the design of a controlling neural network using adaptive resonance theory. In [11], the authors developed a new method based on neural networks that allows learning multichain redundant structure configuration during grasping.

In our previous a work, we proposed a method where the capacities of two specific kinds of neural processors [12], vehicle driving and path planning, were stacked as to control mobile robots. Each processor behaves as an independent trained agent that, through simulated evolution, is encouraged to socialize through low-bandwidth, asynchronous channels. Under evolutive pressure, agents develop communication skill and cooperative behaviors that raise the level of competence of vision-guided mobile robots, allowing a convenient autonomous exploration of the environment. In [13], a neural behavior-initiating agent (BIA) was proposed to integrate relevant compressed image information coming from other cooperating and specialized neural agents. Using this arrangement, the problem of tracking and recognizing a moving icon was solved by three simpler and separated tasks. Neural agents associated proved to be easier to train and show a good general performance. The obtained neural controller handled spurious images, solved acute image-related tasks, and, as a distinctive feature, in prolonged deadlock conditions showed traces of genuine spontaneity.

In this chapter, we have taken these ideas further and propose an all-neural controller specialized in governing the functioning of a multi-joint robot, with many joints, muscles, sensors, and specialized sub-processors. The general problem is to find an ideal balance that guarantees self-motivation and maximizes the learning capacity of the robot in human-robot interaction situations.

Our methodology contemplates the partially supervised training with backpropagation of shallow networks inside explicit scenarios, with specialized tasks, where information about the environment is available and is used as targets for local neural training. The objective at this basal level is to produce reliable abstract representations of the environment, including both short-term and long-term influences and wave-time-related information. This neural set is then stacked together with other internal and external neural signals, creating a fertile ground for the robot to learn new behaviors related with human's interaction. Our macro-objective is to build robots supported by self-motivated, multipart, robust neural controllers.

1.2. Research methods

We have constructed neural models written in C++ that behave or can be trained to behave as different kinds of neural sub-processors including self-activated behavior initiators, wave generator, timing generator, and general purpose predictive units. We also develop C++ model for an expandable mechanical universe where neuro-mechanical nodes composed by muscles, sensors, joints, mechanical structures, and mechanical links can be connected together, creating wormlike robots extrapolable to many components. The robot universe includes other items such as ball, floor, fixed walls, and one flexile moving wall that can be manipulated by humans.

Through evolutive methods, the neural subcontroller learns to share clue information along a few low-bandwidth channels producing a self-motivated robot with a high level of competence. We show that this proactive robot is capable of interacting with humans through appropriate interfaces and learning complex behaviors that satisfy unknown, subjacent human purposes.

1.3. Autonomous neural controller

The proposed self-activated neural controller is developed around the ambient in **Figure 1**. The mechanical assembly is defined by a set of repetitive, neural-mechanical blocks called joints, snapped together to form long chains. The wave generator block is a shallow network directly connected to the actuators, one neuron per muscle. Its function is to massively move the muscle in a coordinate way. The timing generator, position detector, and ball detector blocks are all shallow, three-layer neural networks, trained with backpropagation to do robotic tasks related to sensor activities. The behavior initiator block is an energy-consuming network that satisfied a local, weight-encoded syntactic rule. By evolutive algorithm and through a

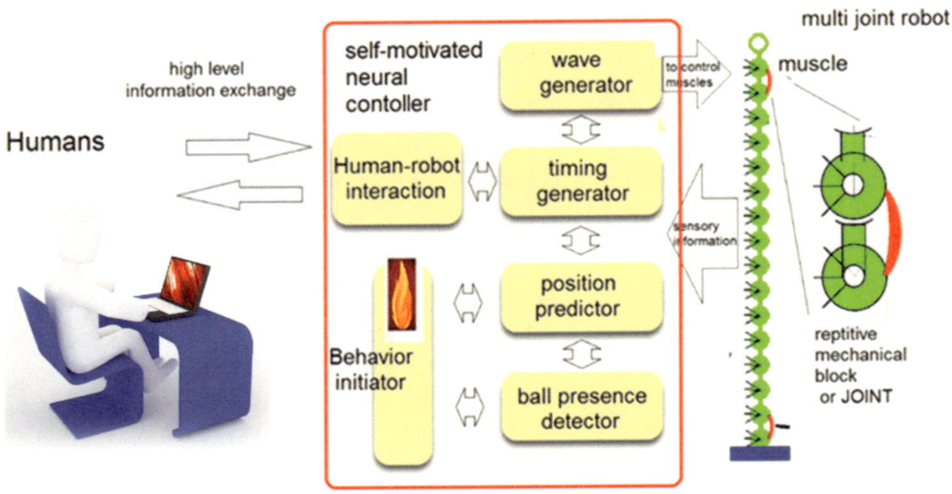

Figure 1. Autonomous neural controller. Modular neural-mechanical blocks called joints are snapped together to form long chains. The resulting structure is controlled by an arrangement of stacked neural controllers. A wave generator massively moves robot muscle in a coordinate way. Other shallow neural networks are trained with backpropagation do specific robotic tasks: handle sensor activities, timing generation, position detection, and ball sensing. The behavior initiator is an energy-consuming, self-activating network that satisfied syntactic rules and pushes behaviors by itself. The genetic combination of all these elements produces a self-motivated robot capable of learning, through human-robot interaction, behaviors that satisfy human's expectations.

convenient interface, human-robot interaction triggers a learning process where some weights are modified, and the robot learns behaviors that satisfy human's expectations. After training, the behavior initiator network behaves as a default mode network (DMN) that assumes the control, burns energy, and uses other subjacent resources to initiate new behaviors, if required.

2. Biological brains

2.1. Brain's wiring diagram

The basic building block of brains is the neuron, which by itself has a very especial nature in terms of energy consumption, higher than any other kind of cell in living creatures [14]. From human to rotifers and very simple worms, neurons group themselves into elaborated networks called brains, where the common factor seems to be carefully knitted structuring complexity, with high job specializations [15, 16].

2.2. A default mode of brain function

"Whilst part of what we perceive comes through our senses from the object before us, another part (and it may be the larger part) always comes out of our own head." William James (1890)

In classical studies of brain function, the main accepted model is based in task-evoked responses. In general, the used experiments encourage a reflexive view of how the brain

http://dx.doi.org/10.5772/intechopen.71958

works, ignoring that brain functions may be mainly intrinsic, connecting by themselves information and processing it to respond to environmental demands. By carefully analyzing the allocation of the brain's energy resources, Raichel [4] argues that the essence of brain function is indeed mainly intrinsic and components of signal transduction and metabolic pathways are all in a continuous state of flux.

Consider this functional aspect of human brain, described in Raichel's research [3, 4]:

"In the mid-1990s we noticed quite by accident that, surprisingly, certain brain regions experienced a decreased level of activity from the baseline resting state when subjects carried out some task. These areas—in particular, a section of the medial parietal cortex (a region near the middle of the brain involved with remembering personal events in one's life, among other things)—registered this drop when other areas were engaged in carrying out a defied task such as reading aloud. Befuddled, we labeled the area showing the most depression MMPA, for "medial mystery parietal area. This cuing — among the visual and auditory parts of the cortex, for instance—probably ensures that all regions of the brain are ready to react in concert to stimuli. Further analyses indicated that performing a particular task increases the brain's energy consumption by less than 5 percent of the underlying baseline activity. A large fraction of the overall activity—from 60 to 80 percent of all energy used by the brain—occurs in circuits unrelated to any external event."

According to [3, 4], the human brain has a default mode of function controlled by a default mode network (DMN) which serves as a master organizer of its dark energy. The DMN is thought to behave like an orchestra conductor, issuing timing signals, much as a conductor waves a baton, to coordinate activity among different brain regions. This orchestrated way of doing things is described in a neat story in [4] where during a quite beach afternoon a placid tourist does daydreaming watching nowhere. In his lap rests a magazine that he's been reading for a while, suddenly a weird looking insect lands in its naked leg, firing a cascade of stimulus. The point is that during the following chains of events, where the human tries to get rid of a potential danger, the brain in fact consumes less energy during daydreaming. Raichel found that the default mode network burns energy and maintains the control of the whole body, while many other powerful neural processors (vision, sense of touch, etc.) return to the borderline of activity and keep on burning energy, ready to actuate.

The lesson about this biological brain story is that to survive in a complex physical world, our robots and robot controllers should have a safe default mode that keeps itself in charge, burns energy, preserves the mechanical structure in a safe condition, and is ready to evocate other behaviors under stimuli.

3. The robot and its environment

The robot is assembled with elements that contain sensors, muscles, rigid joints, and a male-female coupling (**Figure 2**). Each joint has a dedicated neuron that activates the corresponding muscle which, for the sake of simplicity, has both contraction and expansion capacities.

Joints are snapped together to form arbitrarily long wormlike robots (**Figure 3**).

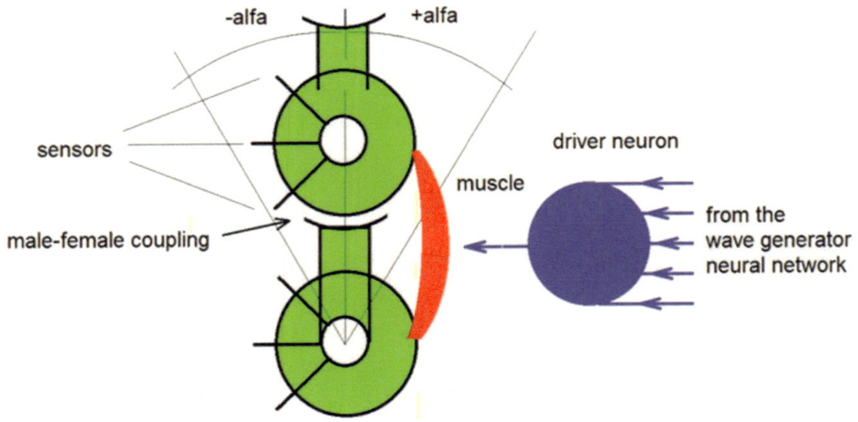

Figure 2. The basic robotic joint with sensors, muscles, and neural driver. The joint can be snapped into long chains. Muscles are driven by the output neurons of an associate network.

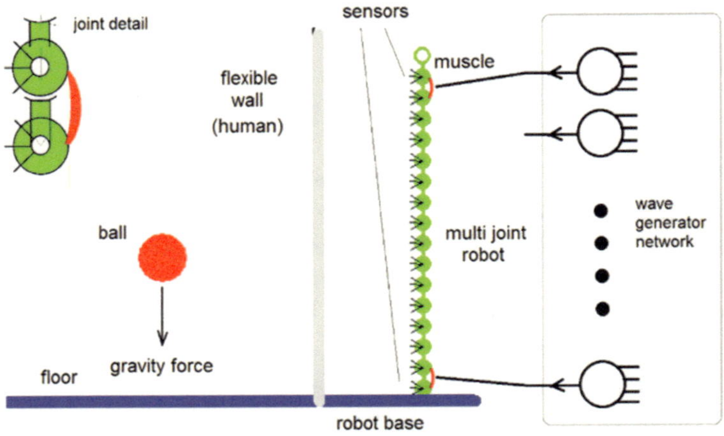

Figure 3. Modular robot with 16 joints and dedicated driven neurons in its working environment.

4. Autonomy

Our approach to autonomous robots is based in autonomous controllers, constructed with artificial neural nets, and incorporating basic rules of living brains in terms of energy usage, default mode network (DMN), and the orchestrated, autonomous transitions forms default mode to other operative behaviors in reaction to stimuli.

4.1. Artificial neural networks

The neural networks used in this chapter are sigmoidal neurons trained with backpropagation [17]. Other functioning details are given in [12, 13].

In both biology and circuit complexity theory, it is maintained that deep architectures can be much more efficient (even exponentially efficient) than shallow ones in terms of computational power and abstract representation of some functions [18, 19]. Unfortunately, well-established gradient descent methods such as backpropagation that have proven effective when applied to shallow architectures do not work well when applied to deep architectures. Our method uses shallow nets trained with backpropagation, but these networks are thereafter stacked with other networks, thus becoming deep architectures.

5. Neural controllers

5.1. Autonomous behavior initiators

As mentioned in the introduction, the *Drosophila* brain involves nonlinearity and the competence of only a few neurons in the final fly's behavior-initiating mechanism, deep buried in its brain. So, we are interested in neural structures with few neurons and genuine spontaneity. In the previous work [12], we presented a solution where the term behavior is defined as a finite sequence of events distributes in the space time. The initiation of these sequences is fired by using an n-flop, a robust network constructed with sigmoidal-type neurons sharing a common self-activating excitatory input K [20]. Being robust, it serves as foundation for other large-scale optimization structures that solve difficult jobs, such as the travel salesman problem (TSP). The n-flop is the basic building block beyond the concept of programming with neurons [20], and the term is derived from the flip-flop, a computer circuit that has only two stable states. n-flops have n-stable states and the rooted capacity to solve high-dimensional problems [21].

In an n-flop, neurons are programmed by their weight interconnections to solve the constraint that only one of them will be active when the system is in equilibrium. To this end, the output of each neuron is connected with an inhibitory input weight (-1) to each of the other n-1 neuron inputs (lateral inhibition). In addition, each neuron receives a common excitatory input K which, on controlled situations, tends to force all neuron outputs toward 1. A solution or desired output is self-activated by rising K and forcing all neurons to some near-equilibrium but unstable "high-energy" state. At this point, K is set to almost zero, forcing the network to seek a low-energy or equilibrium-stable state. The solution given by a non-biased n-flop is a unique but unpredictable winner, which may be used as a behavior initiator, where "behavior" corresponds to a finite sequence of events, distributes in the space time. A unique winner guarantees a conflict-free operation in terms of robotic conduct. A good stabilized n-flop will always satisfy the syntactic rule "only one winner," even when neurons in the n-flop community share input weights with outside-world neurons, including other n-flops. This conduces toward a proactive scenery where it is possible to control, with events that happen inside or outside the robot, the initiation of behaviors that are being pushed from the inside (**Figure 4**).

Like in biological brains, the proposed behavior initiator constantly consumes energy, and since it controls behaviors, it can affect the whole information processing of the robot.

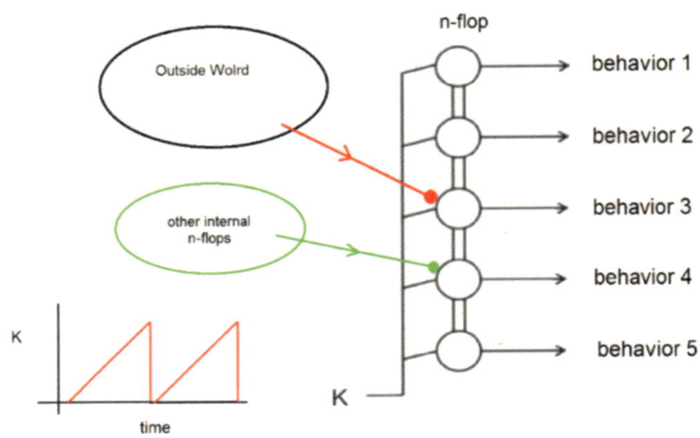

Figure 4. The n-flop as a behavior pusher. A set of sigmoidal-type neurons inhibit each other with −1 value weights and share a common self-activating excitatory input K. Under controlled situations, K raises and forces all neuron outputs toward a 1 output. Once in this high-energy position, K comes down to almost zero, forcing the network to seek a low-energy or equilibrium state. For each K cycle, a new, unique, random winner is generated. Neurons in the n-flop can share input weights with other insider or outsider neurons. This results in a proactive scenery where behavior initiation is being pushed from the inside and all behaviors can be eventually awakened, but it is still possible for events inside or outside of the robot to modify the statistical occurrence of behaviors.

5.2. The wave generator

Waves are important in living creatures, and some forms of contraction waves are always used for locomotion and other activities [22].

We use a wave generator network to control the robot's muscles through a one-to-one assignment so that one output neuron controls one muscle. The net is pre-trained with a set of inputs that produce output values in the range 0–1. This moves the joint associated to the muscle in the range (α, $-\alpha$) where α is a target angle measured in degrees. With the appropriated targets, the net learns to reproduce moving wave forms in its outputs (**Figure 5**).

The training objective is to create a neural moving wave that in turn produces a mechanical moving wave through the robot's body.

5.3. The timing generator

Timing is important in living creatures making it possible to control complex thing, from walking to sleeping [23]. We use a neural timing generator trained with backpropagation so that its output vector behaves as a programmable shift register with left, stop, right commands and a winner-takes-all output; the winner stays near 1, while all other m−1 outputs stay off (near to 0). The training objective is to create neural timing signals that produce mechanical timing through the robot's body (**Figure 6**).

5.4. The position predictor

The position predictor is trained to indicate the position of the ball when it touches the sensors. The predictor receives sensor signals in the range 0–1 as input and predicts the mean position of the detected ball in terms of one joint number. For example, in **Figure 7**, due to

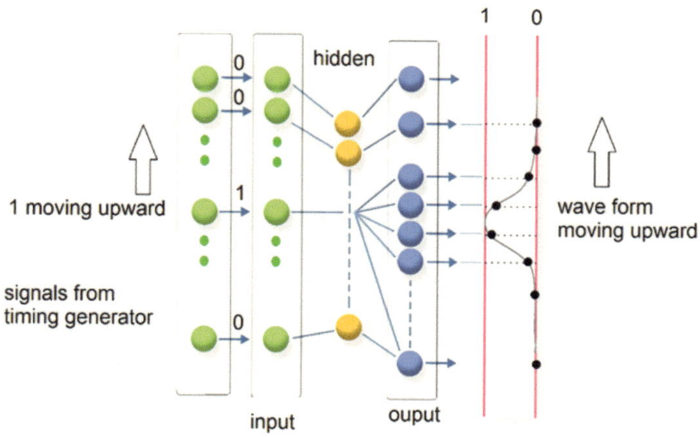

Figure 5. The wave generator. A shallow network receives as input 16 decoded timing signals produced by a timing generator. By using a moving wave form as target, the net is trained to generate the chosen waveform and to move it, when the input timing signal moves. Since output neurons directly drive robot's muscles, moving mechanical waves can be created in the robot's joint structure. The chosen hidden layer has nine neurons so data compression occurs.

spatial interaction between the space sensors and the ball, a complex input pattern is produced. Applying a mass center algorithm, the position of the ball can be estimated in terms of a unique joint number and given as target to the net.

5.5. The ball presence detector

The ball presence is trained to indicate that the ball is touching the sensors somewhere along the robot's body. It is a first front detector, and its training includes white noise as counter example so that the net learns to distinguish the specific sensor excitation pattern produced by the ball (**Figure 8**).

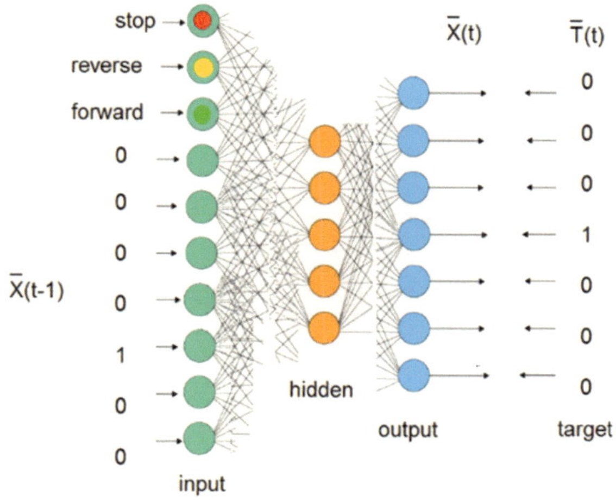

Figure 6. The timing generator. After training, the output vector behaves as a programmable shift register, with left, stop, right, commands and a winner-takes-all output, where only one of n-defined output stays on (near to 1), while all other m-1 outputs stay off (near to 0).

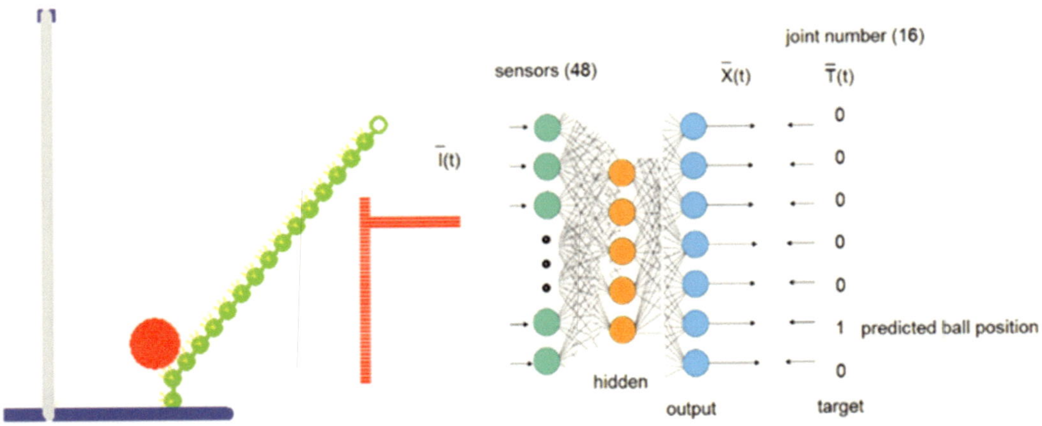

Figure 7. The position predictor is trained to indicate the position of the sensed ball in terms of a joint number. From 48 sensors, 16 outputs are derived.

5.6. The autonomous neural controller

Our next step is to assemble the above-defined neural devices into an integrated autonomous neural controller (ANC) that combines the different capacities of the participant networks. As shown in **Figure 9**, a five-flop is established as a basal behavior initiator, where neuron 1 is connected with a positive weight to a constant output, becoming the neuron with the highest probability to win, assuming the role of a default network. When the ball presence network becomes active, the state 3 may become a winner activating the three-flop, which feeds random values to the wave generator producing a random moving wave. Notice that a single event (ball presence) activates a complex assembly of neural devices that work by themselves, creating a mechanical wave running through the robot's body.

To promote complex behaviors, a set of selected outputs are allowed to have connecting weights with a selected set of neurons (**Figure 9**).

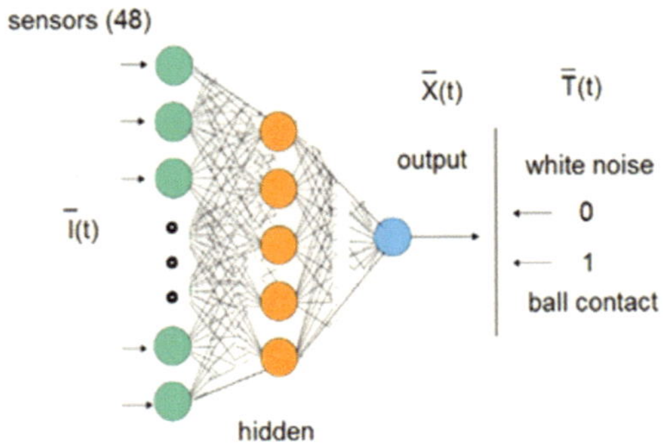

Figure 8. The ball presence detector is trained to indicate that the ball is touching the sensors somewhere along the robot's body.

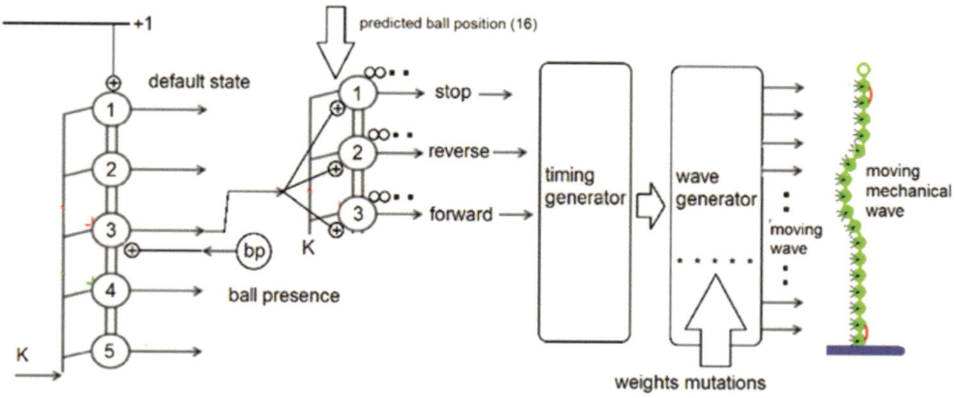

Figure 9. The autonomous neural controller. A 5-flop acts as basal behavior initiator; its number 1 neuron is connected with a positive weight value to the constant 1 line, making the neuron the highest probability to win (default state). When the ball presence network (bp) becomes active, the state 3 becomes a likely winner that in turn activates the 3-flop. Next, random values are fed to the wave generator, producing a random moving mechanical wave in the robot. To promote complex behaviors, selected outputs are allowed to develop connecting weights with other neurons, for instance, the 3-flop neurons have connective input weights with the position predictor network. Through weight mutations, complex behaviors emerge.

Specifically, the outputs of the ball position predictor (16) are weight connected with the neurons of the 3-flop, making possible for the ball position to control the direction of the moving wave. This comprises 16 × 3= 48 weights.

The hidden weight in the wave generator (144 weights) is also allowed to mutate, opening opportunities for different wave forms and wave movements to appear. The overall behavior of the free-running autonomous neural controller is thus governed by these 192 variables.

6. The human-robot interaction

Once the autonomous neural controller (ANC) begins to behave like an orchestra conductor, issuing timing signals to coordinate activities among different control regions, humans begin to interact with the robot through a keyboard and a visual interface (**Figure 10**). Humans are asked to play the coconut dance game, in which a couple tries, without using their hands, to move upward a coconut placed between them at their waist level; in our case, the human player uses the robot as dancing partner. We choose this activity because it requires a close, coordinate interaction between the two participants, and it doesn't have a trivial solution. The coconut (ball) is subjected to gravity force and is released somewhere between the dancers. The human, represented by a flexible wall, must use the keyboard to move toward the robot and trap the ball between the two bodies; he/she then uses the keyboard to manipulate a moving body bending that pushes the ball up. The game is won when the ball is pushed up, out of the body's reach.

Animated by internal n-flops, the robot behaves proactively, burning energy and initiating behaviors independently of the outside world.

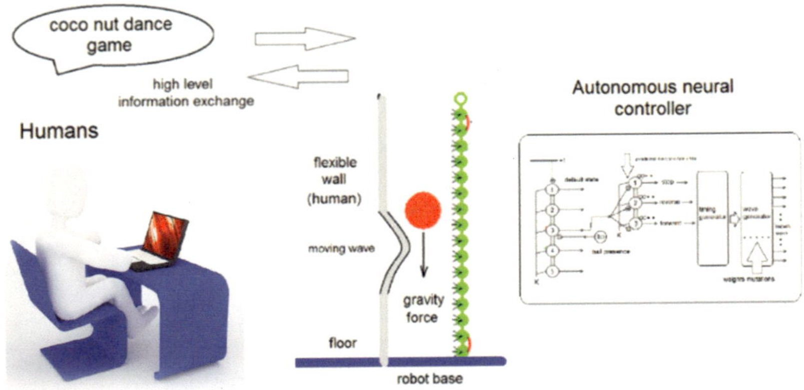

Figure 10. Human-robot interaction. Humans play the coconut dance game by using the robot as dancing partner. This activity requires a close, coordinate interaction between the two participants, and it doesn't have a trivial solution. The coconut, pulled down by gravity, is released somewhere between the dancers. The human (flexible wall) must use the keyboard to trap the ball between the two bodies and then manipulate a moving body bending, to push the ball up and out of the body's height.

7. Genetic algorithms

Genetic algorithms are search algorithms used to find near-optimal solutions in arbitrarily created search spaces [24]. Applications in robot control have been reported in [25]. In this work, the search space is defined by a chromosome formed with the 192 weights defined in Section 5.1.

The 144 weight values obtained in the trained process in Section 5.2, corresponding to the wave generator's hidden layer, are left untouched but subjected to possible future changes. The 48 weight values corresponding to the ball position predictor and the 3-flop are given initial random value between +0.5 and −0.5.

Genetic algorithms have three main operators: selection, crossover, and mutation.

For the purposes of this chapter, we will use an evolutive approach where only mutation and selection are put to work. This kind of process plays a dominant role in bacterial evolution [26] and in pseudo-code can be written as:

```
get fitness
{
    timer=p;
    store initial coconut vertical position hi
   do{
      use stored move
      play
```

timer--

} until timer>0

get coconut final vertical position h_f

}

if (h_f - $h_{i>0}$) fitness= h_f - h_i

else > fitness=0

Mutation is implemented by iterating all bits in the chromosome and randomly adding a small value (positive/negative) to them. The probability of changing one weight is called the mutation rate and is here maintained in 10%.

8. Results: the quick evolution

8.1. Experiment 1. High human activity

Several human players interact with the robot. His/her moves (keyboard inputs) are stored in a vector with fixed time sampling. The fitness is measured in how much the coconut raises in a given time period, in pseudo-code:

get fitness

{

timer=p;

store initial coconut vertical position h_i

do{

use stored move

play

timer--

} until timer>0

get coconut final vertical position h_f

}

if (h_f - $h_{i>0}$) fitness= h_f - h_i

else > fitness=0

After using this fitness formula with the genetic algorithm of Section 7 and after about 5000 accepted mutations, the kind of individual shown in **Figure 11a** evolved. Since humans do most of the active part, the evolved robots learn to stay upright, facilitating the human actions, but show little or null body wave activity.

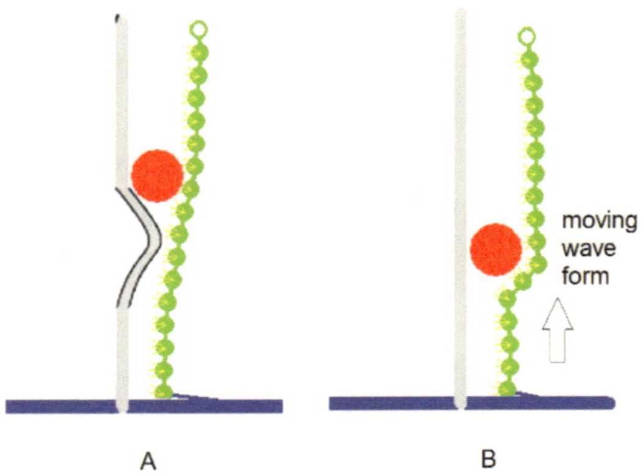

Figure 11. Evolved autonomous robots. (A) When human do most of the active part of the game, the evolved robots learn to stay upright, facilitating the human actions, but show little or null body wave activity. (B) When the human provides little game action and puts the coconut-lifting responsibility in the robot, evolution teaches the robot the connotation of the game. The evolved robot develops an autonomous dynamic response that learned to produce its own mechanical moving body bending and uses it to push the coconut all the way up.

8.2. Experiment 2. Low human activity

For this setting, the human players stay mostly inactive, as a passive wall whose only function is to get the coconut pressed against the robot.

By using the same fitness formula of experiment 1, a quite different outcome is obtained. Although the human provides little action to the game, the fitness formula put all the coconut-lifting responsibility in the robot. In other words, evolution teaches the robot the connotation of the game. The final evolutive result, after about 19,000 mutations, is a robot with an autonomous dynamic response that learned to produce its own moving body bending and uses it to push the coconut all the way up, out of the body's gap (**Figure 11b**).

9. Conclusions

By coupling two self-activated n-flops, we end up with an autonomous behavior initiator system that mimics the functioning of a living brain, in the sense that a default network consumes energy and is ready to initiate other behaviors under specific stimulus. Due to n-flops activity, all behaviors are constantly self-pushed from the inside.

With behaviors pushing from the inside, the robot is quite ready to face the real word and quickly learn new tricks. This is corroborated by the relative small number of mutation required to evolve reliable robots.

Our model incorporates some basic aspect of biological brains: (a) a fraction of the overall activity of all energy used by the autonomous neural controller (ANC) occurs in circuits unrelated to any external event. (b) In terms of structure, the components of the ANC are separated, carefully knitted constructions with pronounced job specializations.

Complex behaviors are codified in one single chromosome with 198 genes.

This satisfies one of the basic rules of evolution: Few genetic information unravels into complex things.

It seems reasonable to conclude that in a compact gene, small mutations produce enormous changes in the mutated individual, which enriches the search for solutions.

At least for our model of ANC, a successfully interaction with humans depends on the human attitude, if the humans put too much emphasis on the robot to learn to stay quiet. On the other hand, if human stays quiet but the basic rules of the game (lift the ball) is passed on to the robot learning, then the robot will pick up to the hard part of the job.

As in biology our robots, concerning behavior initiation, do throw the dice, but they keep and attractively control over when, where, and how this random event will be put into effect.

Author details

Oscar Chang[1,2,3*]

*Address all correspondence to: ochang@yachaytech.edu.ec

1 Yachay Tech. School of Mathematical Sciences and Information Technology, Republic of Ecuador

2 Universidad Central de Venezuela (UCV), School of Electrical Engineering, Graduate Studies Program, Venezuela

3 Prometeo Project, SENESCYT, Republic of Ecuador

References

[1] Maye A, Chih-hao H, Sugihara G, Brembs B. Order in spontaneous behavior. PLoS One. 2007;**10**(1371). (Online). Available: http://www.plosone.org/article/info:doi/10.1371/journal.pone.0000443

[2] Brembs B. Genetic Analysis of Behavior in Drosophila. Cognition and Behavioral Neuroscience. Online Publication. Date: Feb 2017. DOI: 10.1093/oxfordhb/9780190456757.013.37

[3] Ichle M, Marcus E, Snyder AZ. A default mode of brain function: a brief history of an evolving idea. Neuroimage. 2007;**37**(4):1083-1090

[4] Raichle ME. Two views of brain function. Trends in Cognitive Sciences. 2010;**14**(4):180-190

[5] Eban-Rothschild A, Bloch G. Circadian rhythms and sleep in honey bees. Honeybee Neurobiology and Behavior: A Tribute to Randolf Menzel. 2012: Springer Netherlands. pp. 31-45. https://doi.org/10.1007/978-94-007-2099-2_3

[6] Palyanov A, Khayrulin S, Larson SD, Dibert A. Towards a virtual C. elegans: A framework for simulation and visualization of the neuromuscular system in a 3D physical environment. In Silico Biology. August 2012;**11**(3-4):137-147. DOI: 10.3233/ISB-2012-0445

[7] Sharique H, Mall RN. Development of autonomous aero-robot and its applications to safety and disaster prevention with the help of neural network. International Journal of Engineering Research & Technology (IJERT). August – 2013;**2**(8). IJERT IJERT ISSN: 2278-0181

[8] Pessin G, Osório FS, Ueyama J, Wolf DF, Braun T. Mobile robot indoor localization using artificial neural networks and wireless networks. In: Proc. of First Brazilian Conference on Critical Embedded Systems (I CBSEC). 2011. pp. 89-94

[9] Khan M. Imitating the Brain: Autonomous Robots Harnessing the Power of Artificial Neural Networks. Computer Science Honors Papers. 8. 2017. http://digitalcommons.conncoll.edu/comscihp/8

[10] Bartona A, Volnab E. Control of autonomous robot using neural networks. AIP Conference Proceedings. 1863. 070002. 2017. DOI: http://dx.doi.org/10.1063/1.4992224. July 2017

[11] Nasser R, Philippe G. Robotic Grasping: A Generic Neural Network Architecture, Mobile Robots: towards New Applications. Lazinica A. ed: InTech; 2006. DOI: 10.5772/4687. Available from: https://www.intechopen.com/books/mobile_robots_towards_new_applications/robotic_grasping__a_generic_neural_network_architecture

[12] Chang O. Evolving cooperative neural agents for controlling vision guided mobile robots. 2010 IEEE 9th International Conference on Cybernetic Intelligent Systems, Reading. 2010:1-6

[13] Chang O, Campoy P, Martinez C, Olivares-Mendez M. A robotic eye controller based on cooperative neural agents. Neural Networks (IJCNN), The 2010 International Joint Conference on. pp. 1-6. 2010. http://ieeexplore.ieee.org/stamp/stamp.jsp?tp=&arnumber=5898127&isnumber=5898083

[14] Harris J, Jolivet R, Attwell D. Synaptic energy use and supply. Neuron. 2012;**75**(5):762-777. ISSN: 0896-6273, http://dx.doi.org/10.1016/j.neuron.2012.08.019

[15] Collins F. Making the Connections: Study Links Brain's Wiring to Human Traits. National Institutes of Health; 2015. https://directorsblog.nih.gov/2015/10/06/making-the-connections-study-links-brains-wiring-to-human-traits/

[16] Hochberg R. Three-dimensional reconstruction and neural map of the serotonergic brain of Asplanchna brightwellii (Rotifera, Monogononta). Journal of Morphology. **270**: pp. 430-441

[17] Suliman A, Zhang Y. A review on back-propagation neural networks in the application of remote sensing image classification. Journal of Earth Science and Engineering. 2015;**5**:52-65. DOI: 10.17265/2159-581X/2015. 01. 004

[18] Bengio Y, Courville A, Vincent P. Representation learning: A review and new perspectives. IEEE transactions on pattern analysis and machine intelligence. 2013;**35**(8):1798-1828

[19] Bengio Y. Learning Deep Architectures for AI. Foundations and Trends in Machine Learning. 2009;**2**(1):1-127

[20] Shackleford JB. Neural data structures: programming with neuron–technical. Hewlett-Packard Journal. June, 1989:69-78

[21] Serpen G. Managing spatio – temporal complexity in Hopfield Neural Network simulation for large-scale static optimization. Mathematics and Computers in Simulation. 2004;**64**(2) January 2008:279-293

[22] Organismic Biology course (Bi 11), Notes on Animal Phylogeny. http://www.cco.caltech.edu/~brokawc/Bi11/AnimalPhylogeny1.html

[23] Rensing L, Meyer-Grahle U, Ruoff P. Biological timing and the clock metaphor: Oscillatory and hourglass mechanisms. Chronobiology International. 2001;**18**(3):329-369

[24] David E. Goldberg. Genetic Algorithm, — in Search, Optimization & Machine Learning. Addison Wesley; 1989. Google Scholar

[25] Gill MAC, Zomaya AY. Genetic algorithms for robot control. Proceedings of 1995 IEEE International Conference on Evolutionary Computation, Perth, WA, Australia, 1995, 462 p. DOI: 10.1109/ICEC.1995.489192. http://ieeexplore.ieee.org/stamp/stamp.jsp?tp=&arnumber=489192&isnumber=10439

[26] https://www.researchgate.net/publication/20715998_Bacterial_EvolutionBacterial. Evolution Algorithm for rapid adaptation

Section 3

Risk Event Recognition

Chapter 8

Intoxication Identification Using Thermal Imaging

Georgia Koukiou

Additional information is available at the end of the chapter

http://dx.doi.org/10.5772/intechopen.72128

Abstract

In this chapter, seven different approaches are presented for identifying persons who have consumed alcohol. The main concept is to identify a drunk person based on the thermal signature of his face. The thermal map of the face changes as the person consumes alcohol due to the increased activity of the blood vessels. The methods are mathematically supported and present high rate of identification success. The experimental material was based on a systematically created database which includes the thermal images of the drunk persons as well as the thermal images of the face of the corresponding sober persons. This database is freely available on the web and can be used by the scientific community. In each method, different features are extracted for intoxication identification. The advantage of the majority of the methods is that drunk identification can be achieved without employing the image of the sober person for comparisons. Accordingly, a commercial system incorporating some of the presented methods does not require the existence of a database with thermal images of sober faces, thus it will be capable to operate on unknown persons. The achieved identification success for each separate method is over 80%.

Keywords: thermal imaging, drunk identification, intoxication inspection, drunk database, noninvasive drunk monitoring

1. Introduction

Intoxication by means of alcohol consumption is a serious and sometimes dangerous condition that a person may fall into as far as its health, security, and the social security are concerned. Citizens have to be trained not to consume alcohol beyond the permissible limit. However, this is a societal problem and has to be encountered by the society and its mechanisms. The material of this chapter is beyond the social component of intoxication. It elaborates on the capabilities of contemporary technology to identify drunkenness and prevent intoxicated persons to be engaged in dangerous situations, that is, driving or handle critical installation.

IntechOpen

© 2018 The Author(s). Licensee IntechOpen. This chapter is distributed under the terms of the Creative Commons Attribution License (http://creativecommons.org/licenses/by/3.0), which permits unrestricted use, distribution, and reproduction in any medium, provided the original work is properly cited. (cc) BY

Common means of identifying drunkenness is by a breathalyzer or a blood test. Both methods require the person under test to come in touch with the device and to stand for an invasive test. Both procedures are time-consuming, especially the blood test, and they have a considerable cost. These techniques cannot be applied or used to monitor intoxication remotely and prevent drunk persons from being engaged in tasks that require the operator' s attention and are associated with security. For example, it is not efficient to perform a test with a breathalyzer before a football match if it is desirable to prevent the drunk persons entering the stadium. The material in this chapter presents ways for identifying intoxication by means of thermal infrared images of the face.

Specific algorithms are presented in this chapter and their discrimination capabilities are explained [1–13]. The original idea lies on the fact that the blood vessels' network of the face will present increased activity when the person has consumed alcohol, changing in this way, the temperature distribution on the person's face. Accordingly, a commercial system can be derived which could be used for a fast assessment of the intoxication situation. In case of a positive inference, a breathalyzer can be employed for verifying the results. Obviously, it is not possible to obtain a thermal map of the face by means of visible light. Acquiring images from faces in thermal infrared spectrum, information related to the temperature of the face is obtained which mainly depends on the physiological condition of the person (illness, exercises, and drunkenness). The human face being in a mean temperature around 300 K, radiates according to the Wien's Law as a perfect black body, with maximum at 10 μm wavelength.

Drunkenness is a challenging physiological condition to be investigated using infrared imagery. However, most of the publications in the literature refer only to automotive anti-drunk driving systems, which utilize electrical signals from the heart or brain [14]. Extensive review of the relevant literature is given throughout the material which is being developed in this Chapter. Seven different approaches are discussed in this chapter for identifying intoxication by means of thermal infrared images. Specifically:

1. A feature vector is formed for drunk person identification by simply taking 20 different points on the face of each person.
2. The temperature differences which are presented on the face after alcohol consumption are discussed.
3. The activity of blood vessels on the face when the person is drunk is examined.
4. Neural networks are tested on infrared images of faces for discriminating drunk persons.
5. Temperature distribution on the eyes of sober and drunk persons is studied by means of thermal infrared images. The iris and the sclera are of the same temperature for the sober person. For the intoxicated person, the iris becomes darker.
6. Isothermal regions on the face of sober and intoxicated persons are extensively studied for drunk person identification.
7. Markov procedures are employed for the discrimination of drunk persons. This approach is applied only on the forehead.

Initially, basic elements are provided regarding the limits in alcohol consumption posed in different countries, as well as the thermal behavior of the skin is analyzed. Furthermore, an analytical description of the database with sober and the corresponding drunk persons created in Electronics Laboratory Physics Department University of Patras, Greece, is provided and the experimental procedure carried out toward the completion of this database (http://www.physics.upatras.gr/sober/) is described.

The methods for drunk identification were developed independently and the obtained features are different. It is important, in a future work the correlation between these features as far as their common information is concerned to be analyzed so that an optimal identification procedure using all this information can be devised (information fusion).

The final goal of the exposed material is to achieve a drunk person identification using only its thermal images without the need of comparisons with the corresponding images obtained when the person was sober. This is achieved by most methods presented here and constitutes a significant challenge toward building a commercial product. Such a commercial product could scan the face of a person and in case he is identified as drunk, the system will prevent him of being engaged into critical procedures (driving or operating specialized infrastructure).

2. Alcohol consumption limits

Alcohol that enters our body mainly during meals, if of course not too much, do not endanger us, unless there are health reasons that prohibit its consumption. However, excessive alcohol consumption may be particularly dangerous for someone who manages machinery or drives a vehicle and may have consequences on other persons as well. The effects and symptoms that alcohol brings to the human body vary according to the amount of alcohol present in the body (milligrams). The way alcohol affects the human body begins with the absorption of ethyl alcohol into the digestive system and its final appearance in the blood and exhaled air, where authorities can measure with the well-known alcoholmeters (breathalyzers).

Each country has set its own limits on alcohol consumption, and there are countries where zero limits have been established, such as Slovakia, the Czech Republic, Romania, and Hungary. Estonia, Poland, and Sweden have placed the blood alcohol limit at 0.2 mg/mL, while Lithuania at 0.4 mg/mL. In Austria, Belgium, Bulgaria, Cyprus, Denmark, Finland, France, Germany, Italy, Luxembourg, the Netherlands, Portugal, Slovenia, and Spain, the limit is at 0.5 mg/mL. If the blood alcohol concentration exceeds 0.5 or 0.25 mg/L of exhaled air, the driver will be fined in proportion to the level of violation of the permissible limits. These limits are reduced in the case of special vehicle drivers such as ambulances, busses, trucks over 3.5 tons, motorcycles, and mopeds [15–21].

Drinks are categorized according to the amount of alcohol they contain. Blood alcohol concentration (BAC) is different for men and women depending on their weight, the amount of drinks they consume and at different time instances after consumption. The effects on each individual according to the indication of the BAC are as follows:

- 0.2–0.3 mg/mL: The person has a slight euphoria and shyness, a laxity, a loss of coordination and perhaps a little dizziness.
- 0.4–0.6 mg/mL: The person can have a sense of well-being, relaxation, reduction of inhibitions, warmth, and euphoria. It may also present some minor thought and memory dysfunction, attention deficit reduction. Finally, feelings may be more intense and behavior more intense.
- 0.7–0.9 mg/mL: The person thinks he can work better than he actually does (overestimating his potential). There will be little decrease in balance, speech, vision, hearing, and reaction time. He is euphoric. His judgment and self-control are diminishing. Finally, attention, logic and memory are diminishing.

Driving with a blood alcohol concentration of 0.8–2.9 mg/mL is a criminal offense and if the person is legally drunk. Also, if the alcohol concentration in the blood is above 3.0 mg/mL, death occurs from alcohol poisoning.

The relationship between alcohol concentration in the blood and alcohol in the exhaled air should be highlighted. The amount of alcohol contained in 1 mL of blood is the same as the amount of alcohol contained in 2100 mL alveolar air. This corresponds to 0.24 mg/L of alveolar air. According to the above, for an average adult weighing 300–400 mL of pure alcohol, death occurs.

Alcohol contained in a drink is almost absorbed by the gastric tube. The absorption rate of alcohol depends mainly on:

- The fullness or emptiness of the stomach. Full feed slows absorption while full absorption is between 2 and 3 hours instead of 45–90 minutes (most people after 1 hour).
- The type of food in the stomach: fatty foods cause a greater deceleration in albumin absorption while less starch.
- The type of drink: beverages with CO_2 (carbonate) are absorbed faster because carbonate ions accelerate stomach emptying.
- The alcohol content of the beverage: beverages with 10–20% alcohol are absorbed faster.
- Individual factors: alcohol dependence (chronic drinkers), mood, particularity of gastric and intestinal mucosa.

Alcohol is distributed more rapidly to the tissues that have the greatest perfusion, but over time, it is redistributed everywhere. The greater the amount of water contained in a tissue, the more it is influenced by alcohol, for example, blood and nervous tissue. Conversely, it occurs in fat and bone tissues.

3. Skin thermal behavior

The human body emits electromagnetic radiation, like all bodies [22]. Since its temperature is close to that of the environment (~300°C), the entire spectrum of this radiation lies in the area of thermal infrared. At the same time, our body absorbs thermal radiation from the environment. The skin emits as nearly perfect black body (emissivity = 0.98) and based on the Wien's law, the wavelength for the maximum of its emission is at 9.5 μm. Therefore, thermal imaging devices such as thermal infrared cameras designed for human body inspection operate in the range of 7–14 μm.

The use of infrared radiation has become popular as infrared thermography [22] in medicine, since the 1960s to record the temperature of human skin. Infrared thermography is the technique that measures the heat (infrared radiation) emitted by the body and displays the temperature distribution on the surface of the body. Measurements are made with special cameras that detect infrared without coming into contact with the body. The intensity of the thermal radiation is transformed into an electrical signal and this in a color thermogram, in which the hottest spots are presented in stronger colors. An infrared image is an optical map of surface skin temperature that can provide accurate temperature measurement but cannot quantify blood flow on the skin. In order to explain the thermographic images, it is necessary to have a good understanding of the physiological mechanism of blood flow on the skin and the factors that affect the heat transfer to it. From our understanding regarding blood flow on the skin, heat transfer between tissues and skin temperature has changed rapidly over the past 40 years, allowing us to better represent and understand thermal measurements. At the same time, the improvement in camera sensitivity coupled with improved CCD technology and the development of computational imaging systems have improved the noninvasive thermography method.

Modern technology provides accurate temperature measurement with accuracy better than 0.05°C without getting in or touching the skin. These systems produce high-resolution images at high speed and the measurements are quantitative. When measuring the temperature of the skin under the influence of a cold environment, its temperature distribution is heterogeneous. On the contrary, the temperature distribution of the skin is more homogeneous in warm conditions. During exposure to heat or intensive exercise, the blood flow in the skin may be increased in order to increase the consumption potential. When the human being is exposed to a cold environment, the surface of the skin restricts the flow of blood and thus becomes a perfect insulator. In these hypothermic conditions, our skin works to maintain the core body temperature.

Another procedure for controlling blood flow to the skin is dynamic thermography which includes local cooling or heating of the skin [23]. The ability of blood to transfer heat between the various levels of tissues to the skin can be predicted by models. These models are based not only on conductivity, tissue density, specific heat, and temperature of the tissues, but also their metabolic needs as well as the speed flow of the blood. A disadvantage of infrared thermography is that it cannot directly demonstrate that the increase in temperature is due to the increase in blood flow. One way to prove this is to combine infrared thermography with other direct blood flow control techniques such as Laser Doppler.

4. Experimental procedure and the database

The Thermo Vision Micron A10 Model infrared camera was used to capture the thermal images from the face. This camera has an operating wavelength range from 7.5 to 13 μm, and a radiometric dynamic range which adjusts automatically to temperature range. This wavelength region corresponds to the maximum of the Wien curve for blackbody emission with temperature at 300°K. This is exactly the behavior in emitting electromagnetic radiation from the human skin [22]. In our experiment, 41 persons participated among them 10 females. A quantity of half liter of wine which corresponds to 62.4 mL of alcohol was consumed by each subject, in an hour time duration. A first frame sequence of 50 frames was obtained for each person before alcohol consumption. Another sequence of the same number of frames was acquired half an hour after consuming the last glass of wine. The frame rate acquisition was set to 10 frames/sec.

The resolution of the infrared images is 128 × 160 pixels. The camera was quite close to the face of the person so that the thermal image contains the whole face. The experimental procedure requires the availability of the thermal images of an intoxicated person as well as the thermal images of the corresponding sober person so that comparisons can be carried out. The persons that participated in the experiment were alert about the strict requirements of the procedure. Researchers working close to our research group and being sensitized on the experimental requirements took part in the experiment. All of them were healthy and willing to release their personal data to the public (http://www.physics.upatras.gr/sober/). The created database contained all relevant information for the participants (age, weight, sex, etc.). We considered the person who consumed half a liter of wine as drunk or intoxicated. In the experimental procedure, no blood tests were contacted.

Three glasses of wine are enough to bring a person in the intoxication situation which corresponds in exceeding 0.2 mg/L of exhaled air [15]. However, with this quantity of wine, other participants were brought in the limit of intoxication while others were deeply intoxicated. Measurements carried out by the police showed off these differences in persons' intoxication (breathalyzer 0.22–0.9 mg/L). The maximum concentration of alcohol in the exhaled air was reached half an hour after the consumption of the last glass of wine. This concentration was found at 0.22 mg/L for the heavy persons that used to drink alcohol and raised to 0.9 mg/L for the light persons that used not to drunk alcohol. Gradually, breathalyzer indication decreases. Females were more sensitive to alcohol than the males.

Finally, it is worth mentioning that all participants were healthy and calm when the experiment started, and had not undergone any kind of body exercise. All participants were present at the room of experiment half an hour before its initiation. Actually, the purpose of the experiment was to reveal temperature changes caused only by alcohol consumption. No other abnormality is considered.

5. A simple feature vector from face

A simple feature vector is formed for drunk person identification by simply taking the pixel values of 20 different points on the face of each person (**Figure 1**). Therefore, each face image corresponds to a 20-dimensional feature vector:

$$x_i = [181\ 169\ 203\ 166\ 217\ 175\ 171\ 189\ 169\ 206\ 152\ 144\ 243\ 165\ 225\ 147\ 247\ 149\ 247\ 127]^t \quad (1)$$

which corresponds to a point in the 20-dimensional space; since in each single acquisition, 50 images are grabbed and this information corresponds to a cluster of 50 points in the 20-dimensional space.

It is important to find out if the cluster which corresponds to the same person moves in the feature space as the person consumes alcohol [24]. Simultaneously, we have to examine if the cluster of each person moves toward the same direction with alcohol consumption. If the direction of movement due to alcohol consumption is different for different persons, then we would have many directions in the 20-dimensional space, toward which the clusters of the drunk persons are moving. In this case, it would be difficult to demonstrate the space in a simpler way (preferably in two dimensions).

In this paragraph, it is analytically explained that the final problem is of two dimensions since only two of the eigenvalues obtained by means of the generalized eigenvalues problem are of significant value. In these two dimensions, it is evident that the clusters are moving toward the same direction with alcohol consumption (**Figure 2**).

In our case, the feature space dimensionality was examined by the statistics of the clusters of eight persons. Consequently, there exist eight clusters in the feature space for the sober persons and the corresponding eight clusters for the drunk persons projecting onto this 2-D space, the suitable directions for maximum separability, has to be found.

This maximum separability in a reduced dimensionality space is achieved by a linear transformation W. The two most important directions w_i of W are used for projection. This linear transformation is:

$$y_i = w^t x_i \quad (2)$$

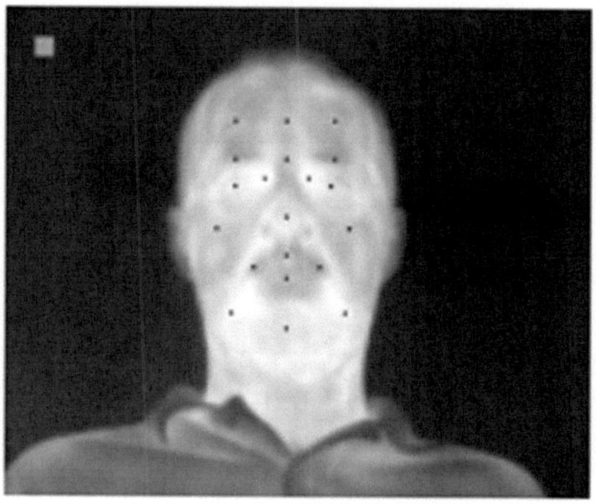

Figure 1. Twenty points were obtained on each face to monitor temperature changes with the consumption of alcohol.

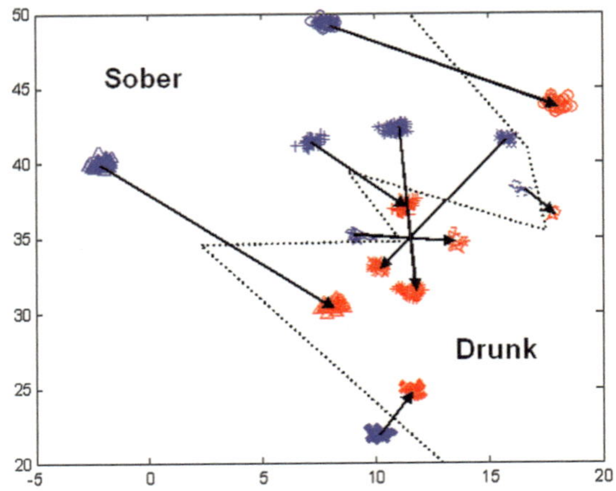

Figure 2. The 16 clusters of 8 persons in the 2-D space formed by the two most important directions (correspond to the first 2 largest eigenvalues). We call hereafter this space, the "drunk space".

An important criterion function that can be used for the separation of the clusters is given by

$$J = \frac{S_B}{S_W} \tag{3}$$

The clusters are moving apart as J increases. The matrices S_W and S_B are called within-scatter and between-scatter matrices, respectively. Eventually, S_W must be small and S_B must be large. The cumulative dispersion of all separate clusters (cluster scatter) can be estimated by the corresponding S_W matrix, which is evaluated by summing up all individual cluster-scatter matrices S_i as follows

$$S_w = S_1 + S_2 + . \ . \ . + S_8 \tag{4}$$

where

$$S_i = \sum x_i{*}x_i^t \tag{5}$$

In the transformed space, the within-scatter matrix (S_W) is given by

$$(S_W) = w^t S_W w \tag{6}$$

The between-scatter matrix S_B reveals how much the centers of the clusters are separated. The evaluation of the between-scatter matrix S_B is realized as follows

$$S_B = \sum m_i{*}m_i^t, \quad i = 1, 2, \ldots 8 \tag{7}$$

where m_i corresponds to each cluster center. In the transformed space, the between-scatter matrix (S_B) will be given by

$$(S_B) = w^t S_B w \tag{8}$$

Therefore, the function J in the transformed space is given by

$$J(w) = \frac{w^t S_B w}{w^t S_W w} \tag{9}$$

The maximization of the function J(w) results in vectors w obtained from the solution of the generalized eigenvalue problem:

$$S_B W_i = \lambda_i S_W W_i \tag{10}$$

The obtained matrix W contains the eigenvectors w_i which show the directions in the transformed feature space on which the original features x_i are projected. From this solution, the eigenvalues which correspond to w_i are also obtained. Each eigenvalue describes the amount of information that the corresponding eigenvector contains regarding each cluster separability capabilities. Actually, the Fisher Linear Discriminant (FLD) method corresponds to the solution of (10). Obviously, in this procedure, the matrices S_B and S_W operate with opposite effect.

The generalized eigenvalue problem was solved, as we mentioned previously, for 8 persons (males) of the same weight. A total of 16 clusters are available in the 20-D feature space, that is, two clusters per person (sober and drunk). The sum of these two largest eigenvalues over the sum of all eigenvalues gives the quality of cluster separability in the reduced (2D) feature space. In this experiment, this ratio was found equal to 70%. The resulting two-dimensional feature space is demonstrated in **Figure 2**, along with the 16 clusters. Furthermore, in **Figure 2**, the direction of movement of the cluster of each person is exhibited. According to **Figure 2**, the new 2-D feature space is separated into two regions corresponding to sober and drunk persons, respectively. Consequently, a person can be easily classified as sober or drunk depending on the position of its cluster in this new reduced space. This space is called, hereafter, the "drunk space".

6. Face temperature differences after alcohol consumption

The thermal differences between various locations on the face are examined in this section [2]. The purpose of this approach is to examine specific locations on the face and find out if the temperature difference between these regions changes with alcohol consumption. Thus we are not interested for the temperature of the eye but if its temperature changes with respect to another location of the face, for example, the lips. In order to apply this procedure, the image of the face of each person was partitioned into a matrix of 8 × 5 squared regions of 10 × 10 pixels each. The position of the regions was exactly the same for a specific person (sober and drunk). The temperature difference of all possible pairs of squared regions is monitored as the person consumes alcohol. A total of 40 values were calculated on the face of a specific person who correspond to the squared regions for a specific acquisition.

The thermal differences among all values of the 40 squared regions were evaluated, thus creating a matrix 40 × 40. We had to compare the difference matrices which correspond to the same person when he was sober and in the case he consumed alcohol (**Figure 4**). The maximum variation between the corresponding differences is monitored and actually reveals the regions which change temperature with alcohol consumption. It was found that for the drunk person the nose and mouth has increased temperature in relation to the forehead.

The main finding of this approach is that two locations, as shown in **Figure 3**, are good candidates for proving intoxication, namely the forehead and the nose. For the drunk person,

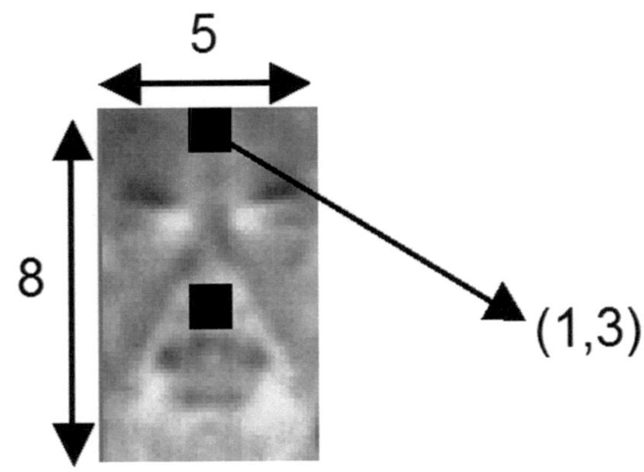

Figure 3. Each of the black regions is of 10 × 10 pixels area. A total of 8 × 5 regions are taken on each face. The temperature difference between the regions is monitored as the person consumes alcohol.

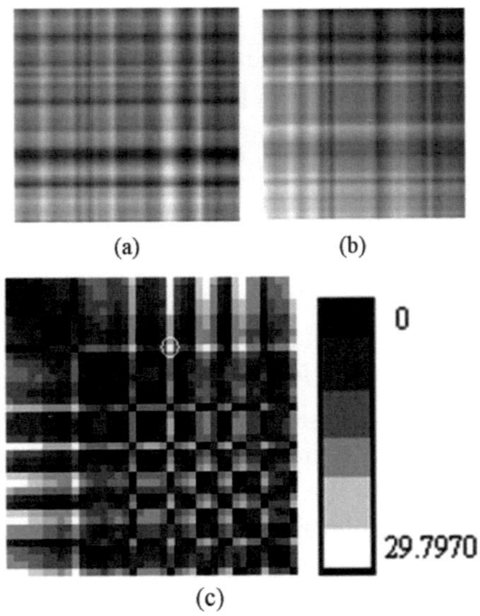

Figure 4. Three difference matrices, (a) for the sober person and (b) for the drunk person, (c) the difference of the difference matrices (values normalized to full grayscale). Large changes for the thermal differences on the face are indicated by white points on this matrix. The white circle corresponds to the largest difference equal to 29.8.

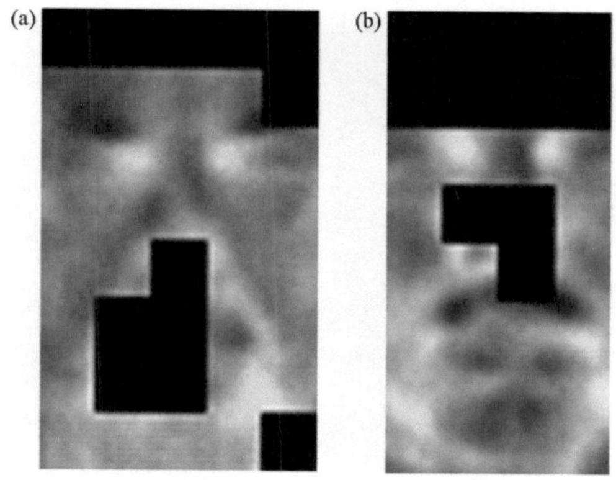

Figure 5. The black regions on faces A and B are those presenting maximum difference with alcohol consumption. These regions were indicated by the difference of the difference matrices.

the forehead appears cooler than the nose while for the sober, the two region are at the same temperature. **Figure** 4a is presented with the thermal difference matrix for the sober person. In **Figure** 4b, the thermal difference matrix for the drunk person is shown. These two matrices differ significantly on the white locations of matrix **Figure 4(c)**. The final matrix which is the difference of the difference matrices is crucial for revealing locations of the face with large temperature variation.

In **Figure 5** demonstration of the described method is given. The black regions on the face are those presenting maximum difference with alcohol consumption. These regions were indicated by the difference of the difference matrices. Accordingly, if the nose of a person is hotter than the forehead, this person should be declared as intoxicated by a drunk identification system.

7. Face blood vessels activity in drunk person

In this section, blood vessels are separated and isolated from the rest of the information on the image of the face by applying morphology on the diffused image. For this purpose, the top-hat transformation is applied [7]. Top-hat transformation is applied to isolate hot or cold features in an image of a specific size. An example is shown in **Figure 6**. The features to be isolated are of 5 × 5 pixels area. This transformation is described next.

7.1. Top-hat transformation

The basic morphological operation is that of erosion [26, 27]. Erosion is a shrinking procedure carried out when a signal A (binary or gray scale) is affected by another signal S, the structuring element:

$$A \ominus S = \{(i,j) \in A : S(i,j) \subset A\} \tag{11}$$

where (i,j) is the position of A on which S lies.

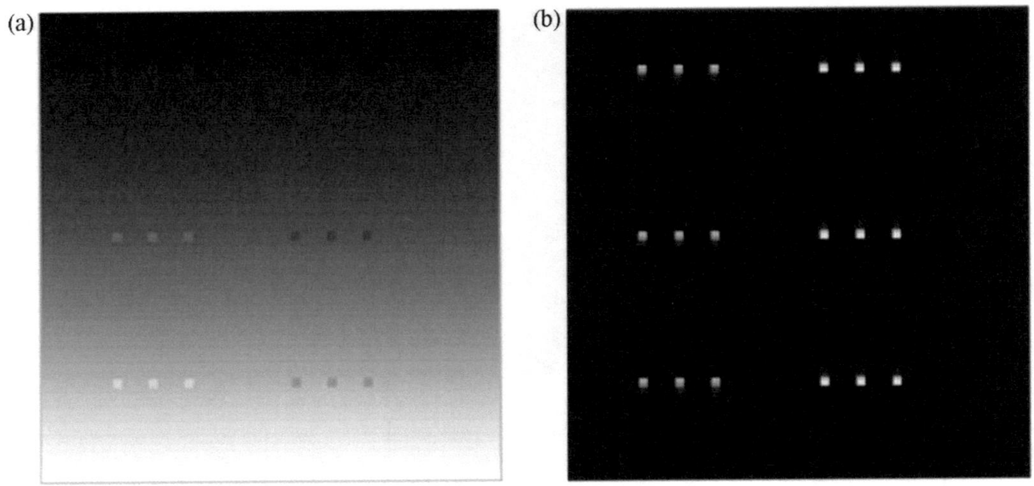

Figure 6. (a) Hot and cold spots of area 5 × 5 pixels on a varying grayscale background, (b) top-hat transformation of image in (a) using the summation of (15) and (16). The structuring element used, was a flat disk of radius 5.

A complementary operation to that of erosion is dilation. It is a kind of expansion of the signal. It is defined as the erosion of the complement of *A*:

$$A \oplus S = (A^c \ominus S)^c \tag{12}$$

When an erosion is followed by a dilation the smoothing-shrinking morphological operation called opening is obtained. Opening smoothes out from the signal A, all details that are smaller than the structuring element S. It is denoted as

$$A_s = (A \ominus S) \oplus S \tag{13}$$

Furthermore, when a dilation is followed by an erosion, the smoothing-expanding operation called closing is obtained. Closing covers (smoothes) all details (intrusions) of the signal A that are smaller than the structuring element S:

$$A^s = (A \oplus S) \ominus S \tag{14}$$

Employing a top-hat transformation (hot or cold), someone can extract small features from a signal *A*. Actually, protrusions in the signal can be obtained by subtracting the opened signal from the original (hot top-hat transformation)

$$Top - hat_{hot} = A - A_S \tag{15}$$

which allows to extract white (hot) features against a dark background. On the other hand, an intrusion of the signal can be obtained by subtracting the original signal from the closed one (cold top-hat transformation)

http://dx.doi.org/10.5772/intechopen.72128

$$Top - hat_{cold} = A^S - A \tag{16}$$

and actually allows to extract dark (cold) features against a brighter background (see **Figure 6** a and b).

However, before applying top-hat transformation on the image, anisotropic diffusion is performed to eliminate noise.

7.2. Anisotropic diffusion

Thermal infrared images contain noise, which many times distorts significant information and details that are important for the interpretation of the image. Anisotropic diffusion technique [28] is capable of filtering out noise leaving significant parts of the image very important in perceptual vision, like edges or lines, unchanged.

The physical background of diffusion is based on the concentration distribution u (pixel distribution), so that its gradient causes flux j according to Fick's law:

$$j = -D \cdot \nabla u \tag{17}$$

where D is the diffusion tensor, which is in general a positive definite symmetric matrix, and is a function of the structure of the image. Diffusion corresponds to mass transport (gray values in images) without destroying mass or creating new mass. So,

$$\partial_t u = -divj = -\left(\frac{\partial j}{\partial x} + \frac{\partial j}{\partial y}\right) \tag{18}$$

where $\partial_t u$ is the time partial derivative of the concentration distribution u. From the above equations, we have:

$$\partial_t u = -\mathrm{div}(D \cdot \nabla u) \tag{19}$$

In anisotropic nonlinear diffusion, the diffusion tensor is not constant over the image smoothing thus only along edges and living the information across edges unchanged. Specifically, if the diffusion tensor D is defined to be a function of the gradient of u, that is,

$$D = g\left(|\nabla u|^2\right) \tag{20}$$

then the diffusion preserves edges since no diffusion is performed vertically to edges but parallel to them. In real problems anisotropic nonlinear diffusion is capable to sharpen edges if the function g(.) is chosen properly.

The implementation of Eq. (19) in the experimental procedure can be carried out in the following way.

Let $u_0(x, y)$ be the original input image and $u_t(x, y)$ the digital image at iteration t. The discreet in time implementation of (19) is carried out by employing the four nearest neighbors and the Laplacian operator which was used in [28]:

$$u_{t+1}(x,y) = u_t(x,y) + \lambda \sum_{i=1}^{4} \left[g(\nabla u_t^i(x,y)) \cdot \nabla u_t^i(x,y) \right] \tag{21}$$

where in the experimental procedure was used $0 \leq \lambda \leq \frac{1}{4}$ and

$$\nabla u_t^1(x,y) = u_t(x, y+1) - u_t(x,y) \tag{22}$$

is the gradient of south direction,

$$\nabla u_t^2(x,y) = u_t(x, y-1) - u_t(x,y) \tag{23}$$

is the gradient of north direction,

$$\nabla u_t^3(x,y) = u_t(x+1, y) - u_t(x,y) \tag{24}$$

is the gradient of east direction and

$$\nabla u_t^4(x,y) = u_t(x-1, y) - u_t(x,y) \tag{25}$$

is the gradient of west direction.

The nonlinear anisotropic diffusion method was applied to all 41 faces corresponding to sober and intoxicated persons. In order the diffusion to take place only along edges the value of k which affects the degree of smoothing was selected equal to 20.

If thresholding is used on images after diffusion and top-hat transformation, the image obtained is richer for the intoxicated person compared to that of the sober person. In our experiments, the threshold was chosen to be equal to 100. In **Figure 7**, two images obtained

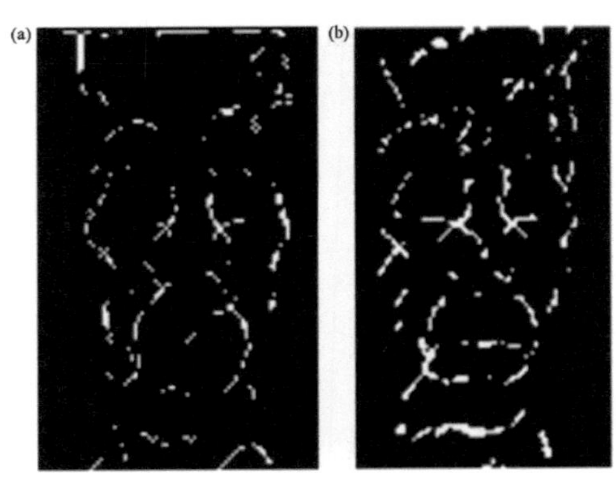

Figure 7. Binary images obtained using a threshold equal to 100. Sober left and intoxicated right. Vessels on the drunk person are more distinct compared to those on the sober person.

for the intoxicated (right) and the sober person (left) are shown. Image registration was applied in order to compare the images. Discrimination between sober and intoxicated persons' images was achieved based on the number of bright pixels. For the intoxicated persons, the number of bright pixels is larger for sober persons. This concept is the main supporting idea that the proposed method that contributes significantly in the forensic science. Brighter vessels constitute a clear evidence to suspect for alcohol consumption and proceed to further check up and inspection of the person.

It is worthy to mention that it is possible using an image like those in **Figure 7**, to infer about intoxication since white pixels for the drunk person are more intense around the nose, the mouth, and on the forehead. The fact that the corresponding image from the sober person is not required for comparison constitutes the substantial forensic contribution of this method.

8. Neural networks for discriminating drunk persons

Neural networks have been used as a classification tool in a variety of machine vision techniques such as face recognition [29] and thermal infrared pattern recognition [30–33]. Especially, a thermo vision application for biometric recognition is addressed in [32], while neural structures are employed in [33] for recognition of facial expressions using thermal maps of the face.

This method offers a way of discriminating sober from drunk persons, using thermal infrared images and neural networks. The neural networks are employed as a black box to discriminate intoxication by means of the values of simple pixels from the thermal images of the persons' face. In this work, the neural networks were used by means of two different approaches. According to the first approach, a different neural structure is used from location to location on the thermal image of the face and the convergence capabilities of the network are monitored. A successful convergence characterizes the corresponding location of the face as being a good candidate for intoxication identification. According to the second approach, a single neural structure is trained with data from the thermal images of the whole face of a person (sober and drunk) and its capability to operate with high classification success to other persons is tested. Its generalization performance is also accessed.

In the first approach, different networks are trained on different locations of the same face. Thus, there will be a serious indication on the suitability of the specific face locations for drunk identification. Consequently, the face of each person is partitioned into a matrix of squared regions of 10×10 pixels each as the one depicted in **Figure 8**. There is a complete correspondence between these locations on the images of sober and drunk persons. **Figure 8** is illustrated one of these square regions of 100 pixels on a pair of infrared images (sober-drunk) of a specific person.

A simple neural network is trained using the data in the two black regions as shown in **Figure 8**. The vectors used as input to the neural structure are of nine elements obtained when a small 3×3 window moves all over each of the two 10×10 pixels regions. In this way, 200 vectors are obtained to train a three-level neural structure of [9 30 1] neurons, for these two specific regions of 10×10 pixels. Furthermore, a larger network of [49 49 1] neurons was employed using as input vectors of 49 elements. These elements were obtained when a window of 7 × 7 pixels moves around each of the two 10 × 10 pixels regions. The back propagation algorithm was employed for training both neural structures.

Successful convergence of a neural network to a minimum value in a specific location means that this face location is suitable for drunk identification. For demonstration purposes, a region for which we have high convergence of the network is given in red in **Figure 9**. For all participants in the experiment and especially when the large neural structures were employed, high convergence was observed mainly on the forehead, the nose, and the mouth as depicted in **Figure 9**. Thus, these locations of the face of a person are the most suitable to be employed for intoxication discrimination.

In the next approach, the whole face of each specific person is examined as a single area of 5000 pixels (50 × 100), as shown in **Figure 10**. Our purpose is to be able to discriminate between the sober and the drunk image of a person using a specific neural structure which has been trained with information coming from the same person.

The big region of 5000 pixels gives 5000 different vectors of 49-elements each, as a window 7 × 7 is moving around the image of the sober person. Another 5000 vectors are obtained from the thermal image of the drunk person. A neural structure of 3 layers with 49 neurons in the first layer, 49 neurons in the hidden layer and 1 neuron in the output layer, that is, a [49 49 1] structure, was trained with the above data. Next, the recognition procedure was tried. The

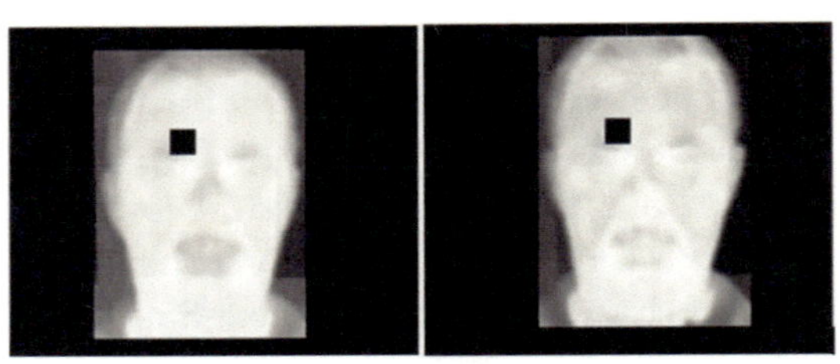

Figure 8. The same square region of 100 pixels on a pair of infrared images (sober-drunk) of a specific person.

Figure 9. Two different persons correspond to the above colored matrices. The employed neural networks with structures [49 49 1] converge at the red areas giving to the areas of the forehead, the nose and the mouth desirable drunk discrimination capabilities.

same trained network was tested with the same data and resulted in satisfactory performance. When the output was closer to zero, the pixel was declared to belong to a sober person (black), otherwise (closer to one) it was declared to represent a drunk person (white). In **Figure 11**, the results of this experiment are presented. The achieved performance for the pixels of the sober image is 89.22%, while for the drunk image, the performance is 87.09%, with even higher performance at the regions of the forehead and nose. In conclusion, the training of a single neural network using information from the whole face can easily point out the regions which better support drunk discrimination.

The case of a neural network trained with the data from the whole face of a specific person (sober and drunk) and tested using the data of the rest persons is discussed also. Accordingly, if the person is sober, his face should be black, while if he is drunk, his face should be white.

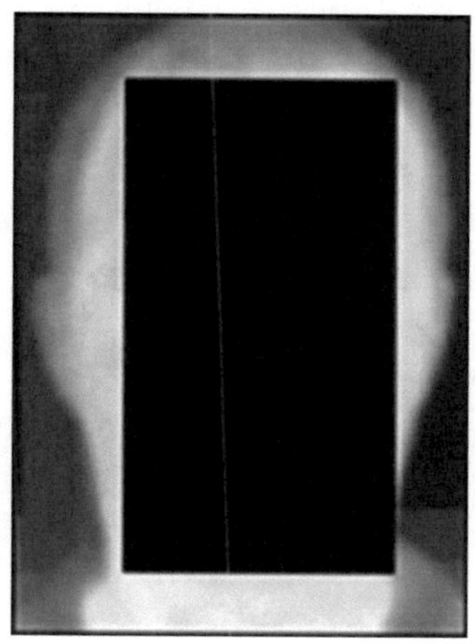

Figure 10. The whole black region drawn on the face of a specific person in the above thermal image was used for training a single network.

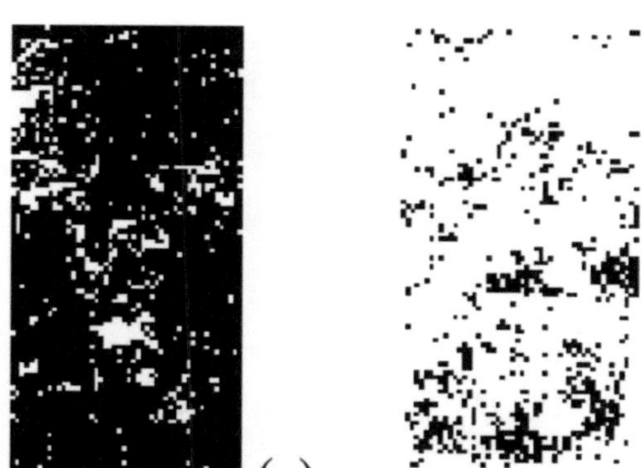

(a) (b)

Figure 11. Discrimination results obtained by a neural structure [49 49 1], trained with the same data from the whole region. The achieved performance for the pixels of the sober image (left in black) is 89.22% while for the drunk image (right in white) the performance is 87.09%, with even higher performance at the regions of the forehead and nose.

Relative results are demonstrated in **Figure 12**. A neural structure of [9 30 1] was trained using data from person 1 and tested using the data from person 2. At the left of **Figure 12** the face should be black recognized as belonging to the sober person, while at the right it should be white since it corresponds to the drunk person. The depicted performance is satisfactory and an operator can discriminate the sober from the drunk easily. It is worth emphasizing that according to the images in **Figure 12**, the pixels on the forehead and the nose are correctly classified in almost all cases.

Since the forehead is a very promising location on the face for intoxication identification, the above procedure was repeated only on the region of the forehead for all persons participated in the experiment. The area employed was shown in **Figure 13**. Accordingly, the neural structures are trained with the data from one person and tested with the data from the rest persons. The use of the forehead area for intoxication identification led to two significant conclusions: (a) The small neural structures have better identification performance since they achieve better generalization behavior during training. (b) Their success is on average 90%.

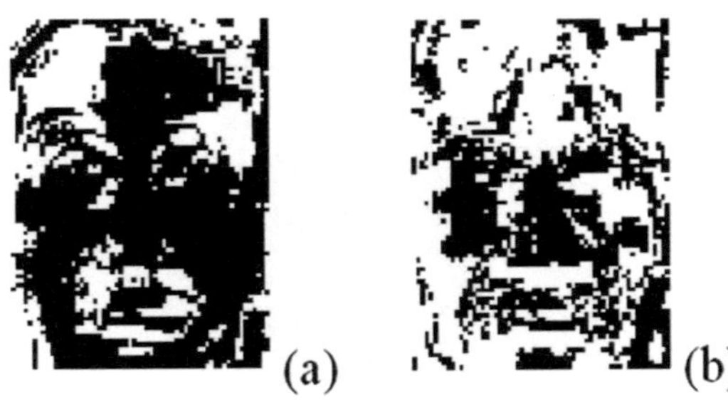

Figure 12. Results obtained when a neural structure of [9 30 1] was trained using data from person 1 and tested using the data from person 2. At the left the face should be black recognized as belonging to the sober person while at the right it should be white since it corresponds to the drunk person.

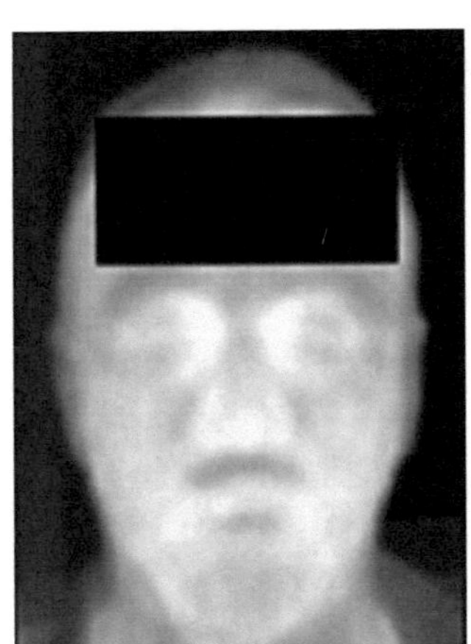

Figure 13. The black region on the forehead of the persons was employed to test the neural structures for identifying drunk persons.

As a general conclusion of this final approach, we can say that we can decide with 90% confidence if a person is drunk or not using a small neural structure. No data records of the inspected persons when they are sober are needed for comparison.

9. Temperature distribution on the eyes

Temperature distribution on the eyes of sober and drunk persons is studied by means of thermal infrared images (**Figure 14**). It is observed that the temperature difference between the sclera and the iris is zero for the sober person and increases when somebody consumes alcohol (**Figure 15**). For the drunk person, iris appears darker compared to sclera which means that the sclera temperature increases. This is something expected since the sclera is full of blood vessels which present increased activity when the person consumes alcohol. Thus, in a screening procedure for drunk identification, the infrared images of the sober person are not needed. Although in most cases the sclera is brighter than the iris for the drunk persons, in case that their gray level difference is very small, histogram modification algorithms can be used to enhance this difference and show off intoxication. In order to express the confidence of the method in drunk person discrimination, the Student t-test was employed. The results gave over 99% confidence of the discrimination inference.

Specifically, for the 28 among the 41 people who participated in the experimental procedure, it is evident by a simple comparison of the thermal images that the sclera becomes hotter compared to the iris after alcohol consumption. The images in **Figure 15**, where the iris is darker than the sclera (right), have not undergone any kind of preprocessing. This difference between the sclera and the iris becomes evident for four more persons when a histogram equalization algorithm is applied. Initially, for all these sober persons the sclera and the iris appeared with the same gray level as being in the same temperature (**Figure 15**, left image). Finally, four more persons presented this difference when a histogram clipping algorithm was applied which clips all values below 0.5 and above 0.75 of the gray level range and after that stretches the remaining histogram to its full range (MATLAB imadjust ([0.5 0.75], [0 1])). For five persons who used to drink alcohol and their breathalyzer indication was below 0.4 mg/L, it was not possible to show off the difference between the sclera and the iris.

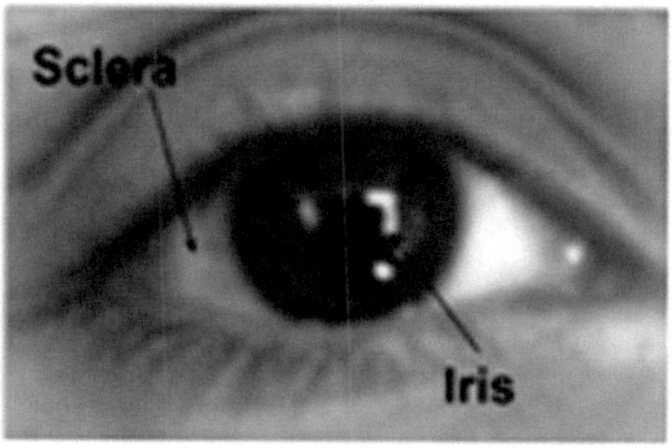

Figure 14. Sclera is surrounding iris which is actually a muscle controlled part of the eye to adjust the size of the pupil. Sclera lies on a net of blood vessels.

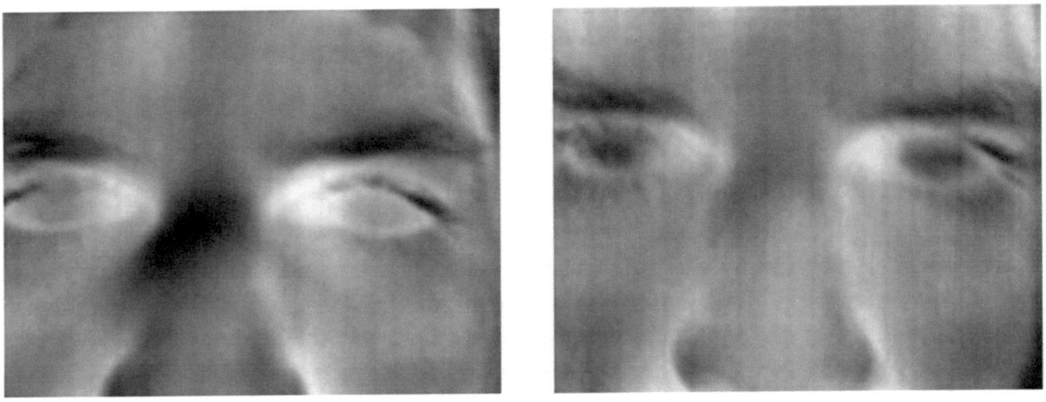

Figure 15. The left thermal image corresponds to the face of the sober person while the right to the face of the corresponding drunk person. For the drunk person the sclera becomes hotter from the iris.

The temperature difference between the sclera and the iris was examined [4, 6] based on the statistics of the pixels in these two regions by means of two different estimation procedures which correspond to two different discrimination features. In the first procedure, the ratio of the mean value of the pixels inside the sclera to the mean value of the pixels inside the iris was calculated. This procedure was performed on the left eye of each participant, both in the case he is sober and when he consumed alcohol. Consequently, two ratios of the mean value of the sclera to the mean value of the iris are available. It is observed that the ratio of the mean pixel value on the sclera to the mean value of the iris increases when the person has consumed alcohol. Specifically, for the 36 from the 41 cases, the specific ratio increases with alcohol consumption while only in 2 cases it decreases, and in the rest 3 it remains almost the same. The results were analyzed using the Students-t test, in order to support statistically the drunk screening capabilities of the proposed method from eye thermal images. In the second procedure, is estimated the variance of the pixels contained in the whole eye. This evaluation was performed for the left eye of each participant when the person is sober and when he is drunk. Therefore, two variances for each participant have been calculated, corresponding to sober and drunk person, respectively. It is observed that the variance increases in case that the person has consumed alcohol. Specifically, among the 41 participants only 4 presented decreased variance in the region of the eye for the drunk person compared to the sober one.

The proposed method presents the advantage that there is no need for comparison with the image of the sober person to infer for the intoxication situation. Simply, if an inspected person presents a gray level difference between the sclera and the iris, it has to be further tested for alcohol consumption with conventional means.

10. Face isothermal regions for drunk person identification

Drunk persons can be discriminated from sober ones using face isothermal regions. For this purpose, the morphological feature vector called pattern spectrum and support vector machines

(SVMs) are employed for feature extraction and classification. Two different approaches are employed for extracting the isothermal regions of the face giving continuous vectors for intoxication identification. In the first one, the histogram of the face is divided (both of the sober and the drunk person) into equal regions. In the second approach, we examine in which isothermal region the whole forehead lies for the sober and the drunk person and which other regions of the face are within these isotherms.

Anisotropic diffusion was applied on the thermal infrared images for smoothing boundaries before extracting the isothermal regions. Specifically, anisotropic diffusion [28, 34] is used for noise removal, homogenization of regions, and detail preservation. The morphological feature vector called pattern spectrum [25, 26, 35] is extracted from the isothermal regions and transferred to the SVMs [36–38] for recognition of intoxicated persons. The identification success is found to be over 80% which is considered satisfactory.

Initially, four different types of isotherms were implemented, as follows:

- Equidistant in the histogram range (0–255).
- Equal populated in the histogram range.
- Isolation of a single isotherm on the image.

Arbitrary determination of each isotherm is min and max (e.g. based on the minima of the histogram).

Figure 16 illustrated one example for each case. Experimentation on these four different types of isotherms revealed that only two of them are suitable for identifying drunk persons. Specifically, the first and the fourth type of isotherms, that is, equidistant and arbitrary determination as stated in the begging of the section. Using these two different types of isotherms in combination with anisotropic diffusion and morphology, isothermal features have been extracted for identifying intoxicated persons.

In the first approach, the histogram of the face, both of the sober and the drunk person, is divided into equal regions. It was found that the best number of isothermal regions is eight. In this case, we have the maximum perceptual information on the different isothermal regions. The majority of the pixels on the face belong to the two higher regions with pixel values from 191.25 up to 255. These two regions (191–223.125 and 223.125–255) occupy almost the whole face and their shape will be used to discriminate between sober and drunk. The shape also of the whole isothermal region 191.25–255 will be tested for identifying intoxicated persons. In **Figure 17(a)** and **(b)**, the regions 191.25–223.125, 223.125–255 and the whole region 191.25–255, respectively, are shown in red. The regions become larger in case of the drunk person as it is easily recognizable. Accordingly, someone can decide which person is the drunk, if both red images are available. The basic problem is that the images of the sober person are never available and thus in real problems, there is not any capability of comparisons.

In the second approach, features that could help to recognize the drunk person without using the images of the sober counterpart, were tested. Accordingly, it is examined in which of the isotherms the forehead lies for the sober person and which other regions of the face are within

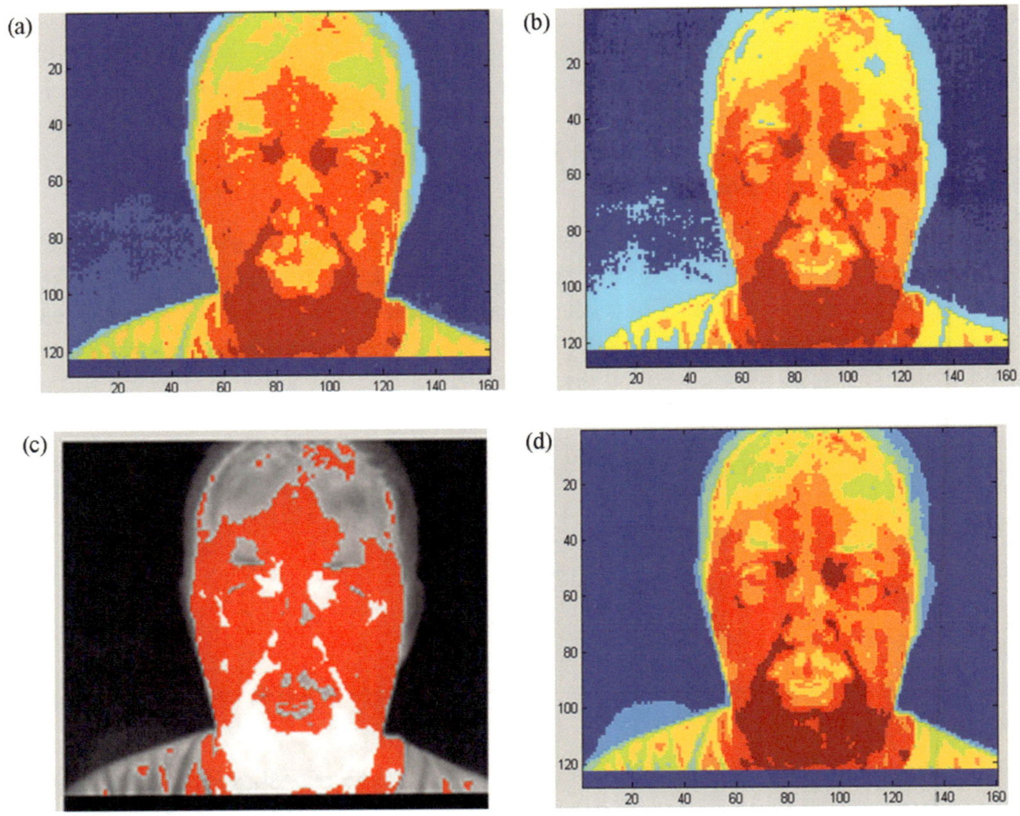

Figure 16. The four different types of isotherms on the face, (a) equidistant in the histogram range (0–255) in eight regions, (b) equal populated in the histogram range in eight regions, (c) isolation of a single isotherm on the image, (d) arbitrary determination of each isotherm min and max (e.g. based on the minima of the histogram).

these isotherms. After that it is examined in which isotherms the forehead lies for the drunk person and which other regions of the face are within these isotherms. Thus, we do not care about the value of each isotherm but we care about the isothermal regions of the face that include the forehead. From **Figure 18**, it is evident that some regions below the forehead are not isothermal with the forehead for the drunk person. The area of the red region decreases. This can be easily monitored in real time problems by an operator (e.g. policemen).

Measuring the decrease of area details is a task that can be performed using morphological granulometria [26, 35], that is, successive openings with an increase in size structuring element (pattern spectrum). All the above procedures for feature extraction using isothermal regions of the face were applied on the infrared images after a light smoothing preprocessing was performed. The smoothing processing which was applied is the anisotropic diffusion. The simple spectrum without diffusion gave the largest success which reaches 86%. These values correspond to Linear and Precomputed Kernel types in the SVMs. This case is the most interesting one, since the drunk person is recognized from the fact that the isothermal region in which the forehead

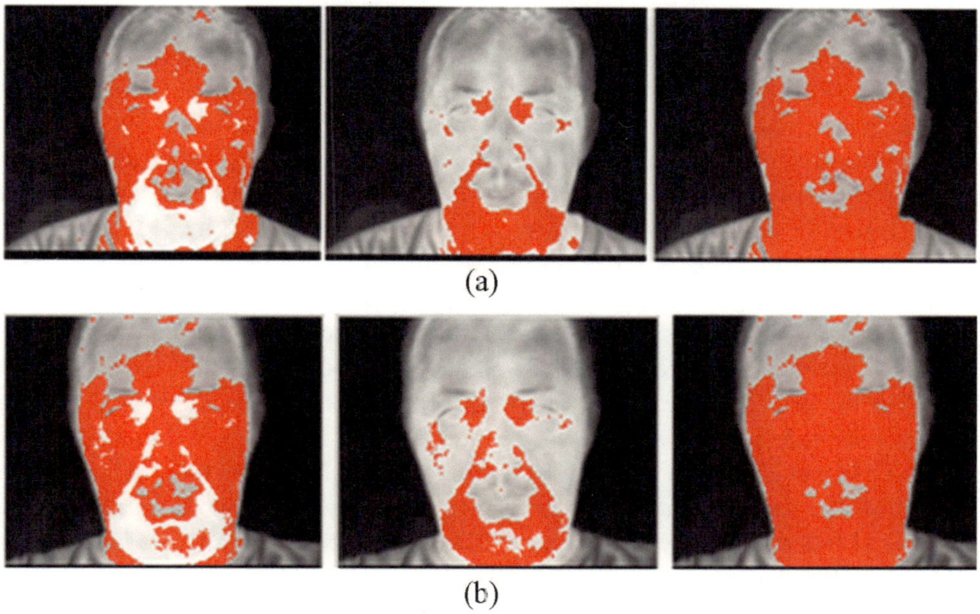

Figure 17. The images on the top row (a) correspond to sober person while in the bottom row to the corresponding drunk one. In the left column the red pixels have values in the range 191.25–223.125, in the middle column the pixel values lie in the range 223.125–255, while in the right column in the range 191.25–255. The regions, as it is easily recognizable, become wider in case of the drunk person.

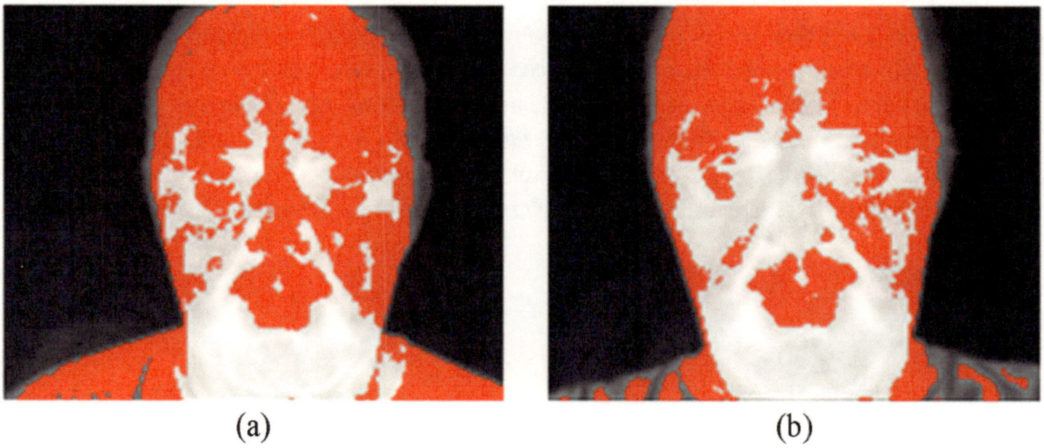

Figure 18. (a) The region of isotherms that contains the forehead, for the sober person includes other regions as well. For the drunk person (b) the forehead is more isolated.

belongs contains actually no other region of the face. Thus, for intoxication identification, the thermal image of the drunk person is adequate to verify the drunkenness, and no comparison with the image of the sober person is needed.

11. Markov chains for drunk identification

In this approach, the features used for intoxicated person discrimination are the eigenvalues of the transition matrices which correspond to Markov chains [39] used to model the pixels on the area of the forehead of each person. In the experimental procedure followed, a region on the forehead of both the drunk and the sober person was obtained, having 25 × 50 pixels size as shown in **Figure 19**, for a specific participant in the experiment. For this region, separately for the sober and the drunk person, the pixels of the forehead were brought into histograms of 8, 16, and 32 equal populated bins, respectively. The reduction of the histogram size from 256 graylevel representation to either 8, 16, or 32 bins were necessary to avoid sparse two-dimensional transition matrices of first or second order, due to small number of pixels (25 × 50) in the inspected area of the forehead. For each person, a total of three transition matrices are created for the image of the sober and three for the image of the drunk. Accordingly, for the face in **Figure 1** a more-or-less equal populated histogram with 16 bins is shown in **Figure 20a**. The transition matrix regarding the pixels of the histogram bins in **Figure 20a** is depicted as a black and white image in **Figure 20b**. This transition matrix of a Markov chain is a special tool for studying second-order statistics on the forehead, that is, co-occurrence properties of the pixels.

Using the 41 × 50 16-D eigenvalue vectors for sober and that many for the drunk as data, a three layer neural network with different neurons at each layer, were trained. It was found that 16 neurons at the input layer are sufficient for the network to converge satisfactorily. In this process, a network was trained with the data from 40 people and its behavior was tested on the 41st (leave-one-out method). This process was repeated by excluding and testing each one of the 41 people. Each time a new network of neurons was trained, it was found that its magnitude is the same as the previous procedure having 16 input neurons. It was found in all cases that the person to be checked was correctly classified. The convergence success gave each time training error less than 2%. This fact shows that only one person out of 41 is not correctly identified, if he is drunk or not. This result is obtained for the case where 16 states have been used and therefore 16 eigenvalues of the transition matrix of each image.

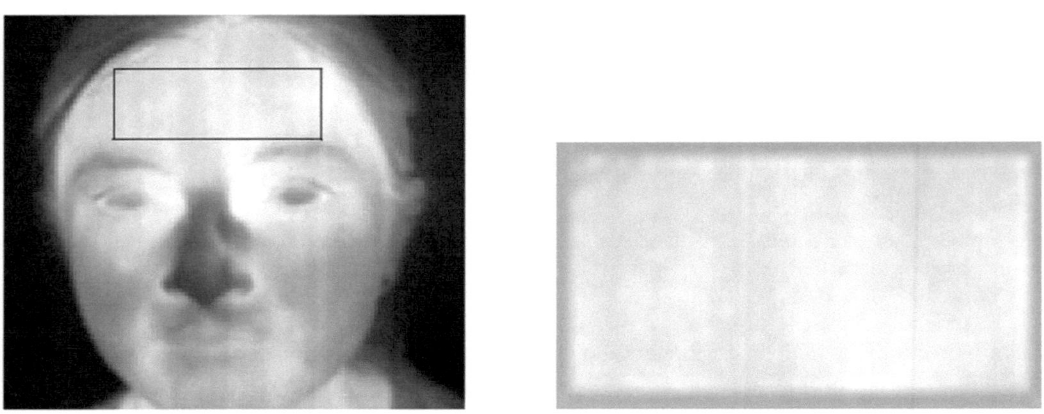

Figure 19. Region on the forehead where the Markov properties of the pixels are studied.

http://dx.doi.org/10.5772/intechopen.72128

Based on these results, a network of neurons of relatively small size may contain all the necessary information for separating the sober from the drunk. This conclusion results from all data obtained from the people participated in the experiment. This network can be integrated into an automatic intoxication detection system, which by using the face image of an intoxicated person end evaluating, the pixel transition matrix from the forehead will employ the vectors of the eigenvalues of the transition matrix for recognition. A 2D representation of the eigenvalues space (from 16D) for a specific person is shown in **Figure 21**. The separability of the sober and drunk person is obvious even in the 2-D space.

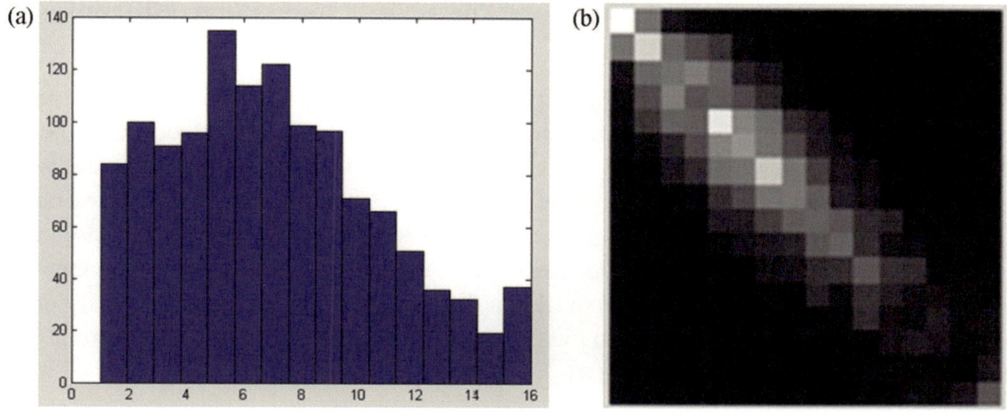

Figure 20. (a) A 16 bin histogram of the pixels on the forehead of a sober person, with 16 bins, (b) the transition matrix of the pixels on the forehead of the sober person in **Figure 1**. Quantization in a 16 bin histogram has been used.

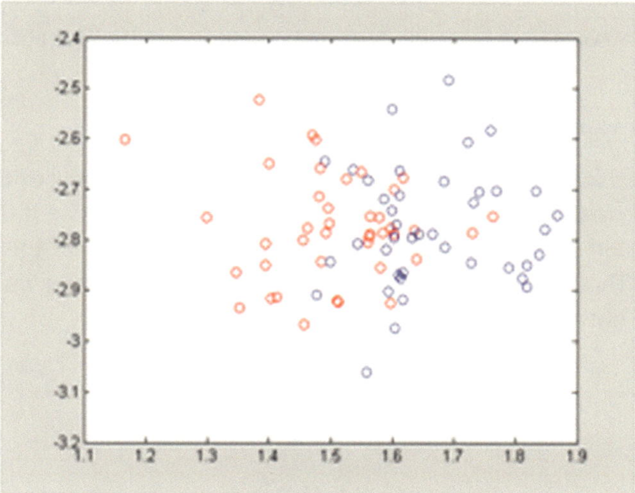

Figure 21. 2D representation of the eigenvalues space (from 16D) for a specific person. The two coordinates correspond to the largest eigenvalues. The separability of the sober and drunk person is obvious even in the 2D space.

12. Future perspectives: fusion approaches

The material presented in this chapter appears in the literature for first time worldwide. It is actually the first approach worldwide to address drunkenness by means of thermal infrared images of the face of the inspected person. This material was based on a PhD thesis carried out in the Physics Department University of Patras, Greece [39]. The whole material incorporates seven different approaches for feature extraction used for identifying drunk persons. All methods have been presented in scientific journals. The scientific work was based on a well-organized experimental procedure based on which thermal images of 41 persons were recorded when they were sober and when they were drunk. A well-organized database and the basic routines are available to access the thousands of images recorded (http://www.physics.upatras.gr/sober/).

All seven methods analyzed present high drunk identification success which is over 80%. It is expected that combining all this information into a unified identification procedure, the success rate will approach 100%. This requires sophisticated information fusion techniques which will employ combination of different kind of information. Work is currently carried out on this interesting topic. An important aspect toward completing this task is to elaborate on the correlation properties of the different features information extracted from the seven methods. In practice, an electronic system incorporating a thermal infrared camera can embody one of the proposed methods and point out to the police to whom an extended inspection for alcohol consumption is due.

The presented methodologies have found great recognition and publicity from the scientific community and the media [10–13].

The main advantages of these methods are as follow:

- They are not invasive and all the information is acquired remotely.
- The images do not depend on the existing natural lightning, but absolutely on the face temperature.
- Infrared images are obtained even in the drunk.
- Most of the drunk identification methods require the images of the drunk persons only to perform. This means that the approaches are independent of the thermal image of the sober person and it is not required in a database the images of the sober persons for comparisons. That is, the inspected person can be any unknown person and its sober signatures are not required.

Author details

Georgia Koukiou

Address all correspondence to: gkoukiou@upatras.gr

Electronics Laboratory (ELLAB), Physics Department, University of Patras, Greece

References

[1] Koukiou G, Anastassopoulos V. Facial blood vessels activity in drunk persons using thermal infrared. In: Proceedings of the 4th International Conference on Imaging for Crime Detection and Prevention (ICDP-11); Kingston, GB; 3–4 November 2011

[2] Koukiou G, Anastassopoulos V. Mint: Drunk person identification using thermal infrared images. International Journal of Electronic Security and Digital Forensics (IJESDF). 2012;**4**: 229-243

[3] Koukiou G, Anastassopoulos V. Face locations suitable drunk persons identification. In: Proceedings of the IEEE International Workshop on Biometrics and Forensics (IWBF 2013); Lisbon, Portugal; 4–5 April 2013

[4] Koukiou G, Anastassopoulos V. Eye temperature distribution in drunk persons using thermal imagery. In: Proceedings of the IEEE International Conference of the Biometrics Special Interest Group (BIOSIG 2013); Darmstadt, Germany; 4–6 September 2013

[5] Koukiou G, Anastassopoulos V. Mint: Neural networks for identifying intoxicated persons. Forensic Science International. 2015;**252**:69-76. DOI: 10.1016/j.forsciint.2015.04.022

[6] Koukiou G, Anastassopoulos V. Mint: Drunk person screening using eye thermal signatures. Journal of Forensic Sciences. 2016;**61**:259-264. DOI: 10.1111/1556-4029.12989

[7] Koukiou G, Anastassopoulos V. Mint: Intoxicated person discrimination using infrared signature of facial blood vessels. Australian Journal of Forensic Sciences. 2016;**48**:326-338. DOI: 10.1080/00450618.2015.1060522

[8] Koukiou G, Anastassopoulos V. Drunk person identification using local difference patterns. In: Proceedings of the IEEE International Conference on Imaging Systems & Technology (IST 2016); Chania, Crete; 4–6 October 2016

[9] Koukiou G, Anastassopoulos V. Local difference patterns for drunk person identification. Multimedia Tools and Applications. 2017. pp. 1-13 (in press). DOI: 10.1007/s11042-017-4892-6

[10] Available from: http://phys.org/news/2012-09-thermal-imaging-camera-scans-drunks.html

[11] Available from: http://www.cbsnews.om/8301-205_162-57505875/drunks-detected-by-thermal-camera/

[12] IEEE Spectrum October 2012, Intoxicam. p. 12

[13] Wu YC, Xia YQ, Xie P, Ji XW. The design of an automotive anti-drunk driving system to guarantee the uniqueness of driver. In: Proceedings of the International Conference on Information Engineering and Computer Science (ICIECS 2009); December 2009. pp. 1-4

[14] International Center of Alcohol Policies. ICAP Blue Book, Module 16: Blood Alcohol Concentration Limits; Washington; 2014

[15] Jones AW. The Relationship between Blood Alcohol Concentration (BAC) and Breath Alcohol Concentration (BrAC): A Review of the Evidence. London: Department of Forensic

Genetics and Forensic Toxicology, National Board of Forensic Medicine, Linkoping, Sweden and Department for Transport; 2010. p. 8

[16] Hunicka B, Laurell H, Bergman H. Mint: Psychosocial characteristics of drunk drivers assessed by addiction severity index, prediction of relapse. Scandinavian Journal of Public Health. 2010;**38**:71-77

[17] Available from: http://www.icap.org/table/BACLimitsWorldwide

[18] Available from: http://www.alcohol.vt.edu/Students/alcoholEffects/estimatingBAC/index.htm

[19] Available from: http://www.alcohol.vt.edu/Students/alcoholEffects/index.htm

[20] Blood Alcohol Content, http://en.wikipedia.org/wiki/Blood_alcohol_content

[21] Diakide NA, Bronzino JD. Medical Infrared Imaging. 1st ed. New York: CRC Press, Taylor & Francis Group; 2008

[22] Hildebrandt C, Raschner C, Ammer K. Mint: An overview of recent application of medical infrared thermography in sports medicine in Austria. Sensors. 2010;**10**:4700-4715

[23] Koukiou G, Panagopoulos G, Anastassopoulos V. Drunk person identification using thermal infrared image. In: Proceedings of the IEEE 16th International Conference on Digital Signal Processing (DSP 2009); Santorini, Greece; 5–7 July 2009. pp. 1-4

[24] Duda R, Hart P, Stork D. Pattern Classification. 2nd ed. New York: Wiley & Sons; 2001

[25] Anastassopoulos V, Venetsanopoulos AN. The classification properties of the pecstrum and its use for pattern identification. Circuits, Systems and Signal Processing. 1991;**10**:293-326

[26] Pitas I, Venetsanopoulos AN. Nonlinear Digital Filters: Principles and Applications. 1st ed. Boston: Kluwer Academic Publisher; 1990

[27] Perona P, Malik J. Mint: Scale-space and edge detection using anisotropic diffusion. IEEE Transactions on Pattern Analysis and Machine Intelligence. 1990;**12**:629-639

[28] Bhowmik MK, Bhattacharjee D, Nasipuri M, Basu DK, Kundu M. Classification of fused images using radial basis function neural network for human face recognition. In: Proceedings of the of The World congress on Nature and Biologically Inspired Computing; Coimbatore, India; 2009. pp. 19-24

[29] Wang MH. Mint: Hand recognition using thermal image and extension neural network. Mathematical Problems in Engineering. 2012;**2012**:1-15

[30] Fang YC, Wu BW. Neural network application for thermal image recognition of low-resolution objects. Journal of Optics A: Pure and Applied Optics. 2007;**9**:134-144

[31] Bauer J, Mazurkiewicz J. Neural network and optical correlators for infrared imaging based face recognition. In: Proceedings of the 5th International Conference on Intelligent Systems Design and Applications; Wroclaw, Poland, Wroclaw; 2005. pp. 234-238

[32] Yoshitomi Y, Miyawaki N, Tomita S, Kimura S. Facial expression recognition using thermal image processing and neural network. In: Proceedings of the 6th IEEE International Workshop on Robot and Human Communication; Sendai, Japan; 1997. pp. 380-385

[33] Weickert J. Anisotropic Diffusion in Image Processing. Stuttgart: B. G. Teubner Publisher; 1998

[34] Bronskill JF, Venetsanopoulos AN. The pecstrum. In: Proceedings of the 3rd ASSP Workshop on Spectral Estimation and Modeling; Boston; 1986

[35] Oliveira LS, Sabourin R. Support vector machines for handwritten numerical string recognition. In: Proceedings of the 9th International Workshop on Forentiers in Handwriting Recognition; 2004

[36] Osuna E, Freund R, Girosi F. Training support vector machines: An application to face detection. In: Proceedings of the Conference of Computer Vision and Pattern Recognition (CVPR 1997); Puerto Rico; June 1997

[37] Pontil M, Verri A. Mint: Support vector machines for 3D object recognition. IEEE Transactions on Pattern Analysis and Machine Intelligence. 1998;**20**:637-646

[38] Therrien Ch W. Random Processes. In: Therrien CW, editor. Discrete Random Signals and Statistical Signal Processing. 1st ed. New Jersey: Englewood Cliffs; 1992. pp. 85-139

[39] Koukiou G. Recognition of Psychophysics Condition using Thermal Infrared Radiation of the Face [PhD Thesis]. Patras Greece; University of Patras; 2014. http://nemertes.lis.upatras.gr/jspui/bitstream/10889/8936/1/PHD_G_Koukiou.pdf